Pendergast!

Missouri Biography Series

WILLIAM E. FOLEY, EDITOR

Pendergast!

LAWRENCE H. LARSEN AND NANCY J. HULSTON

University of Missouri Press

COLUMBIA AND LONDON

5   4   3   2   1   01   00   99   98   97

Library of Congress Cataloging-in-Publication Data

Larsen, Lawrence Harold, 1931–
      Pendergast! / Lawrence H. Larsen and Nancy J. Hulston.
          p.   cm.—(Missouri biography series)
      Includes bibliographical references and index.
      ISBN 0-8262-1145-3 (alk. paper)
          1. Pendergast, Thomas Joseph, 1870–1945.   2. Politicians—
Missouri—Kansas City—Biography.   3. Kansas City (Mo.)—Politics
and government.   4. Political corruption—Missouri—Kansas City—
History—20th century.   I. Hulston, Nancy J.   II. Title.
III. Series.
F474.K253P465   1997
977.8'411042'092—dc21
      [B]   97-33391
                                                                CIP

∞™ This paper meets the requirements of the
American National Standard for Permanence of Paper
for Printed Library Materials, Z39.48, 1984.

Text Design: Elizabeth K. Young
Jacket Design: Mindy Shouse
Typesetter: BOOKCOMP
Printer and binder: Thomson-Shore, Inc.
Typeface: Weiss

To Clayton A. Newton, 1922–1997,
a scholar, a mentor, and
a true Jackson County Democrat

Contents

Preface

Thomas J. Pendergast reigned as the undisputed political boss of Kansas City, Missouri, during the Roaring Twenties and the beginning of the Great Depression. A large body of material, some scholarly and some not, exists on his organization. On the national level, he ascended as a powerful figure in the Democratic party. In Kansas City, even though Tom Pendergast died in 1945, the name Pendergast continues to evoke strong emotions in the 1990s. Some local commentators have called for "a new Pendergast" to revitalize the community. Others have warned against a return to the days of "the notorious Pendergast machine."

More than half a century after Pendergast's death and the demise of his machine, Pendergast's name also continues to arouse interest far beyond the city he once dominated. His mastery of machine politics, his reputation and that of his organization for fostering corruption and flaunting law and order, and especially his role in facilitating the political rise of Harry S. Truman account for an ongoing fascination with his career and his legacy. An important aspect of any attempt to define Truman is his decade as a political leader in Pendergast's machine. Indeed, an understanding of Truman's approach to politics and decision making requires a knowledge of the political environment of the Kansas City area and how Pendergast operated.

Pendergast may bear comparison to various big-city bosses, but his open alliance with hardened criminals, his cynical subversion of the democratic process, his monarchistic style of living, his increasingly insatiable gambling habit, his grasping for a business empire, and his promotion of Kansas City as a wide-open town with every kind of vice imaginable, combined with his professed compassion for the poor and very real role as a city builder, made him bigger than life, difficult to characterize. No previous biographer has attempted to produce a life of Tom Pendergast, so our book covers new ground, placing in clearer perspective a personality demonized by his bitterest enemies and worshiped as a virtual saint by the most loyal of his friends.

In a very real way, Tom Pendergast was the Pendergast machine. When he fell, his machine fell with him, soon disintegrating at the municipal level. The political machines in Chicago and New York survived many leadership changes, but that was not so in Kansas City. Pendergast stood alone as "Pendergast," and his power went down with him.

We have had so much help over a period of several years in the course of producing this book that space limitations prevent a comprehensive listing. However, in particular we want to acknowledge the following individuals and institutions.

Barbara J. Cottrell compiled the index and assisted at every other production stage. David B. Newton, our excellent research associate, researched and organized difficult-to-use runs of newspapers and manuscript collections. A special word of thanks goes to Judge Howard F. Sachs, a fine historian, who generously, patiently, and always courteously answered our questions, adding to our understanding of pre–World War II Kansas City and Jackson County politics. Robert P. Hudson, M.D., contributed a precise analysis of Pendergast's prison medical records. Michael Pendergast and the late Beverly Pendergast both helped us in a number of ways. Nancy Reeves allowed the use of the unpublished memoirs of her grandfather, Judge Albert L. Reeves. People at the University of Missouri–Kansas City who contributed include Dennis Merrill, David Atkinson, W. Robert Brazelton, Louis Potts, James McKinley, and Patrick Peebles. We express gratitude to Harold F. Smith, Fredrick M. Spletstoser, F. Russell Millin, Paul Donnelly, Eugene W. J. Pearce, M.D., Judge Scott O. Wright, Brian Burnes, Robert Willoughby, Fred Slater, Jean Weldon, Neil Johnson, Jack Wally, Matt Devoe, Lenore Carroll, William S. Worley, and John K. Hulston.

We received assistance from many archivists and manuscript librarians, especially David Boutros, Betty Swiontek, and Jennifer Parker of the Western Historical Manuscript Collection, Gerald A. Motsinger of the Johnson County Archives, Ann McFerrin of the Kansas City Parks and Recreation Archives, and Denise Morrison of the Kansas City Museum. A University of Missouri–Kansas City Faculty Research Grant defrayed certain costs. We express gratitude to the staff of the University of Missouri Press and to Gloria Thomas Beckfield for her careful and intellectually challenging editing. The book was the idea of William E. Foley, editor of the Missouri Biography Series. Last but not least, James Cottrell and Marian Cottrell furnished an island in Canada.

Pendergast!

Introduction

Shortly after Thomas J. Pendergast entered the United States Penitentiary at Leavenworth, Kansas, on May 29, 1939, to serve a fifteen-month sentence for income tax evasion, the prison's associate warden blandly understated nearly everything in an initial "Summary of Impressions":

> It appears that this subject is a first offender. He is a nationally known political "boss" who has allegedly engaged in activities of a most questionable nature in connection with the operation of "machine politics" in Kansas City, Missouri. In view of the scope of his political and business activities, he has been regarded by some as a menace to society. The primary motive in the instant violation seems to have been a desire to further increase his already sizeable income. He is alleged to have spent money quite freely with particular reference to a fondness for gambling on horse races. He seems to have become the victim of his own methods and may be properly classified as a victim of temptation and also of the fact that he was somewhat over-confident as to his own personal immunity where prosecution for violation of the law is concerned. Subject will require separation from the general inmate population for his own protection, in order that he may be able to avoid any approaches of institutional inmates seeking favors, etc., which inmates believe he is able to bestow on them. Any problem he presents will be as a result of that fact.[1]

Pendergast arrived at Leavenworth, only an hour away from his home, at 8:45 on a pleasant spring morning. Rather than follow the practice of surrendering directly to the United States marshal, Henry Dillingham, for commitment, Pendergast went behind bars on his own terms. His only son, Thomas J. Pendergast Jr., and a nephew and political associate, James Pendergast, drove him to prison. Pendergast entered unobserved through a side entrance, outwitting the reporters and photographers gathered at the

1

front gate. An embarrassed deputy marshal reached Leavenworth a few hours afterwards, carrying the formal commitment papers. With the paperwork completed, Pendergast experienced the formal "dressing process." After receiving a medical examination, Pendergast supplied a prison clerk with his name, address, and other data. The prison store issued him the standard two pairs of blue denim trousers, two shirts, two pairs of underwear, and a pair of heavy shoes.[2]

The Bureau of Prisons designated Pendergast a "notorious offender," a special classification reserved for corrupt politicians, major white-collar felons, and infamous career criminals, such as Al Capone. In a calculated move deliberately intended to humiliate Pendergast and to emphasize the severity of his crime, Attorney General Frank Murphy authorized the distribution to the media of Pendergast's official prison admission picture and a set of his fingerprints.[3] In a confidential letter, James Bennett, the director of the Bureau of Prisons, had cautioned Leavenworth warden Robert A. Hudspeth to use "a great deal of tact" in answering requests for information, explaining only that Pendergast would be put through "the usual routine" and would receive the same treatment as any other prisoner.[4]

BOSS TOM

Obviously, Tom Pendergast, inmate registration number 55295—L, was no ordinary income tax evader. Rather, right up until the day he went behind bars, Pendergast numbered among the most influential big-city political bosses in the United States, playing a part in sending presidents Roosevelt and Truman to the White House. He led the Democratic organization in Kansas City, Missouri, a regional metropolis located in Jackson County that in the 1930s had approximately 400,000 citizens. He called his faction "my organization," but almost everyone else called it "the Pendergast machine." Relishing his power, Pendergast asserted, "I'm not bragging when I say I run the show in Kansas City. I am the boss. If I were a Republican they would call me a leader."[5]

President-making aside, Pendergast's all-abiding concern was advancing his political and business interests in Kansas City. The only federal activities (other than investigations of his conduct) that he appeared to care about were those involving Missouri. His involvement in the national political arena was a logical and inevitable consequence of his Kansas City operations. As a matter of course, he could never completely divorce Kansas City politics from the state and national levels, so he was drawn into congressional and presidential electioneering.

Within Missouri, Pendergast sought enough power over the governor, the general assembly, and the judiciary to keep them from interfering in Kansas City. He once said, "The Kansas City organization does not need the state

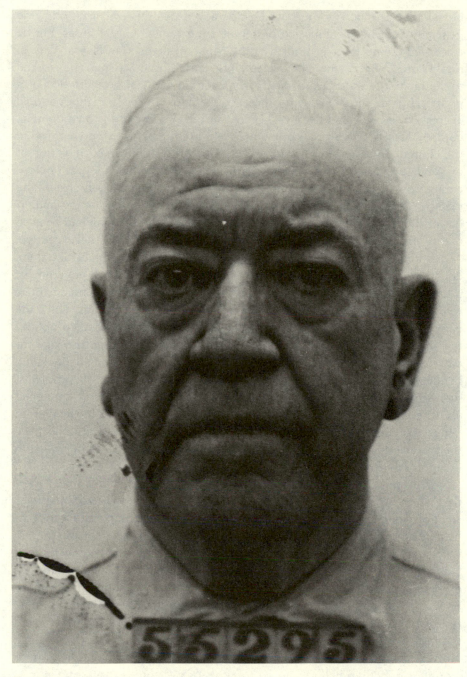

Tom Pendergast in his prison admission photograph. Attorney General Frank Murphy authorized the release of this photograph to the media to humiliate the boss. *(Photograph courtesy the National Archives and Records Administration, Washington, D.C.)*

Democracy as much as the state Democracy needs this organization."[6] He generally kept his machine out of neighboring Kansas City, Kansas, but he cultivated connections just north of the Missouri River from Kansas City in rural Platte County, where he owned land. Throughout Missouri, he worked to dominate the state Democratic party, keeping nominal ties with St. Louis political bosses. He showed little direct concern for national and international events—even wars and famines—except in the context of his own domain. For him, Kansas City was a world unto itself. In spite of his extensive travel in the United States and Europe, he was essentially parochial in outlook, intent on protecting "the House of Pendergast." This aspect of his rule was obvious enough on the national stage that when Harry S. Truman, a high-ranking member of the Pendergast organization, first assumed the presidency, numerous observers feared that his career as a local machine politician had been so narrow in outlook as to inadequately prepare him for the job of chief executive.

In Pendergast's day, the federal government had little direct, let alone effective, control over the more than four thousand local units of government in the United States. Of far more importance in regulating municipalities were state constitutions and measures passed by state legislatures. Until the New Deal, the general thrust of federal court decisions tended to uphold the legislative role of the states.[7] In terms of policy setting and day-to-day administration, local officials and leaders—which, after all, included Pendergast—had little choice except to place their own immediate problems, such as collecting garbage and repairing streets, ahead of what happened elsewhere. As a traditional truism went, all politics was local. In the case of Pendergast, for obvious reasons, the less direct contact with federal authorities, the better. He wanted the freedom to concentrate on running his own version of an orderly town.

Widespread chicanery characterized Kansas City elections under Pendergastism, with untold thousands of fictitious Democratic votes. Sometimes election workers filled out tally sheets without even bothering to count the ballots. Pendergast routinely delivered fantastic margins in the range of 100,000 votes for candidates of his choice in Kansas City and surrounding Jackson County. In the 1934 Democratic primary for the United States Senate, for example, Truman beat his chief challenger, Congressman John J. Cochran of St. Louis, 120,180 to 1,221 votes in Kansas City and 17,349 to 304 votes in the rest of Jackson County, for a resounding margin of 136,004. Cochran carried the rest of the state by 95,259, so Truman's plurality was a fairly comfortable 40,745. Two years earlier, with Pendergast's support in an at-large election for Congress, Cochran had received a total of 92,868 votes in Jackson County, with Kansas City casting 82,972 for him.[8]

Understandably, no matter what aspirants for political office actually thought of T. J. Pendergast, as he preferred to be called, they wanted his support. Hopefuls for offices from governor on down to alderman went hat in hand to see Pendergast at the modest headquarters of his Jackson Democratic Club at 1908 Main Street, "the Power House," a more important address in Missouri than either the state capitol, "Uncle Tom's Cabin," in Jefferson City, or city hall, "the House of Pendergast," in Kansas City. In return for an endorsement, Pendergast expected supplicants to pay a price by showing unfailing loyalty. This meant ignoring widespread vote fraud, criminal depredations, vice rings, and rampant corruption.

Pendergast, despite the fact that he held no elected position, exercised power in a manner comparable to a benevolent and sometimes cruel despot of a medieval European city-state. Gangster elements effectively menaced, cowed, and coerced Pendergast's enemies, providing a significant source of his strength. His minions vastly inflated and manipulated the voting rolls in election frauds possibly unparalleled in American history. He exacted tribute from virtually all legal and illegal businesses in Kansas City, commanding his own economic empire of vast and unknown proportions. He handled almost all private and public welfare functions in Kansas City and achieved a reputation for generosity, dispensing aid to the needy, jobs to the faithful, and holiday turkeys to the hungry. As a Pendergast machine propagandist said, "His heart and soul are devoted to his beloved Kansas City."[9]

Under the New Deal, Pendergast greatly extended his power, garnering huge quantities of the federal money that flowed into Missouri. In Kansas City, his machine engaged the services of thousands of functionaries, many on the public payroll. For obvious reasons, a large number of people held a direct stake in the fortunes of Tom Pendergast and his state within a state, a virtual "invisible government."[10]

In his prime, the hefty Pendergast, who stood five feet, eight inches tall, weighed more than 230 pounds. He had his lunch catered to his 1908 Main Street office from the adjacent Ever Eat Cafe. When the cafe closed in 1975, its longtime owner, C. H. Crocker, discussed Pendergast's luncheon habits: "He didn't want no bone, no fat on it, just as dry as it could be, no salt and pepper. I'd buy a whole pork shoulder, cut it up and put it in the icebox deep freeze. When he wanted a steak sandwich, I'd cook it—sometimes I'd cook two steaks for the same sandwich." Pendergast claimed to drink alcoholic beverages sparingly, if at all. He smoked a special brand of "denicotinized" cigarettes and occasionally enjoyed his own custom-made cigars. He had a coarse and gravelly voice, and reporters quoted him as frequently using in everyday conversation "they was" or "I seen," which offended his sensibilities to the point that he once went out of his way to stress to an interviewer, "I can speak good English when I want to."[11]

Pendergast disliked small talk. While he was often curt and cold in his public demeanor, intimate acquaintances supposedly found him quite congenial and an excellent raconteur, capable of telling good stories and anecdotes, frequently about people he knew. He struck people as having a superior intelligence and cunning. He prided himself on making quick decisions and keeping his word, even if he made a mistake in giving it. He aspired to social respectability, but, even wearing formal dress and expensive tailored clothing, he struck his enemies as being porcine in appearance, an overweight thug. Pendergast had no patience for ideology, and he once asserted that he never listened to political speeches. "I should say not!" he declared. "When I say I never listen to a speech, I mean never. Not on the radio or anywhere else!"[12]

Truman said after meeting Joseph Stalin at Potsdam that the Soviet leader reminded him of Pendergast, and not the other way around. In notes he made on Pickwick Hotel stationery, Truman wrote, "'The Boss' says that, instead of most men being honest most of them are not when they are in a position where they can get away with crookedness. I guess I've been wrong in my premise that 92% are honest." In 1934, Pendergast explained to a reporter what he considered to be the reasons for his success: "I'm where I am today because of my own ability. I know all the angles of organizing and every man I meet becomes a friend. I know how to select ward captains and I know how to get to the poor. Every single one of my ward workers has a fund to buy food, coal, shoes and clothing for the poverty stricken. And when a poor man comes to old Tom's boys for help we don't make one of those —— investigations like these city charities."[13]

Pendergast displayed a quick temper, even in middle age, sometimes slugging or slapping men who dared to disagree with him. Explaining in a 1937 newspaper interview how he had handled two of his toadies when they questioned an order, Pendergast recounted, "One of them hesitated, said he didn't know anything about it. Well, I slapped him with my open hand. The other tried to protest. I hit him with my fist and knocked him through the glass door." A Leavenworth psychologist, after giving Pendergast a formal neuropsychiatric examination, concluded, "His thought processes are quite within the normal sphere, disclosing no delusional trends, hallucinatory experience or special preoccupations. He gives all the impression of having been a dynamic, extroverted personality."[14]

In the 1930s, Pendergast became increasingly reckless, perhaps because he often needed large amounts of quick money to pay gambling debts. His deteriorating health only seemed to spur him on. He openly consorted with criminals, and some authorities believed he sanctioned political assassinations. "Tom's Town" experienced an unprecedented reign of terror for which many citizens refused to hold Pendergast responsible.

Rudolph H. Hartmann, a special agent of the Treasury Department's elite Intelligence Unit, commented on the state of affairs in a letter of June 6, 1939, "Prior to his indictment on April 7, 1939, Mr. Pendergast bore a good reputation among the majority of citizens of Kansas City. Although known locally and nationally as the leader of a political machine, whose henchmen committed many crimes, including vote frauds and were even at times suspected of murder, nevertheless the personal integrity and honesty of Mr. Pendergast were never directly questioned. . . . After these disclosures became known to the public, the major portion of the leading citizens appear to have changed their opinion of him."[15]

When he became aware of investigations launched against him, Pendergast took steps to shore up his support in high places. Harry S. Truman, his man in Washington, D.C., was an old political associate and friend whom Pendergast counted upon. By rigging the Kansas City and Jackson County vote, Pendergast alone had sent Truman, who was sarcastically called "the senator from Pendergast," to the United States Senate. Lloyd Crow Stark, the Democratic governor of Missouri, owed his 1936 election to the Pendergast machine, and Pendergast, along with a select few of his fellow bosses, had played an important role in the presidential nomination of Franklin D. Roosevelt at the 1932 Democratic National Convention. President Roosevelt occasionally demonstrated fidelity, calling long distance from Washington to ask about Pendergast's health.[16]

On the surface, Pendergast seemed unassailable, which made his sudden fall from power all the more surprising. His excesses became so offensively conspicuous that they could no longer be tolerated in a society based on law. In the end, Truman stood aside, Stark plotted against and then attacked the machine, and Roosevelt sanctioned investigations. Federal vote-fraud trials resulted in the convictions of many machine officials. A new state registration act removed countless thousands of names from the voter-registration lists in Kansas City, fortifying Pendergast's opposition and damaging his position in the Democratic party. Finally, though, it was tax evasion that sent Pendergast, like so many other notorious offenders, to prison.

URBAN BOSSISM

Few people felt sorry for the dethroned boss. In the "Age of Roosevelt," as the federal government assumed welfare functions formerly carried out at the municipal level, urban bossism, standard fare in an older America, seemed passé.[17] The time had arrived to sweep aside bosses, who were often depicted as despoilers of the public trust and conventional morality, in a new wave of reform fervor.

The very word "boss" had become an epithet, synonymous with corruption. Of course, one person's boss was another person's leader. In political usage a boss was the manager of a complex organization, sometimes called a "machine" and sometimes a "faction" or a "ring." Bosses frequently held public office, but not always, as in the case of Pendergast during the 1920s and 1930s. The definition of "boss" was broad enough to include just about any political leader who ever exercised power in the United States. So, broadly speaking, Pendergast was hardly exceptional. But he fit into a very special category—a small number of bosses in big cities who exercised great power in the Democratic party for many years.

Bossism had a long history before this century, extending back into colonial times. In Boston, revolutionary leader Samuel Adams molded a faction, the Boston Caucus, into a disciplined popular party that supported anti-British policies and actions, notably the Boston Tea Party of 1773. In New York City, a Jeffersonian political club formed in the 1790s, the Society of St. Tammany, evolved into Tammany Hall, the prototype urban machine. In the first half of the nineteenth century, rings of insiders dominated most city governments. Following the Civil War, when rapidly growing industrial cities required a larger and more costly range of municipal services, bossism assumed more visible—and what reformers felt were more sinister—forms.

Sensational exposés of corruption involving the well-known bosses William Tweed in New York, Alexander Shepherd in Washington, and James McManes in Philadelphia thrust bossism into the forefront as a national issue in the Gilded Age. Samuel J. Tilden, the barely unsuccessful Democratic candidate for president in 1876, came to prominence fighting Tammany Hall, and Grover Cleveland started his rise to the presidency by cleaning up Buffalo. Popular wisdom held that bosses owed their strength to their handing out of welfare to indigents and immigrants in exchange for votes.[18]

Stealing from the public till seemed so common at this time that bribe money, "boodle," was cynically called "honest graft." James Bryce, a titled Englishman and astute student of the American scene, called city government a conspicuous failure. At the turn of the century, Lincoln Steffens created a national sensation with investigative reporting detailing boss-related corruption in several large cities. But despite all the efforts by good-government advocates, powerful bosses persisted into the Great Depression years. Apologists suggested that boss leaders, supposedly fostering ties to all levels of society, created a kind of "community consensus" seen as absolutely essential in running the increasingly more comprehensive city governments. A pro-Pendergast spokesman went even further in extolling bossism, seeing it as part of American government: "We will have machines as long as we have democracy."[19] The more widely held view considered bossism a national disgrace and a serious threat to democracy.

In June 1938, in a speech before a business organization in Nashville, Tennessee, Federal Bureau of Investigation Director J. Edgar Hoover (who was among the most respected men in the nation, according to polls) called the "debauchery of law and order" in large cities a greater threat confronting the people of the United States than hunger, communism, or foreign invasion. "Fifty years of crime in America has culminated into a positive threat to our social order," Hoover thundered. "Corruption begets corruption. One of the worst degenerative forces in American life during the past 50 years has been corruption in public office." He singled out the "gory scenes of multiple crimes" and the "armed fury of entrenched interests" in Kansas City. He referred to "a situation which indeed is not an isolated instance," concluding that "today the throne of the leader of this machine is toppling," accurately predicting the course of events during the coming year.[20] To Hoover, bringing Pendergast down was a blow struck to save the country. Prior to Pendergast's indictment Hoover was the most important national figure to speak out against the Democratic organization in Kansas City.

In the black-and-white mug shot released by Leavenworth officials, Pendergast looks like a stereotypical city boss. After the Civil War, political cartoonist Charles Nast had set the standard by depicting Boss Tweed as a cigar-smoking oaf with a big belly. Tweed was perceived as Irish and Roman Catholic, a combination that nativists found especially threatening to American institutions. That his ancestors actually hailed from Scotland made little difference. Some xenophobes fearfully believed that Irish immigrants banded together in large cities to practice a unique brand of clannish politics, fortified by strong drink. Under this premise, tavern keepers in Ireland were prototypes for Irish bosses in the United States, dispensing to their thirsty customers a combination of spirits and welfare. Another, more plausible, theory attributed the rise of Irish political bosses to large Irish voting blocs. But a 1930 study showed that fewer than half of twenty representative city bosses were Irish.[21] Still, a number of the more important bosses *were* of Irish extraction, including James Michael Curley in Boston, Edward J. Kelly in Chicago, Frank Hague in Jersey City, and, of course, Thomas J. Pendergast in Kansas City.

Boss Curley, in particular, shamelessly played on his Irishness. He spent a long career claiming to champion the cause of Boston's large Irish population against the city's wealthy and dominant Brahmins. A gregarious and sometimes charming man, Curley had great fun running for and holding public office in Boston and Massachusetts. Two prison terms, one for taking a civil service examination for a constituent and the other for tax evasion, hardly tarnished his local image. Curley enjoyed leading crowds in his unofficial campaign song, "Vote Early and Often for Curley." He gave spellbinding orations twisting the British Lion's tail, made conspicuous appearances at Irish wakes, and marched in St. Patrick's Day parades.[22]

Curley was the inspiration for the aging boss character in Edwin O'Connor's popular 1956 sentimental novel, *The Last Hurrah*, which helped change the general image of Irish bosses from unfavorable to favorable, giving the impression that they were more like Curley than Tweed. Indeed, David McCullough, in his Pulitzer Prize–winning biography of Truman, depicted Kansas City as a sort of "Boston West" that featured a rollicking and relatively harmless kind of Irish-style machine politics.[23]

Even if he had wanted to, Pendergast could never have operated in Kansas City the way Curley did in Boston because the two cities' demographics were so different. Kansas City, located in the center of the United States, hard against Missouri's western border with Kansas, had not started to grow until after the Civil War. Centrality and lush agricultural hinterlands made Kansas City an excellent transportation and agribusiness point, with a distinct western rather than eastern flavor. Unlike Boston and many other Atlantic Coast metropolises, Kansas City never had a great number of immigrants. In 1930, the local chamber of commerce arrogantly billed Kansas City as "The Most American City," underscoring its only 6 percent foreign-born population.[24]

There was a rather large Irish constituency, but it constituted a distinct minority, so Pendergast seldom accentuated his Irish background. This did not necessarily mean a rejection of his own heritage; on the contrary, he could become quite sentimental in private about his Celtic roots. Although the Irish constituency was small, it was well represented in politics. Indeed, one student of Kansas City politics concluded that the names of local politicians read like the roster of a unit in the Irish Republican Army.[25]

The times of Tom Pendergast in Kansas City spanned the Gilded Age through World War II. In Missouri, Kansas City competed with St. Louis for supremacy. To the west, Kansas City had a great deal of influence throughout Kansas, Colorado, and Wyoming, and extending down into Oklahoma, Texas, and New Mexico. Great packinghouses and stockyards gave Kansas City a well-deserved reputation as a quintessential cow town.

A steady expansion of western agriculture, fueled by new national and overseas markets, led to continual growth in Kansas City during the first quarter of the twentieth century. World War I did not last long enough to have a significant impact on Kansas City, but Prohibition and the Great Depression had great import. Kansas City never realized the prediction of an early promoter, William Gilpin, who in the 1850s forecast that it would grow into the great "centropolis" of the world, with a population of fifty million within a hundred years.[26] While this vision fell far short of reality, throughout much of Pendergast's life Kansas City was the largest city in the United States between those bordering the Mississippi River and those on the Pacific Coast, a vast region covering more than half the country.

To what extent was Pendergast a product of his times? The answer might be the same as that for any American who grew up and lived in a new modern industrial and urban era. However, what Pendergast did that made him unusual was to seize the moment, shaping the life of his city on his own terms and leaving an indelible mark. In essence, he made his own times.

ONE

Early Years

1872–1894

Thomas Joseph Pendergast entered the world in St. Joseph, Missouri, on July 22, 1872, a typical hot and muggy summer day. On August 6, Father Thomas Walsh of St. Joseph Cathedral baptized him according to the rites of the Roman Catholic Church. A baby picture, probably taken in a St. Joseph studio, shows the future man with a pug nose, little bags under the eyes, a firmly set mouth, and fleshy cheeks and jowls, wearing a ruffled frock dress. In the 1930s, the photograph hung in a black frame, along with baby pictures of many other important Kansas Citians, in an informal gallery on the wall of a former speakeasy, the Cottage Inn, operated by legendary local character Lloyd W. "Speed" Mayhan. When a surprised Boss Pendergast saw the picture, he inscribed in the upper left-hand corner, "Speed, Where in the Hell did you get this?"[1]

Pendergast was the ninth and last child in a family that was large even by the standards of the times. He had three brothers, James, John, and Michael, plus five sisters, Mary Anne, Josephine, Delia, Margaret, and Catherine. All except Delia and Catherine lived into adulthood. When Tom went to prison at age sixty-six he was the only surviving Pendergast sibling. After he became a national figure, writers sometimes confused family relationships, giving the wrong number of siblings or, as one writer did, even identifying Tom as James's son.[2]

Tom's parents, Michael and Mary Reidy Pendergast, both hailed from County Tipperary in Ireland. Mike, born in 1826, immigrated to North America, as did his siblings, Patrick, Edward, Mary, and Margaret. Patrick settled in Illinois, and the family ultimately lost track of him. Edward and

Margaret, after arriving in New Orleans, went directly to St. Joseph. Mary stayed in New Orleans, married Owen McCormick, raised three children, and then moved to St. Joseph in 1870.

Family records do not show the arrival dates of any Pendergast family member, or whether they came separately or together. Mike, according to a Pendergast in Florida who undertook a broadly based family history, first immigrated to Canada. Merchant ships that regularly transported lumber from Canada to ports in the United Kingdom frequently, rather than deadhead back, carried to Canada under notoriously bad conditions multitudes of Irish immigrants escaping the potato famine. Great numbers soon left Canada and went south to the United States. Whether Mike actually followed that course or even whether he soon linked up with any of his brothers or sisters is unknown, but he eventually reached Cincinnati. There, in 1855, he married Mary Reidy, who was born in 1834 and had entered the United States at New Orleans, probably with her parents.[3]

The newly married couple, Mike, twenty-nine, and Mary, twenty-one, started their life together in Gallipolis, Ohio. About 150 miles up the Ohio River from Cincinnati, Gallipolis was a prime shipping center for the coal regions of Ohio and neighboring West Virginia. On January 27, 1856, the couple had their first child, James Francis Pendergast. Mike, a sturdy, well-built man, had little trouble finding work as a teamster, but prospects for advancement appeared limited at best. In addition, Gallipolis had only a few Irish residents. In 1857, the year a financial panic severely hurt the eastern economy, the Pendergasts moved eight hundred miles west, to St. Joseph. Doubtless, the presence of relatives in the Missouri River city influenced the choice. In all likelihood, the Pendergast family traveled west on one of the regularly scheduled steamboats from Gallipolis to the fabled "Middle Border" on the eastern edge of the Great Plains, the jumping-off place for the Far West.

More than 5,000 people lived in St. Joseph in the 1850s, a comparatively large number for a wilderness outpost. During the California gold rush, some 17,000 forty-niners had outfitted for their trek in St. Joseph. The city gained fame as the eastern terminal of the colorful, uneconomical, and short-lived Pony Express. The Hannibal and St. Joseph Railroad that ran across northern Missouri reached St. Joseph in 1859. Unfortunately, the city lost a temporary advantage as a frontier railhead when the Civil War disrupted service. Following hostilities, a decision by the owners of the Hannibal and St. Joseph Railroad dashed hopes that St. Joseph would grow into a great railroad center. Rather than build tracks west from St. Joseph, they decided to divert the main line fifty miles to the south through Kansas City and on into the Southwest, planning to exploit the Texas cattle trade. Even though the leaders of St. Joseph scaled down their aspirations, the city remained a thriving and expanding place, albeit increasingly secondary to Kansas City.[4]

Mike and Mary settled permanently and raised their rapidly growing family in St. Joseph. Mary gave birth to Mary Anne in 1858, followed by Josephine (Josie) in 1860, John in 1862, Delia (Bridget) in 1864, Margaret (Maggie) in 1865, Michael Joseph in 1867, Catherine (Katie) in 1869, and finally Thomas Joseph in 1872.[5]

As employment was plentiful, Mike quickly found work as a drayman. He may have worked for Russell, Majors, and Waddell, a large western freighting firm that, prior to declaring bankruptcy during the Civil War, had a regional headquarters in St. Joseph. At times, Mike, as did many haulers, freelanced as an independent contractor. Usually, however, he labored for others, and not always as a teamster; in 1868 he worked as a farmer and in 1879 he worked at the W. H. Whitaker Starch Factory. In his prime, his oxlike strength enabled him to singlehandedly lift very heavy loads. A large dry goods store employed him as a teamster on a regular basis. Although he never became wealthy, he made a steady living, providing enough money to support his family in reasonably adequate circumstances. Mike drank only in moderation, which was highly unusual for someone engaged in an occupation that frequently attracted hard-living and unreliable transients.[6]

Mike Pendergast, in the style of a typical Irish patriarch, ruled his children with stern yet good-natured discipline. Mary provided the home with loving stability. Tom, in later years, called his home life normal and family relations congenial. He characterized his father as "responsible" and his mother as "devoted."[7]

The family residence, which Mike Pendergast owned, was a substantial two-story frame house at 1715 Frederick Avenue. That location, when the Pendergasts arrived, was on the east side of St. Joseph. As the city extended farther east, Frederick Avenue became the main thoroughfare into downtown. A horse railroad line ran down Frederick in the 1870s; it was electrified by 1887, with an electric power plant at 20th Street. Saloons, eating places, groceries, medical clinics, dental offices, and meat markets, plus residential dwellings, lined Frederick. Many shopkeepers lived in the rear or on the second floors of their businesses. The Pendergast neighborhood included an ethnically diverse mix of Irish, German, English, and some black people. In 1899, a coal, wood, and feedlot was on one side of the Pendergast residence, a barber shop on the other.[8]

The Pendergast home had only seven rooms, so it was fairly cramped for such a large family. All the rooms were comfortably furnished and had rugs and curtains, a mark of prosperity. A small barnyard surrounded the property. In following years, after all the Pendergasts had died or moved away, the condition of the house, still in family hands in 1939, gradually deteriorated. Following World War II, a cemetery monument concern acquired the residence, tore it down, and used the lot for a display yard. Maurice Milligan, the United States Attorney who played a major role in sending Pendergast to prison, said that it was fitting that the house had not been turned into a shrine.[9]

Questioned in prison about his school days, Pendergast recalled nothing out of the ordinary. He remembered playing hooky, but the rolls of the public Webster School, which he attended from first through sixth grades, indicate consistently excellent attendance records, so he must have started playing hooky after grade school. He avoided organized extracurricular activities, but played sandlot baseball. He got along well with his schoolmates, and he kept tabs on them through the years. A streetcar conductor remembered, "Tom often rode my trolley car. He was a friendly and good-natured boy. I liked him." At home, Tom joined in the family chores, tending the horses, milking the cow, shoveling coal, feeding the chickens, and chopping wood. His parents made him and his siblings attend mass regularly. With the usual exaggeration, he told his own children how hard it was growing up in "the good old days," working instead of playing and walking four miles to school each way, frequently through several feet of snow. In reality he lived within four blocks of Webster School, and such a snowfall would be extraordinary for Missouri.[10]

The Rise of James Pendergast

In 1876, Tom's oldest brother, James, left St. Joseph and moved to Kansas City. This was far from a final departure; several trains daily made the trip in under two hours. Jim, a solid, muscular man of over two hundred pounds, built along the same lines as his powerful father, rented a room in one of the hundreds of boarding houses in the commercial, entertainment, and industrial West Bottoms, sometimes called "West Kansas," as the district bordered the state of Kansas.[11]

Following a short stint in a meatpacking plant, Jim toiled as a smelter at the A. J. Kelly Foundry. In 1879, he moved to the D. M. Jarboe Keystone Iron Foundry, accepting a well-paying position as a puddler.[12] Puddling required pouring molten metal into various-sized molds; although it was not especially physically strenuous, it was a hot, demanding, and somewhat dangerous job. Molders ran the risk of being splashed with liquid metal or having sparks fly into their eyes. Work on the molding line, performed six days a week on ten- to twelve-hour shifts, generally paid by the number and kind of molds produced. Few people stayed in the occupation for many years. During his foundry days,

Kansas City's West Bottoms in 1889, showing the 9th Street cable railway from Union Depot, with the 8th Street tunnel at left. *(Photograph courtesy the Native Sons Archives [KC590/N170], Western Historical Manuscript Collection, Kansas City, Mo.)*

Jim lived in a variety of different West Bottoms rooming houses, learning his way around and acquiring numerous friends, among them professional gamblers.

Steady employment at good wages in a foundry set Jim somewhat apart from thousands of other laborers in the West Bottoms, most of whom worked either for the packing plants, the stockyards, or the railroads. The city emerged from its frontier days as an important livestock shipper, a crucial link between the western cattle ranges and eastern packers. With the advent of refrigerated boxcars, large meatpacking companies moved into or expanded existing operations in Kansas City.[13]

Kansas City was home to a large number of unskilled laborers, many without roots in a place with a large transient population. Great numbers of railroad passengers changed trains and laid over in the city; the cattle trade drew stockmen and cowboys from all across the western plains on business and for recreation. A polyglot mixture of native-born white and black people, plus German, Italian, and Irish immigrants, added a colorful and boisterous diversity to life in the entertainment districts of Kansas City in the West Bottoms and the adjacent North End. The North End included downtown and residential districts to the east and west. Wealthy Kansas Citians resided on stylish Quality Hill, with lavish mansions and fashionable hotels overlooking the West Bottoms. All this and more the ambitious Jim Pendergast observed with great interest, for he had no intention of remaining a foundry worker for very long.[14]

In the early 1880s, Jim entered the tavern business in the West Bottoms. According to local and family legend, he named his first saloon after a horse, for he supposedly gained his start-up costs by betting and winning a large amount of money on a gelding named Climax. That story, repeated over the years to the point that it is accepted as gospel truth, has a certain poetic ring of authenticity about it, though no such establishment appears in the Kansas City business directories from that period. Records do indicate that Jim purchased the American House, located at 1328 St. Louis Avenue, from one John Porter in 1881.[15]

The American House, which had a prime West Bottoms location near the Union Station, was a two-story combination saloon, boarding house, and hotel. With thousands of railroad passengers daily passing through and laying over waiting for connections to their destinations, the blocks around the station contained the heart of Kansas City's red-light "tenderloin" district. A mecca for vice, the blocks surrounding the bustling train station kept Kansas City's fledgling police department busy. One short stretch of a commercial street featured twenty saloons, and every morning Kansas City's finest routinely picked up drunks from the gutters for transport to the holding tank at police headquarters.[16]

The West Bottoms, a Kansas City version of San Francisco's famous Barbary Coast and the Bowery in New York, contained large and prosperous vice interests. Cowboys, travelers, transients, and townspeople provided ready customers for numerous bawdy houses and gambling dens. Well-known madams with glamorous images achieved celebrity status. "Hell dances," which featured half- and totally naked women who mingled with male audiences, took place openly night and day in dance halls. Almost anything was available for a price. Gaming was a way of life. Flamboyant professional gamblers were local heroes, routinely fleecing country bumpkins. Bunco, floating crap tables, and even the old shell game flourished around the station. Saloons offered roulette and poker. Almost every evening a carnival atmosphere prevailed along the crowded streets, with barkers and shills tantalizing passersby with visions of all sorts of delights. Here was an environment that the ambitious Jim Pendergast found suitable to his needs.[17]

That Jim won big enough on a horse race to buy the American House seems far-fetched. Probably he either saved the money to start his new business or received a loan from gamblers. Kansas City bankers, a conservative lot, would not likely have loaned money for the purchase of an established business to a young foundry worker who had little collateral and who openly gambled. In any event, Jim must have appreciated the dangers associated with owning a tavern in a rough part of town, for in 1884, at age twenty-eight, he purchased for forty dollars a lot in Mount St. Mary's Cemetery on Kansas City's east side.[18]

From the beginning, Jim Pendergast's American House featured gambling devices and rooms upstairs available for short assignations. He soon enlarged the business, adding the address next door, 1326 St. Louis Avenue. In what was an early manifestation of Pendergastism, Jim's American House acted as an informal bank: a steady stream of packinghouse workers came to either cash their pay vouchers or borrow money.[19]

The banking function proved a shrewd move, for it greatly enhanced the business and gradually yet significantly increased Jim's influence in the West Bottoms. In 1884, "Big Jim," as a growing number of friends and acquaintances affectionately called him, attended the Democratic City Convention and, primarily because he was there, found himself elected as one of eleven delegates chosen to represent the "Bloody Sixth" ward in the West Bottoms. Certainly not the real start of a political career, this represented a minor and temporary honor at best. Nonetheless, it allowed the Pendergast organization to trace its origins back to 1884.[20]

Big Jim focused his immediate attention on pressing personal business and family matters. In 1886, he married Mary Kline Doerr, a woman ten years his senior with a young son, Frank, from a previous marriage.[21] Business boomed, and Jim's younger siblings soon began coming down from St. Joseph to help out. As Jim continued to expand his saloon up the 1300 block of St. Louis Avenue, his brothers John and Michael and his sisters Mary Anne, Josephine, and Margaret all moved into rooms in the American House. Jim and his new family lived close by. John and Michael both tended bar at some point, but by 1889 Michael had obtained a job as a clerk in the Jackson County recorder's office, a post that began his long public career and his practice of law. Jim's sisters and his new wife helped with the restaurant and performed domestic duties in the hotel. Young Tom occasionally appeared on weekends to visit and to do odd jobs at the American House. He later traced the start of his Kansas City experiences to 1889, when he was seventeen.[22]

Big Jim gradually increased his political activity. Kansas City had a cumbersome mayor-and-two-house city legislature system. The mayor appointed key department heads and had a veto. In the city legislature, commonly called the council, under the 1889 city charter, the upper house, elected at large, and the lower house, elected by ward, each had fourteen members.[23] Population increases ultimately caused the addition of two more members to each house. Almost all the West Bottoms was in the reconstructed First Ward, and the

Union Avenue in the heart of the West Bottoms in 1913. *(Photograph courtesy the Western Historical Manuscript Collection, Kansas City, Mo. [KC26/N238])*

business mix there made it the most important ward in the city. Aldermen from the West Bottoms seized the opportunity to exercise influence far out of proportion to the number of permanent residents and registered voters in their ward.

In 1887, Jim became a First Ward Democratic committeeman. As such, his duties involved overseeing rough and ready "mob primaries," so called by the way candidates assembled their supporters for a voice vote, usually on a street corner or in a dance hall. The trick to winning was to manipulate the election machinery, telling only friends the time and place of the meeting. Generally, this exercise in participatory democracy, supposedly intended to give unorganized voters a voice, turned into a rowdy street party. All the well-known madams and gamblers attended, along with all sorts of other lowlifes, with all the ensuing chaos reported in the newspapers. This unorthodox method of polling was great frontier fun.[24]

Jim gradually expanded his business interests and political influence. Around 1890, he purchased a saloon at 520 Main Street in downtown Kansas City, and his brother John operated it. Jim served as a committeeman until 1892, when he ran for alderman in the First Ward. He had used his post as committeeman to assiduously build a personal organization inside the locally fragmented Democratic party. Under a new amendment to the city charter ending mob primaries, party committees put forward slates of prospective candidates, with the actual nominees selected by a primary election. Running unopposed, Jim won the primary 270 to 0 and in the general election coasted to a fairly clean 555 to 180 victory over Frank Heuben, a token Republican.[25]

James Pendergast ran as a friend of the working man. Almost from the moment he took office, he gained a reputation for procuring quick releases from jail of constituents arrested for drunk and disorderly conduct. He also helped policemen in trouble with their superiors keep their posts. Furthermore, he supported police-protected gambling, under which authorities safeguarded illegal games of chance, such as floating dice games, from thieves and interlopers, who were usually from out of town. Jim's friends on the police force infrequently staged well-reported raids on gambling dives, but they usually looked the other way. During an 1897 inconclusive state investigation of gambling in Kansas City, several veteran police officers, including one who had patrolled the tenderloin for eleven years, said the only thing they knew about gambling was what they had read in the newspapers.[26]

In addition to favoring gambling, which he claimed was the harmless recreation of the common man, Jim distributed welfare to the poor, primarily in the form of bags of coal and an occasional holiday turkey. He solidified gambling support by leading a successful effort to block antigambling reforms proposed by the heavily Republican and upper-class Kansas City Civic Federation. Aided by gambling donations, he expanded his welfare activities and rebuilt a crumbling Democratic organization in the North End for his own purposes. He easily won reelection in the West Bottoms, earning the title "King of the First."[27]

Jim never sought a higher office. William Southern Jr., the editor of the *Jackson Examiner* in nearby Independence, Missouri, claimed to know why: "The office was only a means to accomplish other things he liked to do. It gave him patronage and it was patronage he used in politics." Southern considered Jim "a man of force and character" who believed in "hitting blow for blow when in a war, but in always repaying a kindness in kind." According to Southern, an understanding of both people and politics served Jim well: "Sporadic reformers do not often get permanent results. They do not understand human nature, they do not mix with the everyday affairs and understand the springs which move men. Pendergast understood all these things. He was a square man and his word was good. This was true in politics as well as in business."[28]

Kansas City mounted police in the 1890s. *(Photograph courtesy the Western Historical Manuscript Collection, Kansas City, Mo. [KC26/N239])*

Once, reflecting on his role, Alderman Jim discoursed on how a boss operates: "And, by the way, that's all there is to this 'boss' business—friends. You can't coerce people into doing things for you—you can't make them vote for you. I never coerced anybody in my life. Whenever you see a man bulldozing anybody he don't last long. Still, I've been called a boss. All there is to it is having friends, doing things for people, and then later on they'll do things for you."[29] This statement was standard boss fare, and could just as well have been made by any of hundreds of American rural and urban politicians. Yet, Alderman Jim was more than just another local boss. He pioneered the Pendergast organization and taught his style of city politics to a very apt pupil, his youngest brother, Thomas J. Pendergast.

TOM PENDERGAST'S FORMATIVE YEARS

Sometime during the 1880s, Tom Pendergast, watching his brothers and sisters one after another abandon St. Joseph for Kansas City, decided that after finishing his education he would leave home and follow them. Jim's success clearly had a fundamental impact on Tom's future career.

Tom Pendergast claimed that he attended Christian Brothers College in St. Joseph for four years and that he received his high school diploma from the school, which was administered by a Roman Catholic order. Christian Brothers records, fragmentary prior to 1889, fail to list him as either a student or a graduate. However, classmates from the school remembered him as a friendly and cheerful fellow who was a poor student in most subjects, but excellent in mathematics and a good baseball player.[30]

Furthermore, Pendergast said that he went to college for two years, leaving school at age twenty. Maurice Milligan, the United States Attorney responsible for his prosecution, asserted in a 1948 account that Pendergast did not attend "St. Mary's College" in Kansas on a baseball scholarship. Neither of the two colleges of that name in Kansas, one in St. Marys and the other in Leavenworth, list him as ever registering. Similarly, a report that he enrolled at Christian Brothers College in St. Louis proved a false lead. Treasury agents said he graduated from the St. Joseph Christian Brothers at age fourteen and then attended two years of college in "St. Mary," Kansas. And so it goes. St. Joseph had two business schools in the 1880s, but their records have been lost. Some of his friends maintained that for a time Tom enrolled as a student at a business college located in a downtown St. Joseph building.[31]

The conflicting stories about Pendergast's formal education are both confusing and interesting. With no records to be found at any of the schools at which he supposedly matriculated, it appears unlikely that he attended college for two years. However, since he did exhibit some bookkeeping skills, it is quite possible that he attended one of the local commercial colleges for a time. Most likely, though, in order to lift himself and his wife from their social roots in the rowdy West Bottoms, he inflated his educational background to give himself and his family increased validity in a world of the rich and powerful. The problem was that he did not keep his story straight, so different versions of his educational background became embedded in local myth, only to surface later, as new accounts of the Pendergast era were written.[32]

St. Joseph business directories contain some information on Pendergast's early employment experiences. His first real job was working for a railroad at age fifteen. In 1890, at age eighteen, he held a position as a "laborer," a generic term for unskilled workers, on the Kansas City, St. Joseph, and Council Bluffs Railroad. During 1891, he was a "clerk," another generic term, for the Chicago, Burlington, and Quincy Railroad. The 1892 directory does not give an occupation for him, but the 1893 guide lists him as working for the Wyeth Hardware and Manufacturing Company. In 1894, he was again called a "laborer." At some point around 1890, a St. Joseph man recalled, "Tom Pendergast was driving a grocery wagon then for Frank Kessler, who had a store at about Nineteenth and Frederick Avenue."[33]

On June 30, 1893, when Tom still lived in St. Joseph, his father died of a massive heart attack at age sixty-seven. His mother continued to reside at the 1715 Frederick Avenue residence until her own death from heart disease at age sixty-eight on December 27, 1902. The two St. Joseph newspapers did not carry Mike's death notice, but Mary received obituaries, probably owing to Jim's rising importance.[34]

Tom moved permanently to Kansas City by late 1894, when he was twenty-two. He had frequently visited his brothers and sisters at the American House, and now that he was ready to join the family business, Tom began an apprenticeship in politics with his brother Jim. Although Tom always claimed he had never poured a drop of liquor for a living—the task was generally considered below the social standing of a high school graduate with two years of college—the 1895 *Kansas City Business Directory* lists his occupation as "bartender." He lived at 1715 West 9th Street, the address of a new family enterprise, the Pendergast Brothers Saloon, owned jointly by Jim and John.

Tom Pendergast's formative years ended when he permanently departed St. Joseph and took up residence in Kansas City. He had experienced the good fortune to reach adulthood in a stable home with caring parents who helped him achieve the maturity to venture into the world with confidence. The very fact that Tom grew up at the end of the western frontier seemed to bode well, presumably imparting the values of rugged individualism much admired by contemporary observers. The brighter side of the frontier experience encouraged opportunity and experimentation. Another, perhaps less desirable, aspect promoted a live-for-the-moment attitude. Casting off the restraints of society meant a tacit acquiescence to forms of lawlessness and vice. While the Kansas City of the Gay Nineties had officially, according to government demographers, passed out of the frontier stage, it remained very much a wide-open place, exemplified by the obstreperous West Bottoms. Given his brother Jim's business acumen, political sagacity, and growing influence, this was precisely the part of town in which Tom Pendergast intended to seek his fortune.

Two

Apprenticeship

1895–1910

When Tom Pendergast, a robust and stocky youth, arrived in Kansas City to stay in 1894, he impressed people as possessing a remarkable similarity to Jim. Like his older brother, Tom was powerfully built and in excellent shape. A broad nose gave him a pugilistic face; combined with a bull neck, wide shoulders, and a barrel chest, it made his appearance formidable. Muscular arms with matching fists, which he was ready and willing to use, provided a touch of menace. Tom was usually friendly and controlled, but a quick temper always lay just below the surface. He appreciated a good joke, but was not given to small talk. He looked the part of a powerful baseball "slugger," and acquaintances readily accepted his claim that he had turned down a minor-league contract in the Western League in order to attend college to play baseball and football on an athletic scholarship. In April 1936, he told a reporter, "I might have been better off, happier, today if I had gone into professional baseball."[1]

By the Gay Nineties, the Kansas City that became Tom's Town had markedly changed from the roaring, overgrown frontier camp that Jim had arrived in two decades earlier. A rapid population increase had swelled the census figures from the 50,000 to the 200,000 range. Still very much a cow town, Kansas City entertained pretensions of rising to the status of "the Philadelphia of the West." The city proper lay directly south of the Missouri River and east of its juncture with the Kansas River. From the Missouri, it was about three miles to the southern city limits along 31st Street. From the West Bottoms, the city extended five miles to the east. The city's surface, gradually graded into the steep riverbanks above the flat West Bottoms, was undulating and covered with scrub vegetation and thick underbrush. The heart of the West Bottoms was approximately one mile square. Above the West Bottoms was the North End, later called the North Side, which contained downtown and housing areas directly east. Residential districts farther to the east constituted an East Side, and the part of town south of downtown was called the South Side.

Kansas City had a gridiron street design. Comprehensive planning and beautification seemed afterthoughts. There were few open squares and, for all practical purposes, no parks. Other than the downtown buildings, the packing plants, and a few large mansions on Quality Hill, wooden structures predominated, with detached individual dwellings, numerous rooming houses, and some apartments. An obvious characteristic of Kansas City was a jumbled appearance. About the only open spaces were the large and sooty railroad yards in the West Bottoms.

Kansas City maintained the most impressive central business district of any place between the Mississippi River and the Pacific Coast. The city had risen so fast that, unlike many eastern towns, it had no obvious main street. Delaware, Main, Broadway, and Grand Avenue, widened to accommodate commercial traffic, numbered among the principal north–south thoroughfares. Large modern edifices, among them the landmark New York Life Building and the New England Building, lined 9th Street. The Victorian Board of Trade Building attested to Kansas City's role as a grain futures market. There were a number of new playhouses, including the first-class Gillis House and Willis Wood Theater. A one-block-square department store, Emery-Bird-Thayer, attracted patrons from miles around. The best hotels were the older Coates House and the newer Savoy, Midland, and Baltimore. The massive Convention Hall was one of the largest structures of its kind in the United States. Street railroad tracks radiated out of downtown. An elevated transit line connected the North End and the West Bottoms.

Easily delineated ethnic and class arrangements further defined Kansas City, which was very much a blue-collar town. Black people accounted for 9 percent of residents, and while some of them lived in the West Bottoms, they were largely concentrated in a very poor community on the East Side. At a time when the proportion of immigrants in many northern cities crossed the 30 percent line, only 11 percent of Kansas Citians declared places of birth outside this country. Recently arrived Italians in Columbus Park, a North End enclave just east of downtown, were a noticeable and compact group. The bulk of native-born Kansas Citians, black and white, hailed from Missouri or nearby states. Kansas City had only a small middle class. A coterie of Protestant white Anglo-Saxon businessmen dominated and shaped community policy.[2]

Kansas City's business leadership in the 1890s, looking forward from a successful past, demonstrated self-confidence sometimes bordering on arrogance.

A view from a large, specially constructed kite of downtown Kansas City in 1900, with the Convention Hall in the left background. *(Photograph courtesy the Grace and Holy Trinity Cathedral Archives)*

Older entrepreneurs traced their roots back to a turbulent post–Civil War era. New investors came from New England and Chicago to manage railroads, establish regional headquarters, construct packing plants, and develop real estate. They sought to transfer eastern cultural life to Kansas City, establishing social clubs patterned after those in New England. Both old and new capitalists banded together to form the Commercial Club, a forerunner of the modern Greater Kansas City Chamber of Commerce.[3]

The elitist members of the Commercial Club saw their responsibilities almost exclusively in terms of driving Kansas City ahead economically. They exhibited almost a mystical faith in their ability to accomplish seemingly impossible deeds against great odds. A favorite proposition held that Kansas City would continue to advance as long as the men of the Commercial Club remained in control. The members of the club had little interest in politics, beyond supporting those elected officials who were friendly to business. This attitude extended to considering the public welfare. After a prolonged downturn followed on the heels of the national panic of 1893, the club decided its responsibility was to bring about a return of prosperity and did not extend to handing out charity to the unfortunate. The general attitude was that those who objected could always leave town.[4]

The Commercial Club's decision to stay out of relief work was made to order for James Pendergast, for Kansas City had no public welfare department as such, and under the weight of depression conditions, private assistance broke down. As might have been expected, rampant unemployment hit the river wards of the West Bottoms and North End. In response, Jim seized the opportunity to greatly expand his own welfare efforts. Few looked very deeply for the source of the money he used in these efforts; although no one could be sure, more than likely the source was gambling interests. Through an uncharacteristic blunder, the Kansas City business community, almost by default, allowed Big Jim to assume a crucial function and to take credit for saving the city from social disintegration.[5] At the same time, Jim greatly extended the power and prestige of his faction. None of this was lost on brother Tom. He saw firsthand the political benefits of providing relief for constituents and the necessity of getting help from illicit sources, in this case gambling.

Tom's Entrance to Kansas City Politics

Tom soon took a room at Jim's American House, emulating his older brothers and sisters. By his own account, he worked at various temporary and seasonal jobs. For a while, he was a "number catcher" for the Burlington railroad, recording the serial numbers on boxcars in the freightyards. He also clerked in a hardware store and at a wholesale house. In short, he performed the variety of tasks people do when they are just beginning their careers. On many evenings and weekends, he helped out in his brother's saloons. A seasonal task that he found especially interesting involved operating—with another ambitious young man, Casimir Welch, who was considered a ruffian by many people—a liquor and food concession that Jim Pendergast had at a local horse-race track, the Kansas City Driving Club. Here, Tom furthered his gambling instincts and acquired a lifelong fascination with "the sport of kings."[6]

Stories circulated that he was as proficient a bouncer as any of his fellows in the West Bottoms, beating up unruly customers and throwing them out the door. This aspect of Tom's training, whether it was true or not, gave him a reputation for violence that caused people to think carefully before crossing him. Furthermore, it caused people to underestimate his innate cunning and intelligence: one political opponent at first dismissed Tom as a "thick-skulled heavy-jowled oaf."[7]

Patrons enjoy a beautiful day at a Kansas City beer garden in 1903. *(Photograph courtesy the Native Sons Archives [KC590/N98], Western Historical Manuscript Collection, Kansas City, Mo.)*

As a matter of course, Tom soon became an integral part of Alderman Jim's entourage. In 1894, Jim, calling in a political favor, secured an appointment for Tom as a deputy constable in a First Ward city court. While holding this undemanding job that mainly involving ushering petty offenders in and out of court, Tom recalled voting for the first time in Kansas City: "I cast my first vote while I was deputy constable. I don't remember who the candidate was, but I am sure he was a Democrat." In 1896, Tom received a better patronage post, as a deputy marshal in county court, which paid him a salary of $100 a month. Such a handsome salary by 1890s depression standards freed him from needing extra employment to make ends meet. Tom's bailiff duties gave him plenty of free hours for political chores, and Jim championed his appointment to several municipal and county committees.[8] In looking after Jim's interests, Tom began his education on the finer points of politics, Kansas City style.

Jim gradually moved Tom directly into grassroots political work, making him a precinct captain. Tom found nothing wrong with being a ward heeler; he saw the nitty-gritty of dealing with the concerns of constituents as part of his education. He later stated, "My precinct was composed of Negroes, bohunks, and Irish." He came to understand life along old Union Avenue in the heart of the tenderloin, a fading but still colorful reminder of Kansas City's frontier heritage. Clyde Brian Davis, a longtime Kansas City reporter, caught the essence of conditions there at that time: "All was bustle along the narrow unpaved street—bustle and noise. There was the clatter of draft horses and steel-tired trucks and the roar of the elevated trolley cars above. The strangest thing was the chorus of barkers outside the cheap clothing stores and pawn shops and novelty bazaars and saloons along the street. Every doorway had its barkers like those before circus sideshows." Davis quoted one barker, who would yell, "Right here—biggest beer in K.C. for a nickel."[9]

Tom learned how to get out the vote, along with such methods of stealing elections as counting ballots twice and cheating in filling out tally sheets. One important duty of his on election day was to make sure that the homeless from the flophouses went to the polls to vote, usually several times. Another ploy was to make sure that lines of voters favoring the Pendergast side had formed prior to the opening of the polls and then to regulate the pace at which voters cast their ballots, in this way discouraging many potential opposition voters from waiting in the long, slow lines. To make arrangements as comfortable as possible for his people, Tom would provide them with chairs.[10] In performing his tasks, it dawned on Tom that there might be other, easier ways to swing elections than rousing derelicts and gandy dancers out of their quarters and regulating polling lines.

Bitterly fought Democratic primaries convinced Tom that in the rough-and-tumble politics of Kansas City, having a system and planning ahead were more important than ideology in winning elections. Although hardly diplomatic, Tom exhibited far less calculating combativeness than his brother Mike, who considered politics a war. Mike once boldly entered a saloon frequented by his political enemies, invited them up to the bar, bought them a round of beer, raised a schooner in a toast, and, with their guards down, threw beer in their faces. He emerged from the brawl that followed somewhat the worse for wear, as he expected, "But," he afterwards told friends, "it was worth it."[11] That kind of thing simply was not Tom's style. He preferred cutting deals and stacking the odds in his favor. Before long, recognizing talent when he saw it, Jim promoted Tom from precinct captain to captain of the First Ward. In addition, Jim used Tom as floor leader of the Pendergast faction at Democratic city and county conventions.

JAMES A. REED

Quite naturally, the Pendergast brothers sought a talented, respectable, and attractive candidate who could win citywide elections and extend their faction's influence beyond the river wards. They found such a man in James A. Reed. Born on an Ohio farm in 1861, Reed grew up on a farm outside Cedar Rapids, Iowa, briefly attended Coe Collegiate Institute, and successfully read for the law. He moved to Kansas City in 1887 and opened a profitable legal practice. An active Democrat, he professed no interest in elected office, confining his efforts to giving speeches. That was before an evening in 1896 when he attended a gathering in a smoke-filled room at a Democratic club. Thirty years later, Reed, pacing back and forth in his Kansas City law office, lamented to a journalist, "If my life has any turning point, then that is it. Everything started there."[12]

Reed recalled that a friend he called "Tom" approached him and began the recruiting process: "Hello, Jim. I hear you are going to be appointed county counselor." Reed replied, "I hadn't heard about it. I would not take a political office, anyway." Tom handed Reed a cigar to put him at ease and casually asked, "That isn't usually regarded as a political office, is it?" Reed remarked on second thought, "Well, no, I guess it isn't." In retrospect, he decided that right then and there he had made a mistake in judgment. Tom soothingly said, "It is one of those advisory jobs. An opinion when it is needed is all there is to it. Let's go over here and sit down." Right away, another friend joined the conversation. Without preliminaries, he said, "Hello, Jim. I hear you are going to be county counselor."[13] Reluctantly, Reed accepted the job.

As Reed had feared, his decision started a long political career that led down the road to the United States Senate and national notoriety as an opponent of Woodrow Wilson and the League of Nations. Reed recounted, "That wasn't supposed to be a political job but the effect was just the same. Friends had done something for me and expected me to return the favor. Of course that was all right; but I got in deeper all the time." In early January of 1897, Reed, described as a "Free Silver Democrat" and a member of the Knights of Pythias, received a two-year appointment at an annual salary of $3,000 to the post of county counselor, which is equivalent to the modern position of county prosecutor.[14]

In 1898, with the help of Jim Pendergast and considerable gambling money, Reed won his first elective post as prosecuting attorney of Jackson County. After assuming office, he concentrated on dealing with what he considered serious crimes, curtailing his predecessor's crusade against illegal gambling. In two years, Reed tried 287 criminal cases, winning 285. Next, in 1900, again with strong support from the Pendergast faction, he ran for a two-year mayoral term as a "reformer," winning a sweeping victory. Perhaps, at that juncture, Reed failed to fully realize the consequences of a Pendergast connection. Much later, he reflected, "A man who ever takes a political office is mortgaged for the rest of his life." Reed made this candid comment to *Kansas*

City Star journalist Richard Fowler in a 1929 interview intended to result in a favorable feature article. On second thought, Reed asked and Fowler agreed to take out almost all the direct quotations. Reed kept a copy of the draft containing the quotations he wanted cut in his personal papers.[15]

The election of James A. Reed as mayor marked the emergence of Alderman Jim as a substantial force in citywide Kansas City politics. Throughout the 1890s, Jim had expanded his business and political interests more or less in concert to the point that they appeared virtually inseparable. He opened a second saloon, this one downtown at 508 Main Street. Jim used this popular saloon, which at one time had seven dice tables, as his headquarters. At one time or another, five other Pendergast siblings worked directly with Jim: Tom and Mike handled political tasks. Josephine, who married Richard Moore in 1892, and Margaret, married in 1892 to George Klingbeil, helped out in one way or another. So did Mary Anne until she married William Costello around 1903 and moved back to St. Joseph.[16]

JAMES PENDERGAST AND JOSEPH SHANNON

On March 28, 1900, the *Kansas City Star* published a favorable account of how Alderman Jim directed his faction at election time in the "pungent and vitalizing atmosphere" of his Main Street barroom. As election day approached, Jim, very much in charge, offered "wise counsel" to his troops. In dramatic fashion, a *Star* writer commented on the significance of it all: "What need, indeed, has he for halls or stages or rostrums? Here gather the candidates, to learn how the battle is waging. Here assemble the leaders to confer together. Here come the humble toilers in the Democratic vineyard to receive their instructions. . . . It is not necessary for him to move out of his place to find anybody he can use or wants to help. The post of duty is the place for Pendergast. If his ward wants him it has but to call at the back or the front door and he is ready." A campaign rally of ten thousand Reed supporters at the Convention Hall was as much a tribute to Jim's personal power as to the popularity of the candidate.[17]

Jim Pendergast's wider field of operations accentuated growing differences with Joseph B. Shannon over the running of the Democratic party in Kansas City and Jackson County. Shannon, born in St. Louis in 1867, had lived in Kansas City since his twelfth birthday. The tall and suave Shannon learned politics on the street and by working as an aide to a railroad lobbyist in Jefferson City. A self-taught political philosopher, he greatly admired the writings of Thomas Jefferson and had a lifelong thirst for knowledge. Shannon considered himself a Jeffersonian Democrat and loved to quote the Sage of Monticello at length. Despite his scholarly predilections, Shannon was a tough and sometimes inexorable politician. His base of support was the Ninth Ward, southeast of downtown.[18]

Joseph Shannon and James Pendergast had more in common than being Democratic politicians. Jim only drank liquor occasionally and Joe not at all. Both had reputations for keeping their word; both were Irish, about which much was made by the press; and both were native-born Americans. Even though neither was born in Kansas City, both were longtime residents. They had cut their teeth practicing the rough-and-tumble style of infighting that characterized political activity in the growing cow town. At times they cooperated, such as in 1894, when they worked together to oppose the anti-immigrant, anti–Roman Catholic, and anti–Irish American Protective Association.

Alderman Jim's adherents called themselves "Goat" Democrats and Shannon's called themselves "Rabbits." Goat and rabbit symbols appeared at the tops of their slates on primary ballots, ostensively to help illiterates vote straight tickets. The names retained wide usage as shorthand political parlance in Kansas City until well after World War II. Hence, Harry S. Truman was a Goat. No one was sure about the origins of the designations. Possibly, the term "Rabbit" stemmed from an observation by Shannon that his accurate political intelligence came from having "rabbits," meaning informers, on every street corner. Another explanation held that Shannon men flocked to the polls in close elections like scared rabbits. Different versions also obscured the origin of the Goats' nickname. One held that Pendergast cohorts in the First Ward owned goats. A second attributed the nomenclature to Pendergast voters who lived in shanties clinging to the sides of the West Bluffs like mountain goats. A third explanation, much favored by anti-Pendergast people, claimed that the appellation referred to the large number of billy goats that the Pendergasts registered to vote in the First Ward.[19]

Destructive primary clashes between Jim Pendergast and Joe Shannon, starting in 1894, carried over into general elections, frequently to the detriment of both Goats and Rabbits. Now and then, including the 1900 elections for many city and county offices, both sides offered rival candidates in the general election. In a few cases, one or the other of the two sides formed temporary alliances with the Republicans. All the considerable number of patronage positions went to the victor, making the stakes very high. Sometimes the Goats and the Rabbits canceled each other out, bringing about Republican victories and no patronage for either Democratic faction. According to a veteran political observer, the Goats and the Rabbits "hated each other more than they did their common enemy, the Republicans."[20]

On August 29, 1900, following a bitter and divisive Democratic county convention, the Goats formed the Jackson Democratic Club. The new organization spent $4,000 to establish a lodge in the Navajo Building at 716 Delaware

The Aldermen of Kansas City baseball team, with Jim Pendergast, identified as shortstop, third from left in the middle row, ca. 1890s. *(Photograph from the Kansas City Museum Archives)*

Street—only a couple of blocks from Jim's Main Street saloon. The large and ample quarters featured billiard parlors, committee chambers, lunch rooms, and, of course, a wet bar. A twelve-hundred-seat auditorium, a former theater, served as a centerpiece and gathering place for club functions. By 1902, the Jackson Democratic Club claimed twelve hundred members. According to a flattering paragraph in a handbook on Jackson County politics, "The club is now on a firm foundation and grows and increases as a powerful instrument for the good of the party."[21] Left unsaid was that the Jackson Democratic Club furthered the interests of Jim Pendergast—who held no official club office—as the cornerstone of his family political enterprise.

To resolve an increasingly destructive situation, Pendergast and Shannon moved toward a compromise that became known in Kansas City as the "Fifty-Fifty" accord.[22] If they could not agree on candidates, they battled each other in the primaries, usually with great vehemence. However, they presented a unified front in general elections. There was nothing unusual in that, except for the Fifty-Fifty. In theory it ensured unity. No matter who won, a Goat or a Rabbit, the winner divided all patronage equally between the two factions.

Although it looked fine on paper, distrust continued. Double crosses led to under-the-table deals with the Republicans. Both the Goats and the Rabbits cheated on the Fifty-Fifty, and they continued to appear more as mortal enemies than as allies.

Given the common backgrounds of Jim and Joe, they should have qualified as friendly enemies. And, after all, they both belonged to the Democratic party. A reporter who knew them both discounted their differences. "While this may all be true as to jealousies caused by the distribution of political pie, the two leaders did not permit the breach to enter into their personal friendships," he claimed. "They thought the world of each other politically and socially, and although they had their tilts and strife for supremacy at the primaries and conventions, it was forgotten, and on election day they stood shoulder to shoulder against the political enemy."[23] If that evaluation was correct, the two men did a good job of masking their true feelings about each other; except for occasional commiserating and shedding crocodile tears over political matters, for political reasons they gave no public indication that they were friends. Few people knew that Jim Pendergast, in one of his last political acts only four months prior to his death, had secretly directed, with Shannon's knowledge, an aborted effort to make Shannon a congressman.[24]

TOM PENDERGAST'S FIRST POLITICAL POSITIONS

The election of James A. Reed as mayor in 1900 serves as an example of the Pendergast machine's sometimes selecting capable and appealing candidates rather than simply men who would work with the machine. The Pendergasts tried to keep men like Reed "money honest," constraining them away from the temptation of receiving ill-gotten gains. Of course, in return for support, the Pendergasts expected unflinching "loyalty." Reed furthered his own prestige with an eloquent welcoming address before the 1900 Democratic National Convention in Kansas City. The Pendergasts basked in reflected glory, and promoting Reed's career became a project that transcended political advantages. Tom even hung a picture of Reed in his office.[25]

At least in the beginning, Reed was unappreciative, seeing being mayor as a necessary evil in furthering his career. He recounted, "That meant absolutely nothing but sacrifice. I had to resign a $5,000 job for one that paid $3,000. As mayor I had less time for my private practice than I had as prosecutor." In his first term, he experienced what he called "two years of hell." He won a hard-fought reelection in 1902 with the help of about thirty young lawyers, he claimed, neglecting to mention the Pendergasts or Shannon. Reed spent two terms fighting the utility interests and gaining some new regulatory ordinances. He did not seek a third term in 1904, instead making an aborted bid for governor. He remained in politics, and in 1910 a Democratic Missouri legislature elected him to the United States Senate.[26]

One of Reed's first moves as mayor had been to appoint Tom Pendergast, then twenty-eight years old, to a two-year term as the Kansas City superintendent of streets. Reed's zeal for reform did not extend to neglecting to settle his outstanding political obligations. During his first term, for example, he allowed Jim Pendergast to name 123 policemen out of a total force of 173 officers.[27] The superintendency paid Tom $2,000 a year and carried with it 250 jobs for him to fill, a plum for the expanding Pendergast faction. Reed felt there was no way a street superintendent could build a record of success, explaining, "The company that had the paving contract let the streets go to pieces."[28]

From all accounts, Tom took his duties seriously. He did as well as could probably have been expected, given the unpromising circumstances. Not content to sit in his office barking orders, as he easily could have done, he went into the streets to direct operations. "He has given his entire time and attention to the work," according to an admiring observer, "and his figure is a familiar one on the streets, standing in a snow storm in winter, or the boiling sun in summer, superintending the work of his men."[29]

The position was a valuable learning experience for Tom. On one hand, he came to see the possibilities for enrichment from lucrative contracts for street paving and repair. On the other hand, he saw that the public generally paid much more attention to the condition of the streets than to what was going on behind closed doors at city hall. The quick filling of potholes garnered instantaneous goodwill, giving the impression of a well-run city in which officials paid attention to the little things. The *Star*, normally opposed to the Pendergasts, even praised Tom: "The position has been a difficult and thankless one owing to the lack of sufficient funds to do the work. But Mr. Pendergast's record has been highly satisfactory, especially to the business men of Kansas City."[30] Reed reappointed Tom, but he resigned shortly afterwards to run for an elective office.

In 1902, Tom benefited from a newfound harmony between the Goats and the Rabbits. By acclamation, the Jackson County Democratic Convention nominated him for a two-year term as county marshal. In this instance, the *Star* opposed him, citing gambling connections: "His associations have not been conducive to the best equipment for public office." Even so, Pendergast, emphasizing his prior experience as a deputy county marshal, won by more than 5,200 votes, piling up huge margins in the river wards; he carried the First Ward by a vote of 797 to 190. A writer for the *Kansas City World*, with what proved considerable understatement, observed: "He is just turned 30 and there is every prospect that he is going to make a marked impression on the local history of the next decade or so. . . . He is a man of marked executive ability—as he has demonstrated in his conduct of the street department. He is a courteous gentleman, too, and immensely popular with all who know him."[31]

As marshal, Pendergast received a salary of $4,000 a year, double that of street superintendent. His marshal responsibilities included most Jackson County criminal matters, while the sheriff assumed the civil duties. In addition to keeping order in the courts, the marshal's men served warrants, transported prisoners, and ran correctional facilities. The Republican editor of the *Rising Son*, which had a black readership, described Marshal Pendergast as a reformer: "Mr. Pendergast's term as marshal established a new era in penal progress. He stood for the Negro as well as the white man. No cruel treatment of prisoners. No jail scandals."[32] At Christmas in 1903, with his own money, Tom purchased fourteen turkeys for a holiday feast for the prisoners in the Jackson County jail.

Tom lost reelection as county marshal in 1904 and again for the same office two years later. The Fifty-Fifty compromise held both times and the river wards delivered as usual, but massive Republican majorities in both elections swamped Democratic candidates. In 1908, temporarily giving up elective politics, Tom accepted another term as street superintendent from a new Democratic mayor, Thomas T. Crittenden Jr. By then, what had been a big step upward for Tom in 1900 appeared almost a comedown from county marshal. Increasingly, he involved himself in the daily affairs of the Pendergast organization. In commenting on his political skills, a reporter lauded "Brother Tom's" performance in the "copper-riveted" river wards: "He has all the Pendergast attributes of caring for and fostering the interests of the residents of those wards and finds time to keep a careful eye out for the interests of his friends generally."[33] Brother Tom looked more and more like the logical successor of Alderman Jim.

Jim's Departure from the Scene

Alderman James Pendergast had talked about giving up his seat on the city council as early as 1900, when he won a fifth term over token opposition. He told a reporter, "This is my last term in politics. I'm positively going to retire." He said his wife, Mary, wanted a home away from the "midst of the business blocks" in the West Bottoms. But he remained in elective politics, running successfully four more times from the First Ward—in 1902, 1904, 1906, and finally in 1908. Mary died in 1905, and close friends noticed afterwards "a lack of the former liveliness" that had impressed many people as Jim's greatest attribute. He embraced religion and actively tried to persuade young Roman Catholic boys to join the Father Matthew Temperance Society.

His saloons and interests in liquor wholesaling, real estate developing, and paving contracting seemed of less significance to him.[34] So did politics.

Not long after Jim triumphed in his last campaign, 1,333 to 443, he expressed an interest in retiring to a farm he owned close to Kansas City in Johnson County, Kansas: "Here I've been dragging myself down to City Hall, acting like a mule one day and a messenger boy the next for nearly seventeen years and yours truly has had his fill." At age fifty-two, he said that he was "dog tired" of squabbling and fighting, no longer finding politics "great sport." What he planned to do was lie back in a chair and feel sorry for all the "suckers" in Kansas City. "It's me for Johnson County, the alfalfa and the flowing lace curtains," he claimed. "It's going to be Farmer Jim from now on to the end of the race."[35]

Jim left the council in 1910 and turned his seat over to Tom, who won election easily. By then, Jim was too ill to spend time on the farm. He did leave the West Bottoms, though; he moved in with his sister and brother-in-law, Margaret and George Klingbeil, at their home south of downtown at 2307 Prospect Street. Jim had suffered from severe respiratory ailments for a decade, and had taken extended trips to Texas, California, and Minnesota seeking recovery, with only temporary success. To compound matters, he contracted acute Bright's disease of the kidneys. In September of 1911, he took to bed, having little hope of recovery. His brothers and sisters maintained day and night vigils. For long periods, he lay unconscious. On November 10 at 4 P.M., he woke and asked a nurse, "Where is Tom?" Tom hurried to his bedside. Jim looked at him and said in a cheerful and strong voice, "Hello Tom." Those were his last comprehensible words. He sank rapidly and died around 7 P.M.[36]

Within an hour after his death, as word spread, Kansas City political and business leaders began to appear at the Klingbeil home to offer condolences. Friends recalled his support of boulevards and parks, and his acquiescence, apparently counter to his own interests, to relocating the Union Station to a site on the southern edge of downtown, away from the West Bottoms. Obituaries, ignoring his gambling ties, referred to his charitable contributions, praising his generosity to victims of the calamitous 1903 flood. The notices of Jim's death viewed his eighteen years on the council in terms of his lack of demagoguery, his calming influence, and his attempts at compromise. One obituary quoted his favorite philosophical epigram, posted behind the bars in his saloons: "You can't saw wood with a hammer."[37]

Jim's final resting place was beside his wife in Mount St. Mary's Cemetery in the plot he had purchased back in 1884. His will, signed July 5, 1911, left all his property equally to his brothers and sisters, except for $1,000 to his housekeeper "for kindness to me"; $17 per month to care for "Mrs. Doerr's boy," Jim's stepson, Frank Doerr; and $500 to the "Father Dalton Church"

The new Union Station, which Jim Pendergast supported even though it took traffic away from his West Bottoms saloon district, under construction in the early 1910s. *(Photograph courtesy the Howard F. Sachs Collection [KC950/N1], Western Historical Manuscript Collection, Kansas City, Mo.)*

for an altar in his wife's memory.[38] Father William J. Dalton was the Roman Catholic priest of the Church of the Annunciation in the West Bottoms.

WILLIAM ROCKHILL NELSON

Kansas City Star editor and publisher William Rockhill Nelson, a towering figure in Kansas City and a national leader of the Republican party, gave Jim a positive obituary in the *Star*'s morning edition, the *Kansas City Times*. The notice stressed that while Jim had engaged in rough and "sharp" political dealings, particularly in his battles with Shannon and the Rabbits, his code of ethics called for never breaking his word or accepting cash for his votes: "Alderman Jim's political power was established by his generosity, his big heartedness to do favors for the 'boys,' to 'go to the front' for one who was in trouble, get jobs and do various little acts of kindness for those who were in need. Besides there was implicit faith in his honesty."[39]

Nelson and Jim Pendergast were, each in their own way, successful city builders. Both, as practical individuals, arrived in Kansas City ready to grow with the town. Nelson, from Indiana, founded the *Star* in 1880 after a careful study of Kansas City's prospects. His newspaper, championing the business community and civic-improvement projects, soon dominated the Kansas City market. He branched out into real estate, becoming immensely wealthy. Originally a Democrat, he joined the Republican party as a friend of Theodore Roosevelt and as a spokesperson for Progressive Republicanism.[40] Nelson, called the "Baron of Brush Creek" because of the proximity of Brush Creek, four miles south of downtown, to his large mansion, Oak Hall, and neighboring real estate holdings, made the *Star* more than just a successful newspaper. It prospered and became a proud and confident institution considered by Nelson the embodiment of all that was good in Kansas City. Nelson, who privately called his paper "The Daily W. R. Nelson," boasted, "The *Star* never loses." Defining the editorial role of his paper in Kansas City, Nelson once said, "The *Star* has denounced outrages by whomever perpetrated."[41] Critics, though, believed the *Star* displayed a holier-than-thou attitude.

In spite of their political differences, Jim Pendergast and William Nelson cooperated on a number of projects, including the building of a comprehensive park system. Nelson provided the publicity and gained the backing of the Republican leaders of the Commercial Club. Pendergast delivered Democratic votes in a crucial 1893 special bond election. Although both men had an interest in living in an attractive city, other possible reasons for this atypical teamwork merit consideration. Generally, property values rose along parks and boulevards, helping real estate developers such as Nelson. And Pendergast perceived potential benefits in the form of construction contracts and patronage jobs.[42]

The occasional meeting of mutual concerns between the *Star* and the Pendergast organization did not last long after the passing of Jim Pendergast. Nelson learned to dislike and vilify Tom Pendergast and all his works, and used his newspaper to foster bitter hostilities that continued long after Nelson's death in 1915. For the next several decades, the *Star* was hard to separate from the Republican party in Kansas City: the paper was devoted to business interests and even selected candidates.

Tom's Maturing Interests

While a young man, Tom looked and behaved more like a professional gambler and ruffian than an aspiring political and civic leader. He sported a full head of sandy-colored hair and a stylish handlebar mustache. Checkered suits and a derby—the type of dress favored by gangsters and gamblers—accentuated his large muscular frame. He was a familiar figure and something of a local hero in the saloons and bawdy houses of the West Bottoms, and he frequented Sullivan's, a popular pub in the North End, singing Irish songs and drinking

William Rockhill Nelson, editor and publisher of the *Kansas City Star*, ca. 1897. (*Photograph courtesy the Native Sons Archives [KC590/N169], Western Historical Manuscript Collection, Kansas City, Mo.*)

beer. In his early years, Tom spent Saturday nights on the town, and on hot summer Sunday afternoons he especially enjoyed excursions with his cronies to baseball games or horse races. He sought the company of the kind of women who frequented the West Bottoms, but he did not have a reputation as a womanizer and kept quiet about his affairs. He lived rather simply at the American House and with some regularity attended Sunday mass. No stories circulated in later years about any unusual behavior or tastes. Tom later managed to separate his uptown life from that in the red-light district, a circumstance that Nelson and many other prominent Kansas Citians found repugnant and unacceptable.[43]

Details concerning Tom Pendergast's marriage are unclear. Tom always stated that he married in 1907. A 1911 newspaper account, however, reported that he and Carolyn Elizabeth Dunn Snider were married in a civil ceremony in Belleville, Illinois, on January 25, 1911. Tom said the marriage was the result of a long-standing engagement and that they had gone to the Illinois city, near St. Louis, to avoid publicity. "Carrie," as Tom's new wife was called, was from a West Bottoms family.

In February 1911, the Pendergasts were married again in a private Roman Catholic ceremony performed by Father Frank T. Walsh. Their first daughter, Marceline Cecelia, was born in April 1911. A son, Thomas Joseph Pendergast Jr., arrived the following year, and their third child, daughter Aileen, was born in 1919.[44]

Tom told prison authorities in 1939 that he had married Carolyn Elizabeth Dunn in February 1907 in Kansas City, but the recorder of deeds in Jackson County failed to find a wedding date. In 1933, Tom had given the same month and year, February 1907, for his marriage in an interview with Jerome Beatty of the *American Magazine*. Tom had confided, "I never can remember the exact date." Beatty wrote, "I checked up later and found out that his memory was even worse than he thought. The date isn't in February. It's January 25th."[45] Further complicating the matter, death announcements for Carolyn Pendergast in 1951 reported that she married Tom in 1910.

In a "Preliminary Social Abstract" prepared when Tom entered Leavenworth, he claimed that he had known Carolyn since childhood. He said that she had attended high school for four years and that she lived at home at the time of the marriage. Details of her background are obscure, but it is clear that she was born in 1882, the daughter of a saloon keeper, Luke Dunn, and his laundress wife, who lived within a couple of blocks of the American House. Carolyn kept quiet on the subject of her marital history. Even her children knew little about her early life.[46]

By the period of his marriage, Pendergast had already embarked upon a business career that went hand in hand and grew in scope in direct relationship to his rise as a political boss. Working for his brother, especially as a book-keeper, had supplemented his formal commercial education. Even though he was, from all reports, conscientious about performing his duties in elected office as county marshal and in the appointed position of city street super-intendent, he also found enough time to pursue private interests. And from 1904 until 1908, during which time he rose toward political leadership, he held no public post. While he ultimately built a business empire, he had to begin somewhere; as it turned out, rather improbably in retrospect, his business start was operating a venture dependent on the services of teenage boys.

In 1902, Tom and Casimir Welch, his old colleague from race-track concession days, operated the Hasty and Hurry Messenger Service, which was actually unreliable and quite slow. Later, the two partners acquired the rival Speedy Service and combined the two as the Hasty, Hurry and Speedy Mes-senger Service, which delivered throughout Kansas City from two downtown locations. Hurry advertised, "Wake up, lunch, carriage, parcels, all promptly attended to. Open day and night." Cas Welch's entrance into politics was as an enforcer and street fighter for Shannon's Rabbits, so between the two men they had connections with all the city's Goats and Rabbits. Competitors argued, perhaps with reason, that the two business partners enjoyed an unfair advantage.[47]

Supposedly, in addition to political clout, Pendergast and Welch also used strong-arm tactics in running their business. There is no record of whether Hurry Messenger Service ran numbers or performed other services for gam-blers, but such services seem likely. The firm employed hundreds of what an advertisement called "reliable boys." The youths were a rough lot—"veritable gorillas," according to one source—kept in line by the fists of their two bosses. In 1908, Welch and Pendergast restructured Hurry under a new name, Hasty-Speedy-Hurry Messenger, Automobile, Transfer and Livery Co.[48]

The *Kansas City World* praised Tom as a friend of the youth in the river wards for keeping in close touch with hundreds of newsboys, either prospective or former employees of his messenger service, one of the biggest employers of young boys in the Kansas City area. According to the paper, the "spectacle" of "Brother Tom" buying a newspaper on a busy street demonstrated his humanity: "A big hand dives into his vest pocket and drags up the first coin it touches. It is placed in the outstretched palm of the boy. Meanwhile Pendergast is taking a leisurely survey of the horizon. He waits several moments for the boy to make his 'getaway.' When that happens, as it usually does, Pendergast strides along with a contented grin, happy that the boy has discretion enough to 'duck' with the change."[49]

Surely, such a depiction of Pendergast as a budding Father Flanagan must have been read with amusement by even the most ardent of his admirers.

One altruistic deed that Tom and Cas did perform was to provide large and lavish Christmas dinners for their youthful workers. They also cosponsored the annual Messenger Boys Benefit Ball, at which a delivery boy voted most popular by his peers received the prize of a new bicycle.[50]

Before his 1910 election to the city council, Tom withdrew from the messenger business. Emulating Jim, he went into the saloon trade with Edward J. McMahon. They operated a popular buffet, Pendergast and McMahon's, on West 12th Street, in a growing new upscale entertainment district. Tom described the place as "high class," contrasting it with the numerous increasingly rough and seedy dives in the West Bottoms. McMahon and Pendergast expanded their holdings, soon owning five saloons in the space of only a couple of blocks. Tom kept the books, feeling that tending bar and bouncing drunks were beneath him. As another consequence of his changing status, he moved out of the West Bottoms to a suite in the new Baltimore Hotel.[51]

Thomas J. Pendergast accomplished a great deal during his two-decade apprenticeship in Kansas City politics, yet his credentials as superintendent of streets, county marshal, and alderman, plus his increasingly impressive business connections, were all secondary to assuming leadership of the Pendergast faction. A year and a half before he died, Jim remarked to his political intimates, "Brother Tom will make a fine alderman, and he'll be good to the boys—just as I have been."[52] But those words did not necessarily mean an automatic nomination of Tom as the next leader of the Jackson Democratic Club. That vital nomination needed to come from a consensus among the ward leaders, and it meant passing over Mike Pendergast, also politically ambitious and the Tenth Ward captain and city licensing inspector, for his younger brother. That is what finally happened.

Thus, Thomas J. Pendergast took over a highly successful family political organization with continuing strong ties to illicit interests. Although the faction had a solid base in the river wards and tentacles reaching throughout town, it did not have a power monopoly inside the local Democratic party. The question remained whether Tom was up to his new responsibilities and whether he had a broader design and more ruthless lust for power than Alderman Jim. Tom soon laid down basic laws to his precinct captains: politics is a 365-days-a-year job, elections are won at registration time, you must get people registered and see that they vote, most people are only politically conscious on election day, and, above all, you must keep in mind that the goal is always to win elections.[53]

THREE

Rise

1911–1925

For the first thirty years of the twentieth century, Kansas City continued to experience rapid expansion. The depression of the Gay Nineties gave way to prolonged prosperity driven by a golden age of agriculture on the central plains. Wheat production climbed steadily, making Kansas City one of the nation's leading grain markets. Concurrently, Kansas City's stockyards overflowed from a deluge of beef cattle, and the packing plants doubled in size and capacity. Kansas City's centrality continued to serve it well. The city claimed honors as the country's number two railroad center, after Chicago. More than 250 passenger trains a day pulled in and out of Union Station. Suburban components—neighboring Kansas City, Kansas, plus Independence and two new industrial suburbs, North Kansas City and Sugar Creek in Missouri—provided the basis for a modern regional metropolis. The population of municipal Kansas City reached 248,381 people in 1910 and moved up to 399,746 in 1930. The proportion of immigrants steadily declined, and the segregated African American population stabilized at slightly less than 10 percent of the total number of inhabitants.

Kansas City's physical and spatial features changed markedly in those thirty years. Downtown, the Convention Hall stood at the center of the urban core. A large new hotel, the Muehlebach, became an instant landmark. The magnificent new Union Station opened in 1914. Annexations more than doubled the city's size, extending the municipal limits almost eight miles south of the river to 79th Street and giving the city a rectangular shape. Even though the fashionable Hyde Park, Roanoke, and Rockhill subdivisions, along with the old towns of Westport, Marlborough, and Waldo, joined the city, the greater number of Kansas Citians lived within a few miles of downtown. After a brief period of development toward the northeast, almost everyone assumed the population would spread in a southerly direction, apace with real estate projects and the extension of streetcar lines. From the river bluffs, new boulevards snaked south, converging at the large Swope Park reserve, donated by and named after Thomas Swope, a real estate and transportation-system magnate.[1]

Yet, despite pretensions of refinement and modernity—the giant new Union Station, the imposing Liberty Memorial to World War I soldiers, the busy downtown, the impressive avenues, the stately residential neighborhoods, the steady population growth, and the general feeling of optimism and well-being—Kansas City, to outsiders, if they thought of it at all, continued to have the image of a big cow town.

J. C. NICHOLS

A man of energy, vision, and strongly held ideas, Jesse Clyde Nichols made his life's work the building up of south Kansas City, Missouri. Born and raised on a Kansas farm and a graduate, Phi Beta Kappa, of the University of Kansas, Nichols had moved to Kansas City after taking courses at Harvard College and traveling in Europe. In the early 1900s, he started purchasing land in a roughly six-square-mile area along the state line and south of Brush Creek. Nichols gradually subdivided his holdings in what he promoted as the Country Club District, building substantial and attractive homes with beautifully landscaped yards. He placed small park squares throughout the area, created tree-lined residential streets, and put statuary bought in Europe at street entrances. Directly across State Line Road, he founded Mission Hills, Kansas, as an exclusive suburb for the wealthy.

Along Brush Creek, he erected a shopping district of Moorish design, the Country Club Plaza, intended to act like a boundary, protecting what he called his "swank" developments from uncontrolled growth from the north. On the western edge of the Country Club District, in what he envisioned as an area of large mansions, he cut a grand avenue, Ward Parkway. He planned another grouping of fine homes, Crestwood, just south and east of the Plaza.

Nichols anticipated the wants of an emerging middle class. Noticing an interest in recreational pursuits that had previously been the preserve of the very wealthy, he placed tennis courts and golf courses in and around his projects. He gambled on the continuation of prosperity, the wide impact of mass advertising in influencing social patterns, and motor vehicles' freeing people from having to live either in the "walking city" or close to transportation lines. Displaying a sense of social order, Nichols, in general terms, envisioned homeowners progressively buying larger and more expensive residences, perhaps even culminating in a Mission Hills or Ward Parkway mansion. He established country clubs with differing class levels in mind. Taking great pains to hold up real estate prices, he required restrictive covenants, denying access to minorities. His business entailed courting political leaders regarding easements, electric and gas lines, sewerage, and the like.[2]

Reports had it that in the course of developing the Country Club District J. C. Nichols talked frequently on the telephone with Thomas J. Pendergast. Nichols's wife supposedly related to a close friend, "From time to time he has had to call on the city for help, especially in this big new development. The city for years has been Pendergast. Pendergast *is* the city. For favors given, he is sucking our blood. He knows everything we do. Clyde has come to a point where he doesn't move without first calling Pendergast. He knows how Clyde votes, has a spotter in every precinct."[3]

Kansas City Ward Lines

Given the composition of the city council, Nichols had little choice except to inform Tom Pendergast of his plans. Ward lines, redrawn as of 1904, had strengthened the Pendergast faction. A significant change incorporated much of the North Side portions of downtown into the First Ward, adding to its importance as a Pendergast stronghold. The new parts of the ward extended eastward from Quality Hill several blocks to Grand Avenue. The Missouri River formed the north boundary and the north side of 7th Street, the south.

As honky-tonks proliferated in the West Bottoms, a new entertainment district developed downtown, especially along 12th and Main. The Pendergast holdings numbered among a galaxy of drinking places. In a very personal era of tavern ownership, many bars bore the names of their owners: Frank Bryant, Pat Donahue, M. Flynn, C. L. Porter, Seymour Schiel, and Frank Wachter. Joe Shannon was a partner in Tookey and Shannon. The Al Campbell Buffet, Rank and Snyder's Buffets, Schuri's Buffet, and World's Buffets all in the classic fashion of the day featured free lunches for their patrons. The Diplomat, the Monte Cristo, the Germanis Saloon, the Sapphire Cafe, the New Atlantic, the Billiard Room, and various sample rooms afforded thirsty customers a wide variety of alternatives for a night on the town. The Stag Barber Shop, proclaiming, "We Never Close," was a combination barber shop and bath house. All in all, the "high-class" establishments of downtown and the "low-class" dives of the West Bottoms marked the continuing importance of the First Ward to Kansas City's growing economy.[4]

A reorganized Second Ward encompassed the southern half of the central business district, containing the Convention Hall. To the east of downtown, the boundary changes further subdivided the North Side into the Sixth, Seventh, and Eighth Wards. Shannon's Ninth Ward shrank in size and suffered a corresponding loss in influence. Of the other nine wards (of fifteen total), five were in lightly populated sections. The Country Club District was in the large Fifth Ward, running all the way south from 39th Street to the city limits at 79th Street, and east from State Line Road about a mile and a half to Holmes Street.[5] Among the four midtown residential wards, Mike Pendergast's Tenth Ward was solid Goat territory. The ward boundaries ensured Pendergast control of roughly half or more of the membership in both the lower and upper houses of the council. Later alterations of ward lines between 1912 and 1924 further cemented the position of the Pendergast organization.

In the Sixth Ward, running east from downtown, Cas Welch was the ward captain, in command of an efficient organization he proudly designated "Little Tammany." Although a Rabbit, he worked closely with Tom, a carryover from their days as active business partners. Welch, born in Jackson, Michigan, in 1873, of Irish parents, grew to manhood in Kansas City. Named after a Polish Roman Catholic saint much admired by his father, Welch, a stocky brute of considerable brawn, had few saintly qualities. At the apex of his power, Welch led his own force of street brawlers and retainers, several of whom were former Hurry messenger boys. Over the years, many of his band met violent ends, among them Jimmy Howard, purportedly the first hoodlum machine-gunned to death in Kansas City. Welch once actually shot and wounded a political rival in a gun battle on a busy Kansas City street.

Joking about his limited education, Welch claimed he stayed in primary school only long enough to reach the page in a textbook that contained the sentence "Ned had a sled." Yet he was more complicated than he pretended. He became an elected justice-of-the-peace judge from the Sixth District in 1910, and in 1922, to thwart a state proposition requiring all judges to be lawyers, he read enough Blackstone to pass a probably rigged bar examination. By then, Welch had already served as a judge for twelve years. The inhabitants of his "bunkhouse" ward, many of whom were African Americans, consisted of rooming-house floaters, manual laborers, artisans, and the city's poor. Welch regarded politics as a ruthless game, and in his own ward he acted as satrap and final arbiter.[6]

In the Second Ward, Miles Bulger, a wealthy and blunt-speaking paving and building contractor, plotted to expand his domain. Bulger, born in Kansas City in 1878, had learned to use his fists at an early age. A plumber at seventeen, he aspired to bigger things. A friend recalled, "When I first saw him he was a kid. He was strong and wiry, with more grit and git-up than the other Irish youngsters. Just to show how he handled himself, I recall that before he was 20 years old he had built a duplex. . . . Nothing could down him.

And even in those days he would crash right through to his objective."[7] Bulger entered politics as a Democrat and, using as a base the city council, where he represented his ward in the lower house for a decade, built a strong organization. The press called the short and wiry man "the Little Czar."

Basically, Bulger was an unreliable maverick, a thorn in the side of both Pendergast and Shannon. In 1914, he won a four-year term as presiding judge of Jackson County's three-judge county court. Bulger was elected at large, and the other two judges in the eastern and western divisions of the county were elected by district to two-year terms. Once installed in office, Bulger handed key patronage positions to Pendergast while at the same time working to undermine him through Shannon. The *Kansas City Journal* accurately evaluated Bulger's approach: "He has loitered in both the Shannon and Pendergast camps and in an effort to cater to both he has had some sad, but beneficial experiences."[8]

THE CITY COUNCIL IN ACTION

The kind of questions that concerned J. C. Nichols rarely received detailed notice in newspaper reports of proceedings of the lower house of the city council, where Tom Pendergast represented the First Ward. Routine questions seldom caused controversy or evoked interest. Usually, proposals relating to technical changes in existing ordinances passed automatically, with the language crafted beforehand in committee. A typical session in March 1913 forwarded to the public service committee a letter from Mayor Henry Jost regarding the municipally owned electric power plant, passed an ordinance governing the erection of a downtown theater, asked the aldermen concerned to review twenty different street repair ordinances, dispatched a proposed ordinance on advertising for bids on contracts to committee, and approved an ordinance widening a street. Pendergast supported a "special privilege" measure requesting approval for the placement of advertising signs and barber poles on sidewalks in the First Ward.[9] Always attentive to detail, Pendergast handled such hardly momentous constituent problems in good stead.

In the fall of 1913, what the *Kansas City Journal* called "verbal pyrotechnics" blazed in the council over an ordinance "regulating and restricting" the location of saloons in relationship to public libraries, churches, and public and parochial schools. Apparently, the ordinance was in response to the location of a saloon in the Washington Hotel, directly across the street from a Roman Catholic school and the diocese bishop's residence. Republican alderman Albert Beach argued against the ordinance on the grounds it was a sham that actually loosened restrictions: "The question is what is this council going

Tom Pendergast in his official alderman's photograph in 1911. (*Photograph courtesy the Archives of the United States District Court for the Western District of Missouri*)

to do here tonight—vote for the saloons or for the women and children of this city? This ordinance will effect no reforms. This is a great moral issue. Under this measure a saloon can face on one street with a side entrance on another opposite a church or school and still not be in violation."[10]

Beach's attempt to link the issue with the morality of saloons sparked a heated debate. After a Democratic alderman said the people of Kansas City opposed saloons, Pendergast, who usually kept quiet, responded, "The people of the state, by a majority of nearly 300,000, defeated prohibition, and it was defeated in Kansas City by 20,000 votes." He then asked, "Are you speaking for the people or just the element which is opposed to saloons?" The alderman defensively replied, "I am speaking for those who are opposed to saloons and I maintain that the great majority of thinking, moral people are opposed to them."[11] Because Pendergast approved of the ordinance, the alderman ended up voting for it and it passed fourteen to two, with Beach registering one of the dissenting votes. A given in Kansas City politics held that a Pendergast was not going to support any form of legislation intended to hurt the liquor traffic.

Reformers, meaning Republicans, came in for disdain and ridicule. Nichols's wife once commented, "They are a broken-down party sitting around like a bunch of hungry dogs waiting for a crumb to fall off the table." When Alderman Beach supported an antigraft proposal, Pendergast made an elaborate show of presenting him a brass bell. With mock solemnity, he told Beach to be the Paul Revere of Kansas City, tinkling the bell in public whenever he found evidence of wrongdoing. Beach's wife, Marjorie, referred to herself and her husband as "a couple of lambs among the goats and rabbits."[12]

Kansas City Democrats painted Republicans as jackals of William Rockhill Nelson and the *Star,* heaping abuse upon the proud newspaper. Pendergast, bitter over *Star* opposition to his slate in a primary-election campaign, growled at the end of a policy statement on another subject, "I may add that if I had been repudiated as often as the *Star* has in the last twenty years, I'd have quit a long time ago. All that the public has to do when it is tired of me is to give me one good licking. I won't linger to bother or embarrass it."[13]

THE TRANSIT RAILROAD AFFAIR

When he thought it expedient, Pendergast had no qualms about consorting with Republicans. In 1914, the Metropolitan Street Railway Company of Kansas City wanted to change its city franchise. Its new franchise proposal, which required a vote of the people, had little popular appeal. The existing thirty-year agreement still had eleven years to run, and what the owners really wanted was a tax reduction and permission to raise fares to shore up their inefficient and generally unpopular transportation business. The argument went that the "Met" needed money to extend streetcar service throughout town. Critics contended that the company already had the right to lengthen its tracks and that if the new franchise passed the company stood to gain millions of dollars. Pendergast and Shannon cut a deal with Republican business interests, apparently in return for a large amount of money, to support the franchise change, giving it a bipartisan facade.[14]

On a special election day, the charter, needing only a simple majority, passed by 7,000 votes out of 46,000 cast. Pendergast delivered a huge favorable vote in the river wards, carrying one precinct by an improbable 258 to 1. The *Star* charged that "election crooks of all political parties, the unprincipled ward heelers, the thugs, the roughs, the daredevils were gathered together under the leading politicians of the crooked class in secret gatherings throughout the city" to steal the election, "being roundly paid" for their services.[15]

"No intelligent man can doubt the existence of fraud on a huge scale," William Rockhill Nelson editorialized. "It is perfectly apparent that there was a purpose, backed by large resources, to put over the franchise—and put it over by any means at hand." No investigation by any public agency followed, despite such an obvious fraud as sixty-three registered voters' claim that they lived in a single small room in a First Ward apartment.[16]

In the Met franchise campaign, Pendergast discovered he could work closely with Conrad Mann, a Republican leader, general manager of the Kansas City Breweries Company, and future head of the Kansas City Chamber of Commerce.[17] The arrangement that Pendergast agreed to set a troubling pattern that he followed as his power and influence rose in Kansas City and Missouri. As later evidence showed, he pursued a very pragmatic policy in making both legal and illegal business transactions. The price of his protection and influence fluctuated in relationship to his own personal desires, with the interests of those who trusted him in Kansas City a cynical afterthought. In classic manner, power corrupted Thomas J. Pendergast absolutely. Placed in that context, the Met affair represented one step in his long march to the penitentiary.

"BOSS TOM" AND "BOSS JOE"

When Tom Pendergast assumed leadership of the Jackson Democratic Club, an uneasy alliance existed between the Goats and the Rabbits. On paper, "Boss Tom" and "Boss Joe" were equals, neither able on their own to control city or county politics. In Jackson County they had to work with local Democratic politicians as yet unbeholden, but needing both men. Inside Kansas City, they had to contend with two rising sub-bosses, Miles Bulger and Pendergast's old business partner, Cas Welch.

Boss Tom and Boss Joe continued to comply with the Fifty-Fifty rule, with occasional temporary variations based on such factors as the weighted importance of certain appointed positions. In 1912, the two men successfully backed mayoral candidate Henry Jost, a lawyer and a Rabbit. They both professed not to care who Governor Elliot Major, a Democrat, appointed as the two commissioners on the state-appointed Kansas City police board. Shannon actually claimed, "The police force is a liability instead of an asset in the political game." Pendergast agreed: "It will not make a particle of difference with the organization of the branch of the party with which I am identified."[18] In reality, needless to say, both men cared a great deal about who Major appointed.

The police were a rough lot of patronage appointees accustomed to helping elected officials in return for a relatively free hand in carrying out what they perceived as their primary duties. While they took a tolerant attitude toward vice of all kinds—for example, they would help certain streetwalkers designated as friends by Tom Pendergast—they frequently acted harshly in enforcing the law. The police board routinely defended officers about whom the public complained. In 1915, a commissioner pointedly praised a policeman found guilty of using undue force: "I admire an officer who sticks up for himself."[19]

Governor Major tried to achieve a balance. He gave Pendergast the right to pick Jackson County's delegates to a Democratic state convention and reduced Shannon's previous domination of state jobs in Kansas City. In a measure of compensation, Major appointed Shannon as a police commissioner, and as such he soon committed acts that illustrated the uneasy nature of the Pendergast-Shannon alliance. Shannon used the police to harass gamblers allied with Pendergast and even to raid one of his saloons for alleged liquor violations. For his part, Pendergast, learning that President Woodrow Wilson wanted his postal appointees to drop all ties with local politics, advocated Shannon as the next postmaster of Kansas City. The "boss rabbit," enamored with the thought of all the federal patronage involved, actually went to Washington to make quiet inquiries before it dawned on him that accepting such an appointment would mean retiring as boss. A newspaper report pointed out that he would have been a "canceled stamp."[20]

In 1914, Shannon and Pendergast agreed on Jost for a second term and on some candidates for other offices. They wanted to present a united front against the so-called nonpartisan ticket strongly backed by William Rockhill Nelson, who envisioned the election of his slate as an important first step toward having Kansas City adopt a commission form of government. During the campaign, the Democrats tried to terrify voters by equating commission government with corruption and claiming taxes would go up. In the April city election, Jost won an easy reelection by 6,500 votes, and the Democrats triumphed for most other offices. Jost piled up a more than 5,900-vote margin in the First, Second, and Sixth Wards, carrying the First by 2,000 votes. Pendergast, winning his council seat for a third two-year term by a 2,080-vote margin, filed a required report listing his campaign expenditures as $25. For the swearing-in ceremonies of the new council, well-wishers placed banks of flowers on and around his desk in the council chambers. Pendergast dispensed the flowers to decorate Jim Pendergast's grave and the statue of his brother raised in his honor in Mulkey Square along Kersey Coates Drive, overlooking the West Bottoms.[21]

In the wake of Jost's return for a second term, the carefully crafted Fifty-Fifty compromise started to unravel. On August 7, 1914, following rumors that the Rabbits intended to wage war on the Goats, Pendergast held a private meeting with the mayor and apparently received assurances that Goat appointees would stay in place.[22]

A week later, Pendergast and Shannon went to Independence, the second largest city in Jackson County, to form a new Democratic county committee. In a love feast of sweetness and light at the Jackson County Courthouse, it took the "Tomjo" Democrats only seven minutes to complete the organizational work and to leave the county Fifty-Fifty in place, without a dissenting vote. The press sensed trouble, however, noting that the two bosses came and went in separate automobiles. With no mention of the colors, a *Kansas City Journal* reporter described Tom's arrival and departure in a "huge" touring car: "Tom's clothes matched the color of the car and in this harmonious blend of color harmony was spread over Tom's face with an expansive smile, for had not the Pendergast forces carried the county? . . . Smiles appeared on the faces of the committeemen as they filed out and filled the autos, and the crowd melted away on the fifty-fifty basis of division."[23]

Early in January 1915, trouble between the bosses erupted into the open. Jost dismissed two Goats from the important patronage-dispensing jobs of president of the board of public works and member of a city-appointed fire and police board, which primarily administered the fire department. In the county, Judge Miles Bulger, who was on the surface allied with Pendergast, removed several key Rabbits.

With a factional war imminent that had the potential of engulfing thousands of city and county patronage workers, Boss Tom and Boss Joe released the transcript of their last-ditch attempt over the telephone, rather than face to face, to restore a semblance of harmony:

Shannon: This is Shannon. How do you feel?
Pendergast: I'm feeling as good as any man could expect to feel that had been kicked from every possible angle.

Shannon: I'm sorry. I want to have a talk with you.

Pendergast: Now don't get the impression that I am complaining. I can take my medicine with the best of them when I am in the wrong, and if you can convince me that I am in the wrong in this case, I'll surrender like a man.[24]

The only thing the two men truly agreed on was that they could not settle their differences over the telephone. Both bosses felt they had enough strength to fight a battle for command of the Democratic organization. Like the leaders of two nations using the media to communicate, the two opponents took their dispute to the press.

Pendergast disclaimed to a reporter any responsibility for the turmoil in a conversation meant to send Shannon a signal: "I am not going to have it loaded on my shoulders that I disrupted the Democratic party in Kansas City. I have faithfully kept every agreement I ever made, have been loyal to Mayor Jost and have been subservient to his every wish. I feel that I have been unfairly treated, but I do not want to air my grievances through the newspapers." Of course, that was exactly what he was doing. He conveyed the message that restoring the two fired city hall Goats to their former positions represented his terms for restoring peace, ominously adding, "I'm not looking for trouble. I'm for peace, but there can't be peace if agreements are to be cast to the four winds and I must be kicked from every angle. I couldn't be expected to stand for such a thing, neither could my friends."[25]

Shannon and Pendergast soon called a summit at city hall to have a heart-to-heart talk. A temporary truce was all they could agree on before Pendergast left near the end of January 1915 for a planned three-week vacation in New Orleans.[26]

Upon his return to Kansas City in February, T. J. Pendergast immediately declared war on Shannon and Jost. He charged them with breaking political promises and threatened that he and his Goat friends would either win the next primary and control the destiny of the local Democratic party or quit politics. "If myself and my friends are defeated in that primary we are out of politics," he claimed. "We will not bore the public by remaining in sight. We'll quit. If we win, I'll see to it that the public won't be bored by the presence of any Shannon men nor any of the *Star* fellows." Shannon declined to comment on Pendergast's declaration of war.[27]

The *Kansas City Journal* concluded that Democratic politics faced a "slaughter" over the next two years unless someone could induce Pendergast to change his mind. Pendergast reiterated that the whole affair was not his fault, and he promised to fight as hard as he could: "I didn't want to fight. I was for peace. But they have given me no choice. They broke faith with me. Now there's going to be a fight. And in that fight I'm going to land all the licks I can the best I know how."[28]

Like all wars, this one had unforeseen results, proving to be a crucial step in the Pendergast faction's taking over Kansas City. Even such a skilled political strategist as Joe Shannon vastly underestimated Tom Pendergast's resolve and growing strength in determining the outcome of civic elections. Shannon apparently failed to comprehend that no Democrat opposing Pendergast had any chance of cutting into his increasingly large recorded majorities in the First and neighboring North Side wards.

PENDERGAST'S RESIGNATION

Before a full realization of the meaning of the Goat versus Rabbit war had set in, on May 3, 1915, Pendergast surprised just about everybody by abruptly resigning from the city council. He took pains to downplay the political implications, explaining that he and his wife had planned for more than a year to move from a cramped downtown apartment at 1301 West 13th Street, a block from the Convention Hall, to a spacious new home in the Country Club District. Asked why he resigned, he told a reporter, "I moved into my new home at Fifty-fourth and Wyandotte streets and I could not represent my ward and not live there very well, so I resigned. There could be no other reason." In tribute to his service, the council gave him a standing ovation.[29]

In an editorial, the *Kansas City Post*, owned by Denver, Colorado, interests, suggested that Boss Tom would no longer have as much influence in the First Ward and that his resignation marked an end to old-style politics in Kansas City. The *Post* called him an "easy boss" who helped "down-and-outers" in their time of need: "For the most part he has given aid when aid was really needed to down-and-outers. In the dead of winter it was Pendergast money that paid for the meals given at various eating houses, and Pendergast money that paid for lodgings for men who had no place to sleep."[30]

Obviously, this favorable evaluation of Tom Pendergast differed diametrically from that promoted over the years in the columns of the *Star*. If nothing else, it demonstrated that another Kansas City newspaper held a more favorable view of Pendergast than William Rockhill Nelson's. Nelson and the *Star*'s depiction of Boss Tom, for partisan reasons, was one of unmitigated evil. So the Tom Pendergast of the 1910s came across the same as the Tom Pendergast of the 1930s.

Boss Tom, it cannot be emphasized enough, changed over time, like all people. As an alderman, he was still learning the ropes and perfecting a style. At that point, he operated much as did many other American machine politicians. An argument can be made that his corrupt practices and voting tactics were well within a normal range. Tom's occasional personal use of both calculated and sudden violence clouded the picture. Once he called a fellow alderman

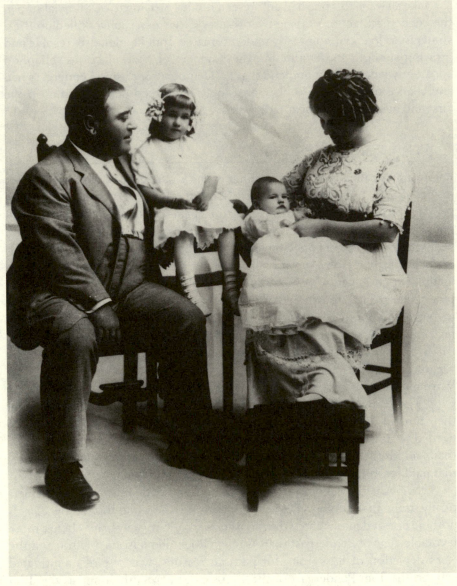

Tom and Carolyn Pendergast with daughter Marceline and baby son, Tom Jr., 1913.
(Photograph courtesy the Pendergast Collection)

with whom he had a disagreement into his office, locked the door, and worked him over with his fists.[31]

As did just about everyone else in Kansas City, the *Post* editorialist speculated on why Tom left the council and on what he planned to do next: "Just why Pendergast has chosen to quit the ward where he has lived so long and go far out to the south is not made public. It may be he has grown tired of the game and wants to devote more time to business. And it may be he has looked into the future—and there has seen the closing day of bossism! Only 'Tom' Pendergast knows the motive."[32] It is worth speculating what Pendergast's image would have been in Kansas City history if he had left politics at this point and devoted the rest of his life to pursuing a business career.

THE ELECTION OF 1916

Boss Tom had no intention of leaving politics. The war of the Goats and the Rabbits reached a climactic stage with the spring 1916 city election for mayor, which well illustrates the machinations and back-stabbing complexities of Kansas City political affairs at that time. In a bitter Democratic City Convention, the Rabbits renominated Jost and subjected a flush-faced and angry Pendergast to jeers and catcalls. In retaliation, Pendergast refused to back the Democratic ticket and ordered the Goats to vote for George Edwards, the Republican mayoral candidate. Even though early on election day Shannon, still a police commissioner, sent Goat police officers to the city limits and used Rabbit policemen to round up more than three hundred Pendergast campaign workers,[33] Edwards won and all the Rabbit candidates for alderman lost. A separatist Pendergast Goat ticket elected five men to the council. This was a disastrous defeat for Shannon, and Boss Tom emerged as the number one Democratic leader in Kansas City.

The power of the Pendergast machine continued to assert itself during the rest of 1916. In Jackson County, the Goats won the summer 1916 Democratic primary, gained control of the party machinery, and swept to a fall victory in the general election. Pendergast strongly supported Frederick Gardner, the successful Democratic candidate for governor of Missouri. In appreciation, Gardner replaced Shannon with a Goat on the police board. Pendergast also gained control of other key state-appointed bodies, including the Kansas City election commission. In 1918, Pendergast won absolute control of city hall, forcing Shannon into an alliance. The Fifty-Fifty returned on paper, gradually moving toward a seventy-thirty Goat advantage.[34]

The political factions rarely used outright violence in winning elections. By informal agreement, the Goats, Rabbits, and Republicans stayed out of each other's tightly regulated wards. A dramatic change came in the divisive February 1916 Democratic primary, however, when Pendergast assistant Denny Costello defected to Shannon. Early on a cold election-day morning, prior to the opening of the polls, Costello and a band of his ruffians rousted out two hundred "poorly clad and hungry denizens" of the flophouses and herded them into a line to vote for Shannon candidates at a polling station located at 405 Delaware, deep in the First Ward. Within memory, nothing similar had ever happened in a Goat stronghold. Pendergast hench-men soon appeared, escorting a large collection of a "wretched agglomeration of humanity," sitting them on camp stools in a rival line.[35]

Inevitable violence followed between the rival enforcers, with the com-mandeered voters innocent bystanders. "The respective belligerents fought like demons and blood smeared the sidewalks and sides of buildings," an eyewitness recorded. One man received a stab wound in the hand, another suffered a broken nose, and the rest of the participants incurred a great many black eyes and bruised scalps. The Costello warriors withdrew for a spell and then resumed the attack, temporarily routing their foes. "The camp stools on which the Pendergast forces were calmly seated were claimed as trophies of war by the 'Costellista's' and a second fierce battle was on," the witness said. The police finally arrived, restored order, and helped work out a compromise that provided for alternate voting by the two lines. The Rabbit voters had to stand, and the Goat voters reclaimed their stools.[36]

In the aftermath, Pendergast took steps to prevent similar disruptions in the future. He formulated a harsh policy of using thugs, both local and imported, to work the polls on election days. Ruffians lurked in front of the ballot boxes, and roving bands of hoodlums moved throughout town fright-ening and intimidating honest voters. On occasion, they demonstrated their prowess by indiscriminately beating up innocent victims. Once Pendergast had the police in his pocket, he stationed officers at polling stations to protect and help the criminals. Many election judges were patronage employees from the fire and water departments. Outright election thievery saw the routine last-minute switching of real ballot boxes with similar-looking ones, right down to scratches and chipped paint, filled with illegal ballots.[37]

ROUGHER ELECTION TACTICS

The new methods manifested themselves in the general election of 1918. Albert L. Reeves, the Republican candidate for the office of U.S. represen-tative, thought he had a good chance of winning by sweeping rural Jackson County and garnering an expected substantial Republican vote in Kansas City proper. In the wake of World War I, sentiment ran strongly against the Wilson administration. On election day, an unusual number of underworld characters—plug-uglies, ex-convicts, and hardened women—appeared at the polls throughout Kansas City. They intimidated election judges and clerks, official ballot challengers, legally registered voters, and especially people bold enough to register complaints. When a voter complained, he was beaten unconscious, left bleeding from the nose and mouth. Witnesses carried him out, as the police watched impassively. On the outside, another hoodlum menaced any journalists or onlookers seeking to gather information about voting irregularities.[38] In a very overt manner, the Pendergast machine moved in the direction of forming an invisible government under which the elective franchise meant nothing in Kansas City.

John Kennish, a distinguished Missourian who had served as a Republican state senator and as a state supreme court judge, saw firsthand what was happening when he served on election day as an accredited challenger in a precinct considered important for the Republican cause. On his arrival at the voting station, a ruffian called him filthy names as election judges, precinct captains, and police officers watched. When Kennish made a challenge, the officials ignored him and the thug, obviously in charge, cursed him. With contempt, the judges threw the ballots of honest voters in a wastebasket and replaced them with ones already prepared by the Pendergast machine.[39]

Reeves, defeated by 12,000 votes, charged that at many polling stations Pendergast election officials switched ballot boxes or added votes. He lost one precinct by a vote 700 to 1, but only thirty people had voted in that precinct up to the time the polls closed. "It was a matter of common knowledge that thousands of voters were disenfranchised at the election and thousands of fraudulent votes cast," Reeves said. He protested the election results, to no avail. Politics was so rough that fraud was simply taken for granted, especially in the bunkhouse wards. Anyway, congressional posts were not considered a paramount concern since they carried with them few jobs and little influence. And, except for the usual outcry, the election irregularities took a backseat to the euphoria that accompanied the end of World War I.[40]

Reeves came away from the campaign with the most repugnant of memories: "With a heavy expense, and with bitter abuse, he could understand why so many men declined to offer themselves as candidates, and why good men would refuse to engage in any kind of political activity. This is one of the weaknesses of democratic government. A citizen hesitates to offer for public office because of the heavy expense and personal abuse to which he is subjected. It was the policy of the boss to make opposition pay a heavy price. His hoodlums were able to carry out this policy."[41] Reeves never again sought an elected public office after his defeat. But it would not be the last time that Tom Pendergast encountered him or his strongly held convictions about the sanctity of the ballot.

The 1918 general election also saw a fractious dispute between Goats and Rabbits erupt in the "Bloody Tenth" Ward, Mike Pendergast's stronghold, which was notorious for long, Goat-regulated polling lines. In a pitched battle on election-day morning at a firehouse polling station, Goat enforcers routed a party of Rabbit bully boys. Andrew Gallagher, a Shannon lieutenant and leader of the defeated Rabbits, speaking from a hospital bed the next day, charged Mike Pendergast with having launched a surprise attack. The aftermath of the affair proved that it had been more than just another election-day street clash: The Rabbits never again mounted serious opposition to the Goats in the Tenth Ward. Gallagher eventually moved to Independence to build a strong Rabbit organization in eastern Jackson County. Mike moved up in the Goat organization and became more bitter than ever against the Rabbits and all their works.[42]

Pendergast's Growing Business Interests

Pendergast had no problem using his political connections to enhance his business interests. Along with two political and gambling associates, John J. Pryor and Philip H. McCrory, he founded the T. J. Pendergast Wholesale Liquor Company in 1911. In 1912, he sold his saloon interests to his partner, Edward J. McMahon. Pendergast coerced First Ward saloons into buying liquor from his company by threatening them with code and license violations, automatically creating a very lucrative market for his new business. He further arranged for the Ross Construction Company, operated by William A. "Willie" Ross but controlled by his father, Michael Ross, a Pendergast ward captain, to receive lucrative city and county road paving contracts.[43] In all likelihood, Pendergast owned part of Ross Construction.

During his alderman days, Pendergast's two best-known business enterprises were both downtown in the First Ward: the Oriental Cafe at the corner of East 8th and Walnut and the Jefferson Hotel on West 6th Street. There was nothing special about the Oriental, which was just another successful First Ward restaurant. The Jefferson, an old six-story firetrap approaching the end of its useful life, was neither a high- nor a low-class hotel. Many of the out-of-town customers stopping there were traveling salesmen. Pendergast employed a manager to operate the hotel, but he kept a small office just off the lobby. From there, he ran the Jackson Democratic Club.

The hotel had a notorious and colorful reputation as an assignation center, with rooms available at hourly rates. Even though the Jefferson Hotel may have warranted a red light, it technically was not a house of ill repute, although anti-vice crusaders claimed a brothel operated on the lower floors. A Pendergast business associate, Booth Baughman, a former Missouri River gambling boat owner, presided over stud poker games at the Jefferson on the sealed-off fifth floor. Occasionally, newspapers carried tantalizing stories about happenings at the Jefferson, such as the account of a woman attempting suicide in apparent grief over the unhappy ending of an affair. In another incident, a Baughman henchman shot and killed a man.[44]

A distinguishing feature of the Jefferson was a basement cabaret featuring popular music, burlesque routines, and beautiful "showgirls" who mingled with the male audience. Under a city ordinance, it was against the law for a woman not working in a place that sold liquor to enter it. Legend held that "torch songs" originated at the Jefferson. Drinks were expensive. A wine list with a colorful blue peacock on the cover offered a wide variety of alcoholic beverages. Imported Cliquot champagne sold for $4.50 a bottle, Hennessey "3 Star" brandy for $1.25 a pint, Old Crow whiskey for $1.75 a quart, absinthe cordials for $.20 a glass, and Budweiser beer for $.25 a bottle. The provocatively named "Chorus Girl" and "Leading Lady" each cost $.20; the "Wild Irish Rose" sold for $.25.[45]

What helped distinguish the Jefferson from competitors was that it seldom closed. An exposé in the *Star*, which probably helped business, reported, "Cabaret entertainers wandered from table to table, singing sensuous songs. Midnight passed and the crowd of the underworld habitués became hilarious. At one o'clock, the hour required by law at which to stop selling liquor, the orgy was at its height." One night Rabbit-controlled police made after-hours harassment raids on the Jefferson and another popular downtown establishment, the Blue Goose Saloon, located in the Puritan Hotel, a notorious prostitution center. The Blue Goose raid netted eight sleepy drinkers, while the Jefferson was so crowded that the police made sixty arrests. Another late-night police foray on the Jefferson resulted in the apprehension of forty patrons, all released from any charges the following morning in what a *Star* reporter called a comic opera proceeding.[46]

Pendergast, who gave up his carousing days at some point after his marriage, was rarely present at a late hour. A self-proclaimed family man, he routinely went home at 5:00 P.M., going to bed by 9:00 P.M. After 1916, his physicians aggressively treated him for syphilis for the rest of his life. He also suffered from a serious ear problem that required him to go east for an operation.[47]

The advent of Prohibition in 1919 forced Pendergast to make business adjustments. That year, he abruptly closed the Jefferson Hotel and arranged to have the city buy the property for $79,555 for a street-improvement project. The same year, he sued unsuccessfully in federal court to have the Volstead Act, which governed the enforcement of Prohibition, declared unconstitutional. Without a legal alternative, Pendergast and his partners closed their wholesale

Downtown Kansas City in 1924, looking north toward the Missouri River. *(Photograph courtesy the Native Sons Archives [KC590/N171], Western Historical Manuscript Collection, Kansas City, Mo.)*

liquor company, stored the remaining spirits in government warehouses, and reorganized as a medicinal-water and soft-drink dealership, the T. J. Pendergast Distributing Company.[48]

With no intention of leaving himself open to any possible federal liquor violations, Pendergast scrupulously avoided any direct or easily traced involvement in rum-running throughout Prohibition. He later claimed that he turned down a chance to sell his bonded distillery liquor for a $2 million profit after learning that the buyers intended to divert 14,000 barrels and 1,500 cases to Cleveland, Ohio, bootleggers. He said that even though he considered Prohibition violations "conventional crime," he rigidly observed the law.[49]

HARRY S. TRUMAN AND THE MACHINE

Even as Pendergast solidified his power inside Kansas City, Jackson County remained a battlefield characterized by shifting factional alliances. In 1918, Pendergast had backed Bulger's successful reelection to a second term as presiding judge. But in 1920, Pendergast had allied with Shannon to defeat Bulger's candidates for eastern judge and western judge. How long the Democrats could afford to fight among themselves and still win seemed somewhat problematic, given a resurgence in Jackson County by the Republicans, long a minority. This Republican growth was marked by the election of Warren G. Harding to the presidency in 1920 and the "Return to Normalcy." In eastern Jackson County, where elections were reasonably honest, Pendergast felt the Goats were strong enough in 1922 to elect the eastern judge, which could be accomplished by finding and running an attractive, able, and reputedly honest candidate.

In Jackson County, the Western Division encompassed only municipal Kansas City, the Eastern Division all the rest of the county. The presiding judge and the two division judges each had one vote in determining county affairs, and the court decided issues by a majority vote. Despite a much smaller body of voters, the eastern judge had as much power as the other two judges. Approximately 400,000 people lived in Kansas City and 70,000 in all the rest of Jackson County, of whom 8,000 resided in Independence. The court oversaw the road system, managed a hospital, ran segregated homes for delinquent children, operated a mental health facility, administered correctional institutions, and issued court orders on the county treasury. All county jobs were patronage positions. The court maintained courthouses in both Independence and Kansas City.[50]

Much patronage was involved, and county politics essentially constituted an extension of Kansas City politics, which meant that Pendergast was interested in county politics as well as Kansas City politics. So, despite titles, Harry S. Truman, the man Pendergast selected as his candidate for the eastern judgeship, was just as much a Kansas City politician as Pendergast, Shannon, or Bulger. Many of Truman's followers tried, incorrectly, to divorce him from Pendergast by turning him into a rural county politician, and, as he moved up in politics, Truman never went out of his way to set the record straight. As a matter of history, Pendergast found exactly the right person in Truman. According to legend, Mike's son, James Michael Pendergast, who had served with Truman in World War I, first suggested him. Truman recalled, "Mr. J. Pendergast came into my store one day and asked me if I'd like to run for Eastern Judge. I told him I'd be delighted to do so. He didn't know I was busted."[51]

Truman had much to recommend him. Born in Lamar, Missouri, in 1884, he had grown up in Independence and had farmed for most of a decade in Jackson County. Truman came from an old Jackson County family. His paternal grandfather, Andrew S. Truman, was an organizer of the county government and substantial landowner. His wife, Bess Wallace, also hailed from an old Jackson County family, and her father had been county revenue collector. Truman had long been on the fringes of local Democratic politics, having held appointed positions as postmaster of Grandview and as a county road overseer. He had a good World War I record as a captain in Battery D of the Thirty-fifth Division of the regular army, and he had been reasonably popular with his men, many of whom came from Jackson County. He carried strong support in fraternal organizations, especially the Masonic Order, and had flirted briefly with a Jackson County chapter of the Ku Klux Klan, until it became clear that the patronage views of the Klan were in total conflict with those of the Irish Catholic bosses.[52]

Truman, on the verge of failing in the haberdashery business, sought a new undertaking in the judgeship. Pendergast cared only for votes, and Truman proved an excellent candidate. Without mentioning Pendergast, Truman later wrote, "In July or August 1921 a meeting of the leaders in Eastern Jackson County was held and it was decided that I should be a candidate for Judge of the County Court for the Eastern District." He won what he called a "hot" primary race over a Rabbit and swept to victory in the general election in the fall of 1922. According to Truman, "The election was a walk."[53]

It could be argued that by lending his name to the Pendergast machine, Truman helped further its corrupt and unscrupulous practices. It could also be argued, perhaps, that he had no choice except to go with Pendergast if he wanted a political career in Jackson County. But Pendergast hardly had a lock on Jackson County. Truman could have gone with Shannon or Bulger. Truman wrote privately in the 1930s, "I am obligated to the Big Boss, a man of his word; but he gives it very seldom and only on a sure thing. But, he's not a trimmer. He, in past times owned a bawdy house, a saloon and gambling establishment, was raised in that environment but he's all man."[54]

THE 1924 ELECTION

A bitter factional struggle badly split the Democratic party in the 1924 city and county elections. In the spring, Republican reformer Albert Beach upset an unpopular Rabbit mayor, Frank Cromwell.[55] Rightly or wrongly, Shannon received the blame for Cromwell's candidacy for reelection, which Cas Welch used as an excuse to complete a shift of his Little Tammany faction from the Rabbits to the Goats. In the fall general election, Shannon, who may have commanded enough votes in eastern Jackson County in a Republican year to swing the contest, refused to back Truman and the rest of the Pendergast county ticket for reelection. Truman and a fellow Goat western judge, Henry McElroy, worked together against a Rabbit presiding judge, breaking the Fifty-Fifty arrangement. Bulger had stepped down voluntarily to run in 1922 for the General Assembly; he was elected. Truman said, "We promptly took all the jobs, but we ran the county on an economy basis which was a real one." Truman lost in what proved the only defeat of his political career, a victim of

Presiding Judge Harry S. Truman uses a check-signing machine. (*Photograph courtesy the Harry S. Truman Library*)

a Republican sweep in Jackson County that was nothing short of a disaster for the Democratic machine.[56]

Miles Bulger, who was temporarily allied with Shannon, experienced Pendergast's wrath after the election. Bulger was waiting for a streetcar when a grey limousine, tires screeching, pulled up and out of the driver's side lunged Pendergast. "Hello," Pendergast said eerily, and then he charged bull-like at the slightly built Little Czar. Bulger, after giving a mocking gesture with a thumb at his nose, turned and ran, outdistancing the bulky boss. A terrified Bulger gasped to onlookers as he ran, "Tom Pendergast. He's got a gun." Pendergast did sometimes carry a revolver; the quick Bulger escaped.[57]

Shortly after that incident, Pendergast's Goats completed their takeover of the Democratic organization in Bulger's Second Ward. Earlier in the year, shortly before the city primary election, Pendergast's ruffians had won a bloody battle over their Bulgerite counterparts during a Second Ward primary meeting.[58] Bulger, virtually destroyed politically, lost what was left of his county patronage after Truman returned to power in 1926, winning as presiding judge.

Bulger retired from active politics in 1930 following eight years of service in the Missouri General Assembly, which he found unrewarding because he had few jobs to hand out. He sold his construction business to devote the remainder of his life to patronizing the arts and playing bridge at the Kansas City Club. On July 30, 1938, Bulger, writing on Kansas City Club stationery, congratulated Governor Lloyd Stark for openly opposing the Pendergast machine: "There was plenty opposition here, but the old economic situation made everyone knuckle to them, if a man wanted a job with a shovel or a man wanted to be a United States Senator, he had to talk to them. Talk about dictators, Mussolini had nothing on these birds here." Bulger died on January 3, 1939, at age sixty-one, following a heart attack suffered while walking on the lawn of his mansion at 5850 Ward Parkway, only two blocks away from the T. J. Pendergast residence.[59]

THE REFORM CHARTER

Even as Boss Tom dealt with schisms inside the Democratic organization, well-meaning reformers unwittingly laid the stage for him to seize vast power, beyond the wildest of dreams, in Kansas City. The leading altruist in trying to turn the community into a city of light was William Volker. A wealthy professed Christian Socialist and philanthropist, he believed the poor needed something more enduring than turkeys on Thanksgiving and similar handouts. He tried to break the Pendergast welfare grip by donating money, persuading the city government in 1908 to establish a model welfare department. He brought in experts from the "Chicago school" of sociology, trained at the University of Chicago in the latest scientific methods of charity work. A bureaucracy was put in place, and the new agency, primarily financed by Volker, started to make inroads into the Pendergast organization.[60]

A prominent Kansas City lawyer, Frank Walsh, who had close ties to Shannon, helped protect the new department from political interference. All that changed during World War I. Walsh went off to Washington to advise President Wilson on labor matters; his departure coincided with Pendergast's general counterattack on the Rabbits. Boss Tom virtually eliminated the welfare department under the guise of a cost-cutting move, and the situation went back to where it had been, with the Pendergast machine retaking control of charitable functions.[61]

Volker was anything if not determined. In 1918, he funded the small Public Service Institute, which had an elite board of civic leaders and was directed by Walter Matscheck. Matscheck, a former Cincinnati official and holder of an advanced degree from the University of Wisconsin, sought to apply political science to city government. He phrased his message in the form of lofty common wisdom: "The point is that the real business of government, particularly local government—the unit of the city—is not governing in any strict sense. It is administering. . . . It's administrative science, and that's where democracy is working." Matscheck professed to lead a crusade to carry forward and perfect on the local level ideas that had stirred the yearnings of free people since the greatest days of Greece and Rome: "These are really revolutionary processes. They are triumphs of democracy."[62] In short, he equated his version of city government with mother love.

His recipe for an urban millennium called for a modified city manager form of government. He said that his plan, which included hiring college-educated, career-professional managers, would lead to an efficient, honest government and would eliminate patronage, thereby stopping the lifeblood of boss rule. Matscheck proposed dividing Kansas City into four wards and having a council with four members elected by ward and four elected at large. An elected mayor would, in effect, be a cheerleader for the city—essentially a figurehead. The mayor and the members of the council would each have one vote in deciding on questions before the council. By a simple majority, they would appoint, in addition to a city auditor and city clerk, a city manager to administer the city government. The city manager would fill the rest of the administrative offices with directors, who on paper would have considerable independence in running their departments. To avoid any hint of partisanship, all candidates for the mayor and council would run as independents in both primary and general elections.[63]

Pendergast historically resisted changes that went significantly beyond the form of the old 1889 city charter, and his initial inclination was to oppose the Matscheck plan, which was put into the form of a proposed new charter in 1925. Voters had passed a new charter in 1908 that strengthened the mayor, but had rejected fundamental alterations in 1905, 1917, 1918, and 1922. After studying the proposal, Pendergast changed his mind. Referring to the existing two-house, thirty-two-member legislature, he told a reporter, "It ought to be as easy to get along with nine men as thirty-two."[64] Consequently, an unholy alliance of the *Kansas City Star*, the Republicans, and Pendergast's machine supported the proposal. Of significant local politicians, only Shannon, realizing the potential for a Pendergast advantage, remained in opposition. On February 24, 1925, the charter passed by a vote of 37,504 to 8,827, and the next day, the *Star* predicted an end to boss rule in Kansas City. This proved vastly premature.

PENDERGAST IN CONTROL

The first city election under the new charter came in a special election in the fall of 1925. Pendergast's slate (supported by Cas Welch, who, despite his affiliation with the Pendergast machine, entertained unrealistic hopes of becoming the boss in his own right) beat Shannon's in the supposedly nonpartisan primary, earning the right to face what were really Republicans in the November general election. At first, Shannon, still commanding several thousand votes, threatened to either sit out the election or support the Republicans. In a dramatic, much-reported "chance" curbstone confrontation that attracted a large crowd, Pendergast shook a finger at Shannon and a fellow Rabbit, growling, "I don't give a damn what you do."[65]

Another Rabbit, former mayor Henry Jost, by then a member of Congress, made a deal with Pendergast to restore peace. In a revealing 1939 letter to Shannon, Jost commented on what happened: "Let's get a few facts. I think everyone who has any knowledge of local politics at all—certainly you— must concede that it was I who fixed up the political peace . . . and you will remember that I did it over your protests. You wanted to bolt. I was more concerned in getting jobs for people who had been fighting for us, and I went over to the Gumble Building, where Mr. Pendergast then maintained his office, and fixed up a peace treaty."[66] As one part of the agreement, Shannon supported Pendergast's slate. As another, the Rabbits retained the right to name the Democratic candidate for Congress. Five years later, Shannon accepted the congressional nomination himself, and Pendergast helped elect him, delighted to see him go off to Washington.

Shannon's support proved crucial in the special 1925 city election. A Republican governor, Sam Baker, had appointed members of his party to the police and election boards in Kansas City, so the contest was reasonably clean by Kansas City standards. The police actually discouraged the use of ruffians at the polls. Election-board officials struck an estimated 6,000 names from the voting lists, mostly from the river wards, and tried to ensure a semblance of honesty by the election judges. These measures resulted in a very close contest. Mayor Albert Beach, formerly a Republican, squeaked through by 534 votes in the supposedly nonpartisan election. Pendergast clearly won four seats and the Republicans three on the new council. In a race not decided until the early hours of the morning, George L. Goldman, Pendergast's man, won the other council position by a majority of 304 votes. A court challenge of the result failed, and Goldman received certification as elected, giving Boss Tom a five-to-four majority.[67]

At a meeting in the office of banker William T. Kemper, with Matscheck and other reformers present, Boss Tom dictated the choice of Henry F. McElroy as the first city manager. Not unexpectedly, the reformers wanted to bring in an expert from out of town, but they reluctantly deferred to Pendergast's decree. McElroy, a real estate executive and former western county judge, was a partisan member of the Pendergast machine, but he bragged about his honesty and made no bones about how he intended to administer Kansas City:

City Manager Henry McElroy demonstrates the operation of a construction machine in the 1930s. (*Photograph by Jack Wally, courtesy the Western Historical Manuscript Collection, Kansas City, Mo.*)

"Listen: I've got half a million dollars of my own. Nobody can expect favors from me. The people are going to get a hard-boiled business administrator." He soon gave a dramatic demonstration of who was in charge, appropriating Beach's spacious office as his own and essentially relegating the hapless mayor to a very small room he would share with a secretary.[68]

Tom's Town had started to take shape. On January 11, 1926, the directors of the Public Service Institute, in what must have been a glum meeting, decided against any official connection with the new municipal government, agreeing to keep "the same attitude of independence which it previously had"—in other words, virtually assigning the organization to political oblivion.[69]

Thomas J. Pendergast had arrived in Kansas City three decades prior to his 1925 victory. After a lengthy apprenticeship, he had ventured on taking a successful ward organization and expanding it throughout the city and county, which proved a very good gamble. Except for an occasional unforeseen political disaster, he could always pull back to the First Ward. As it was, his great political and organizational ability, combined with the help of criminal elements, the acquiescence of the business community, the emphasis on votes rather than ideology, and the use of ruthless tactics, created the powerful Pendergast machine. An increasing willingness to embrace the underworld raised unsettling concerns, and two pressing questions loomed as Boss Tom stood on the threshold of great power in Kansas City: Would he or did he want to escape from his criminal and gambling connections? Was he, no matter the facade, simply a thug who had made good in politics?

Four

Power
1926–1932

During his golden years of power, Thomas J. Pendergast took pains to project an image of himself as a benevolent, kind, and compassionate political and business leader and a devoted family man who wanted only to serve his city and its people. Disclaiming any lust for power or personal gain, he stressed in an interview, "My interest is only in Kansas City—and in my family." He claimed to toil day in and day out for the good of his constituents: "I don't wait until three weeks before an election. I'm working all the time. I'm kind to people—I like to be kind to people. I never give an argument when a man comes in for a dollar or wants help. Maybe he's having trouble with his wife that he wants settled—you'd be surprised how many men come in to get things like that fixed up." Boss Tom tried to help in other ways as well: "Maybe he wants a job. I always go out of my way to help."[1]

He blustered that his morals were "as good as any bishop's, archbishop's, preacher's, reformer's—anybody's." As a guardian of community values, he showed great compassion: "Suppose there's a man who got drunk or had trouble with his wife or got into a fight—a minor police case. We investigate, and if we think he should have help we try to get the case dismissed, or if he's poor we help pay his fine." Pendergast maintained that he opposed crimes against public morality to the point of waging war on lewd conduct by women and on purveyors of narcotics. "We won't have anything to do with helping drug peddlers or prostitutes," he sternly emphasized. "We put the whole strength of the organization to work to slug those people. And to slug them hard."[2]

Pendergast's actual connections to prostitution had been tenuous but assumed to exist for years. In 1918, concerned by the sudden rise of venereal disease among soldiers at Camp Funston in eastern Kansas, Samuel J. Crumbine, the head of the Kansas State Board of Public Health, discovered that the infected men often spent their leave time with Kansas City prostitutes. Crumbine, in what he described as "the most astonishing and exasperating series of conferences I have ever held," visited the Kansas City mayor's office, only to be told that prostitution was a police matter, and then visited the police department, only to hear them blame the problem on the city courts.[3]

When Crumbine inquired about whom he should talk to at the courts he was told, "Why not see the man who owns them?" and was directed to Pendergast's office. To Crumbine's surprise, "The boss saw us at once . . . and seemed to know all about us." Threatening to make Kansas City off-limits to service personnel, Crumbine told the boss, "I will give you just one week, Mr. Pendergast, to have the City Courts hold all arrested street walkers and bawdy-house inmates for examination. If diseased they are to be quarantined and treated. If free from infection, they should be given a stiff jail sentence and kept out of circulation as long as the law will allow."[4]

Pendergast, perhaps reflecting on his own ongoing predicament with syphilis, responded, "You won't have to wait a week, doctor. If the courts aren't doing as you wish by this time tomorrow, let me know. But don't put the city in quarantine, for I promise that your wishes will be carried out to the letter." Upon following up ten days later, Crumbine discovered that Pendergast had indeed kept his word.[5] This incident raises questions about the true nature of Pendergast's relationship with prostitution in Kansas City.

As a practical political philosopher, Pendergast ruminated on the role of government,

> What's government for if it isn't to help people? They're interested only in local conditions—not about the tariff or the war debts. They've got their own problems. They want consideration for their troubles in their house, across the street or around the corner—paving, a water main, police protection, consideration for a complaint about taxes. They vote for the fellow who gives it to them. If anybody's in distress, we take care of them—especially in the poor wards. If they need coal or clothes, or their rent is overdue, we help them out—in and out of season. We never ask them about their politics. We know pretty well how they'll vote after we help them.[6]

In a rare reflective moment, Pendergast called himself an "ordinary fellow" who hated braggarts. Holding that he always kept his word, he admitted, with a fist clenched, that when crossed he struck back. "I haven't obeyed the Bible in that—I haven't turned the other cheek," he snarled, adding menacingly, "I never started a fight—but once the other fellow started, I slugged." He balanced that by telling how close he was to his wife and children, including a married daughter who, "rain or shine, snow or sleet," came by the family home every night to "kiss Daddy and Mother good night." How could voters turn their backs on such a righteous, charming, and warmhearted man? Even a bitter enemy supposedly said, "If we must have a boss, I'd rather be bossed by Tom Pendergast than anybody else."[7]

Tom Pendergast's most obvious charitable activity involved providing Thanksgiving and Christmas dinners for the needy and indigent. At a typical holiday meal in 1930, more than three thousand homeless men of all races formed a line of several blocks leading to Kelly's restaurant at 603 Main in the First Ward. Every diner feasted on large portions of turkey, cranberry sauce, mashed potatoes and gravy, mince pie, and other holiday delicacies. For the Christmas dinner, Pendergast underlings performed duties as Santa Claus's proxies. With the usual efficiency the machine took pride in, a functionary organized the line and handed out tickets. Many of the guests were from nearby flophouses and rescue missions.[8] These down-and-outers or their fellows were the bedrock of the machine, individually voting several times on election day.[9]

Pendergast, in what might be described as a redistribution of graft, made a show of helping individuals in dire financial straits, providing food baskets and buckets of coal and paying medical bills. Pendergast usually carried a pocketful of quarters that he handed out to broken-down derelicts out of generosity and in recognition of their election-day services. Before the New Deal emergency programs began, he ordered a produce company that he had a share in to donate foodstuffs to the city-operated General Hospital, which had temporarily lost its credit. Pendergast made it clear that he expected others to help shoulder the cost of his charitable activities, stating in early 1933, "Every office holder must stand ready to contribute his share toward the relief work carried on by the Pendergast organization."[10]

Many decades later, loyalists praised Pendergast, detailing how he had aided them and their families in times of great need. They remembered him as a generous man, sidestepping the question of the actual source of the money for the good works. His critics and bitter enemies, refusing to find good in anything he did, passed off his actions as cheap politics and rank posturing. In 1930, the *Star* noted the Pendergast Christmas extravaganza but gave far more coverage to parties sponsored by business and religious groups, including one for a mere 103 girls at the Interdenominational Home for Girls in Kansas City.[11]

1908 MAIN STREET

Pendergast the boss was not reclusive. Indeed, he went to the limit to make himself accessible to just about anybody who wanted to see him. In 1927, he moved the office of his Jackson Democratic Club from the downtown Gumble Building at 8th and Walnut to the second floor of a modest two-story yellow-brick structure at 1908 Main Street. The new base of operations on the southern fringe of the commercial core fronted on an important north–south thoroughfare. The Southwestern Linen Company rented the building's first floor.

To reach the Jackson Democratic Club on the second floor, one had to walk up a narrow stairway. "The steps are worn," a journalist wrote. "They have borne the weight of United States Senators, governors, mayors, councilmen, bankers, beggars, and gangsters—yes, and the lame, the halt, and the blind." A long meeting room lined with plain wooden chairs was at the top of the stairs. Large photographs of Woodrow Wilson and James A. Reed, along with a pen sketch of Boss Tom produced by an admirer, graced the walls. A small secretary's station connected with Pendergast's modest office overlooking the street. The inner sanctum was plainly decorated; a distinguishing feature was a framed old political cartoon of James Pendergast carrying away a First Ward ballot box.[12] The whole aspect was that of an austere but adequate business, rather than that of a raucous political gathering place. The decor and atmosphere made clear that Pendergast considered politics a form of business enterprise devoid of any frills.

The address of 1908 Main became synonymous with Tom Pendergast. He held court regularly three days a week from 6:00 A.M. to noon. During absences or to spell him, his nephew James Michael Pendergast, Mike Pendergast's son, usually occupied the throne. Of course, supplicants hoped to see Boss Tom. Frequently, when he reached his office via a back entrance, fifty to sixty people waited in a line extending back from the anteroom, down the stairs, and out along the sidewalk. Telephones rang constantly as a tall weather-beaten old river pilot, Captain Elijah Matheus, a combination receptionist, factotum, and bouncer, briefly interviewed applicants. Almost all, job seekers, vendors, and politicians, easily passed muster. They stood patiently waiting their turn to see the great man. The first in line waited for the boss to call out in a heavy voice, "All right, who's next?" Then Captain Matheus would usher the person in.[13]

Pendergast wasted no time on preliminaries. Invariably, he sat on the edge of a chair in front of a rolltop desk, a soft felt hat on his head and a cigarette fitted with a rather long holder in his right hand. "It's hard to define the impression he made," Matt Devoe, a ward leader, said. "You didn't forget him. He was sturdy, with those huge hands and shoulders. He looked very capable, you know. I think he was a little suspicious of everybody. There was no chitchat at all. You went in and stated your business. He met you alone."[14]

Pendergast expected a visitor to get right to the point with no hemming or hawing, and usually the interview was short, lasting only a couple of minutes

The 1908 Main Street headquarters of the Jackson Democratic Club. (*Photograph courtesy* St. Louis Post-Dispatch)

and seldom more than ten. He interrupted long-windedness with, "What you want to say is this," summed matters up, and terminated the interview.[15] From political aspirants right up to the governor, Pendergast's suppliants received quick yes or no answers.

Pendergast claimed to always keep his word. Once, after he gave a yes answer by mistake to a potential political candidate, he continued to back him. Pendergast dispatched people wanting jobs with the city to see the appropriate supervisor with notes written in one of three different colors: red meant hire immediately, blue signaled to wait until a background check, and black, hire under no circumstances. Someone once heard him tell an old woman, "Now Auntie, you stop crying now, you'll get that job, I promise."[16] Yet Pendergast was far from humanitarian in handing out positions. "Nobody gets a job or an appointment because he's a nice fellow," he said. "He must deserve it politically. It's the same as in any other business."[17]

Bernard Gnefkow, a personal secretary for the boss from 1932 until 1939, claimed that no one received preferential treatment, even senators and governors, except women: "We had orders . . . that I would not make the ladies wait out with the rest of 'em, and if they came alone to put them in as quickly as possible. He was of the old school and believed that ladies came first."[18]

Critics warned that it was all a sham, that Pendergast actually played hard to see when it suited him and that the whole purpose of the mornings at 1908 Main was to deceive the public into thinking of him as a legitimate political leader. But it was obviously more than a mere publicity stunt. Pendergast rose early, arrived at the office on time, and followed the same routine year after year, constituting a unique and, even in his day, very attractive political style. Inescapably, he enjoyed doing it and considered it a necessary part of his job that enabled him to learn a great deal at a personal level about life and conditions in Kansas City.

Without complaint, Pendergast diligently ran his own employment agency for city positions, especially for the water department and the parks department. In addition to job seekers who came unsolicited to his door, he received a constant stream of letters from his political allies. Senator James A. Reed wrote dozens of letters in support of applicants for public employment. The tedious correspondence included such phrases as "an old acquaintance," "very fine fellow," "a very good friend," and "a valuable man in party work." In one letter, Reed requested help for the widow of a deceased Cole County sheriff, describing her as a person of "refinement, intelligence, and highest character." In another, he said Joseph Neschese, a "good conscientious work-man," had been laid off and needed a job to support a "sick wife." The long stream of letters slowed in 1934, when Reed came out so strongly in opposition to New Deal job programs on the grounds that they wasted money that he decided it was inappropriate to seek these jobs for his friends.[19]

On rare occasions, Pendergast wrote Reed in behalf of a constituent:

> I wish to introduce you to Mrs. Ruth J. Rubel, who has a proposition I feel sure will be of interest to you, and I take this opportunity of recommending her ability. She is well qualified in her line of business and capable of handling all of its phases and has had a very successful experience. She has as her clientele the representative business and professional men of Kansas City, many of whom are our friends and associates. I am sure you will be pleased with any business you do with Mrs. Rubel.

Pendergast thanked Reed in advance "for your courtesies to her and the cooperation you may give her."[20]

Some observers found it hard to understand why Pendergast, powerful enough to make or break senators and governors, spent so much time on duties that many other important people would have considered beneath them. Pendergast, however, knew exactly what he was about. Just about any favor, especially bestowing a job, that he delivered in person made him a friend

Tom Pendergast talks on the telephone in his 1908 Main Street office. (*Photograph from the Kansas City Museum Archives*)

for life. Reformers never seemed to understand that more was involved than blindly handing out largess to supporters. William Reddig, a journalist for the *Star,* caught the broader implications of what transpired at 1908 Main in his 1947 book, *Tom's Town:* "The boss was able to operate openly without apology, and he busted himself making a reputation as a substantial citizen—the man of property, the good family man, the friend of the masses, the Jacksonian of large simplicities who hadn't been spoiled by wealth."[21]

THE PENDERGASTS' LUXURIOUS LIFESTYLE

In the summer of 1927, Tom Pendergast felt politically secure enough to take his wife, Carolyn, and their three children, Marceline, sixteen, Thomas Jr., fifteen, and Aileen, seven, on a three-month tour of Europe. Pendergast left brother Mike in charge of the machine during his absence. His followers treated the excursion as a great event, sending enough flowers on the family's departure from New York to fill their three state rooms.[22] Perhaps for the first time since he had entered politics, Boss Tom put the cares of running Kansas City behind him and, like any other tourist, set off to enjoy his first overseas vacation.

Pendergast called the trip a wonderful experience. He and his family visited England, France, Germany, Scotland, Ireland, Wales, Italy, Switzerland, Austria, and Belgium. From the standpoint of industry and beauty, England, Germany, and Austria impressed him the most. "I did not see an acre in Germany and Austria not under cultivation," he reported. "It seems they are utilizing every available foot of ground in those countries in cultivation. There are scarcely any scars of the war left."[23]

Of three great cities visited, London, Paris, and Rome, he especially liked Paris: "London is a wonderful city—big, but has nothing like the ornamentation of Paris. In Rome we saw the great works of art. St. Peter's Cathedral, there, is a magnificent edifice."[24] The Pendergasts spent eight days in Paris, finding, contrary to what they had been warned to expect, no evidence of price gouging.

Tom remarked that he felt well treated everywhere: "Throughout our trip we found no prejudice existing against Americans. People were kind and helpful. I'm glad we went. The trip was beneficial to the children and to all of us." A disagreeable aspect of the trip was an airplane flight from London to Paris. The roaring engines left the Pendergasts deaf for twenty-four hours, and they were the only passengers who did not become airsick. Upon his return to Kansas City, a large delegation awaited Tom at 1908 Main. After telling his listeners about his trip, Tom felt compelled to add, "I would not trade Kansas City for ten places like any of those I visited."[25] All in all, the Big Boss sounded like any other tourist fondly remembering a vacation but happy, after a long trip, to be back home. A new task at hand, building a dream home, occupied the refreshed Pendergast's mind.

Tom and Carolyn decided to construct a stately new mansion in the highest-priced section of J. C. Nichols's Country Club District. Tom called on Nichols, and after being told that the lot he wanted to buy at 5650 Ward Parkway would cost $5,000, he pulled out his wallet and with no hesitation peeled off five thousand-dollar bills. Nichols had never been offered that much ready money before and was afraid to have it around. He feared, moreover, that he might be robbed on the way to the bank. So Nichols persuaded the boss to go get a money order. The story, possibly embellished, became part of Nichols family lore.[26]

The planning of the house left the Pendergast children with vivid and hilarious memories. In France, on the European excursion, Tom and Carolyn, deciding they wanted a residence along the lines of French provincial design, made their children spend hectic days in an automobile laden with luggage touring the French countryside and studying the elaborate chateaus and estates of the landed gentry. Carolyn, in particular, looked for ideas to design a showy mansion, a place she felt would more accurately reflect her perceived station in society. Surely, Tom Pendergast as a serious student of rural European architecture was so out of character that both his friends and his enemies, if they had been told about it, would have found it very difficult to believe.

A Kansas City architect, Edward H. Tanner, designed the Pendergast mansion, completed in 1928, according to Tom and Carolyn's specifications in a prairie version of symmetrical French regency, with a hint of Italian Renaissance style. Tanner headed the J. C. Nichols department of design. The large dwelling had an attractive and tasteful appearance, without being ostentatious. An enraptured architectural reporter for the *Star* wrote, "The massive wrought iron door with its vertical panes of glass, the cut stone cornucopia placed above the stone frame that encloses it and three sturdy chimneys attract the eye of the beholder." A combination of rose-hued bricks laid in white mortar and soft-shaded slate marked the exterior.[27]

Interior decorators chose expensive wood paneling and wall-to-wall carpeting, then a new but trendy embellishment. French gilt and glitter of the Louis XV period prevailed, complete with delicate chairs and objects of art. A master suite, featuring an informal living room, dressing room, and bath, occupied one-third of the second floor. The basement recreation room had a large ornate back bar and a marble front bar with a marble counter and a terrazzo step. Tom bought the bar, a true white elephant, in New York for a profoundly inflated price. The artifact became a great conversation piece among the Pendergasts, so Tom felt he got more than his money's worth.[28]

The Pendergast mansion at 5650 Ward Parkway. (*Photograph courtesy* St. Louis Post-Dispatch)

The Pendergast opposition had great fun with the mansion, which Tom initially staffed with two African American servants, a house man and a maid. Mayor Albert Beach gleefully told his fellows, "Go out on Ward Parkway and there you will see the wonderful mansion of T. J. Pendergast—said to have cost $100,000 with furnishings costing $75,000. . . . My friends, the Republican party is no longer the silk stocking party. The Democratic party is now."[29] The mayor speculated that Tom even wore silk underwear.

Outwardly, Pendergast appeared much like many other successful Kansas City business and civic leaders. But he assiduously avoided the regular noonday luncheons popular among many wealthy Republicans in Kansas City, observing, "They do the resoluting and we get out the votes."[30] He liked prestigious cars, especially Packard sedans and coupes. He occasionally used a driver, but usually drove himself. Probably because of Carolyn's influence, his taste in clothes had become quite refined, leaning toward expensive and conservative tailored suits and ties. His ensembles favored blue and grey. He liked felt nobby hats and sometimes wore spats, the mark of a gentleman; he wore a pocket watch with a gold chain. Seldom, if ever, did he pose for pictures

T. J. Pendergast looking like the popular image of a political boss at the wedding of his daughter Marceline in 1929. (*Photograph courtesy the Western Historical Manuscript Collection, Kansas City, Mo.*)

dressed informally. He assumed a statesmanlike pose in an oil painting he sat for, looking a very distinguished middle-aged man.[31]

Unfortunately, in full figure, his increasingly overweight and bulky shape did not photograph very well. When the *Star* printed a picture of him, the editors usually selected an unflattering one, making him look as bad as possible. The single occasion that he wore a top hat and cutaway jacket, at Marceline's wedding to William Burnett in 1929, constituted a minor catastrophe. He looked for all the world like a goon in fancy dress. Republican campaign workers gleefully cropped and retouched the unflattering picture, distributing thousands of copies. The image became, at least until the release of his prison mug shot, perhaps the most familiar depiction of Boss Tom. The writer of an editorial in a Joplin, Missouri, newspaper, who called Tom a "silk-hatted, fawn-spatted Olympian Jove," undoubtedly had the photograph in mind. "And it was the only time I wore that damn monkey suit," Tom complained. Even so, he offered no apologies, even promising, "And if my other daughter ever wants me to wear that hat to her wedding, I'll do it."[32]

TOM PENDERGAST AND HIS FAMILY

Pendergast took considerable pains to keep his home life as private and unobtrusive as possible. Outside of close relatives and a few intimate friends, the Pendergasts seldom entertained. Hardly any of his political associates saw the inside of his home or met his family; Harry S. Truman never did. In 1937, Tom told an interviewer, "I have never discussed politics at home or with my family. My family life is a thing apart from my political and business activities." The Pendergasts did, nevertheless, warmly welcome those trick-or-treaters who raised the courage to ring their doorbell. A woman who as a girl roller-skated past the mansion recalled seeing Tom wave pleasantly as he sat on the running board of his automobile smoking a cigarette.[33]

Carolyn once refused to accept an urgent long-distance telephone call from Louis Howe, a key aide to Franklin Roosevelt, because it was slightly after Tom's 9:00 P.M. bedtime. Matt Devoe, a machine official for several decades, never saw Carolyn. Like Bess Wallace Truman, the wife of another Jackson County leader, Carolyn stayed in the background, politically speaking, at least in Kansas City. She aspired to be socially accepted, but the very nature of her husband's work was frowned upon by the local social elite. Since a much-coveted listing in the *Social Register* eluded her, Carolyn threw her energies into shopping sprees and lavishing attention on her and Tom's two daughters, Marceline and Aileen.[34]

Carolyn liked expensive gems, and in 1929 burglars stole costly jewels, mostly diamonds, from the Pendergast mansion in what the police described as the largest residential theft in Kansas City history. Pendergast told a reporter: "The jewelry had been collected over a period of twenty-five years. I can't say exactly what the value of the jewelry was. I would say the jewelry could not be replaced today for $150,000."[35]

Tom Jr., Marceline, and Aileen had a good family life. The family favored Boston terriers as house pets and kept other animals on a farm in Johnson County. Boss Tom had a love of animals, which probably would have surprised his enemies, and he passed it on to his children. All three Pendergast children finished high school; only one completed a college degree. The Pendergast daughters both attended private high schools. Marceline graduated from National Park Seminary in Forest Glenn, Maryland, in 1927, and Aileen from the French Institute of Notre Dame de Sion in 1936. Tom Jr. earned a B.A. degree from Rockhurst College, a Jesuit institution in Kansas City, in 1933.[36]

Marceline and Aileen, neither of whom showed any interest in politics, were so close to their mother that Tom Jr. felt Carolyn favored them at his expense. An animosity developed between him and his mother, festering so badly over the years that Carolyn, when she died in 1951, left her son only $1,000 from an estate of more than $800,000. Tom Jr. was close to his father, though; he revered him and tried to protect his memory in the decades after his death. Tom Jr. said in 1989, "Most people didn't understand my father. I only know him as a father and he was perfect. We got along great." Boss Tom often took his son with him to 1908 Main and carefully taught him urban machine politics from the ground up. Even though Tom Jr. proved an apt student, he turned his back on a political career and went into the liquor wholesale business. In 1935, at St. Peter's Church in Kansas City, he married Mary Louise Weyer, the daughter of a wealthy cosmetics manufacturer and business leader, George H. Weyer. No one ever questioned Boss Tom's devotion to his family. Matt Devoe, observing that the Pendergasts were "very, very, very clannish," said of Tom, "His family was his whole life."[37]

Tom remained close to members of his extended family, even as his circle of brothers and sisters grew ever smaller. John, the manager of Jim's old saloon at 508 Main, died in 1914. Michael, who in effect retired from the political arena after a nervous breakdown in 1925, was in ill health for the next four years and died in 1929 from a stroke at age sixty-two. An obituary, noting that old Jim had passed him over for the leadership of the Goats, described Mike as a "tenacious fighting type of the old school," who, unlike Tom, never understood when to compromise and was "not temperamentally fitted" to rise to boss.[38]

Of Tom's sisters, two died before they reached adulthood. Mary Anne died in St. Joseph in 1938. Margaret passed away in 1934 and Josie in 1935, both in Kansas City. Tom and his immediate family were very close to "Aunt

Tom Pendergast Jr. and Mary Louise Weyer's 1935 society wedding. *(Photograph courtesy the Pendergast Collection)*

Josie," who was considered by them to be the heart of generosity and human kindness. Tom Jr. thought she had a great influence on his father's charitable activities: "Her two key words were 'helping' and 'giving'. . . . My Father's involvement with the poor and needy was a twenty-four hour day [sic], seven-day-a-week activity. I heard him repeat Aunt Josie's key words many times."[39] Boss Tom saw part of his obligation as helping his many nieces and nephews, a number of whom held public jobs or worked for one of his businesses.

In addition to Marceline, Tom Jr., and Aileen, a fourth child, Margaret Ann, lived with the Pendergasts. Carolyn claimed her as her half-sister. Margaret Ann, who went by the last name of Morton, was older than the three Pendergast children but twenty-four years younger than Carolyn. Growing up in the home, but never quite treated like a genuine family member, she always suspected that Carolyn was actually her real mother. Whenever the Pendergasts went on vacation, she was left behind. Margaret Ann "always felt something was wrong," as she could not accept the difference between her age and the age of her half-sister, whom she called Carrie. In 1966, a private investigator hired by Tom Jr. said of Margaret Ann, "When she grew older, she wondered about it and tried to learn something about the death of her mother and father but Carrie wouldn't tell her. She feared to ask any of the others."[40]

Margaret Ann remembered being with Carrie up in the attic of the Pendergast home at 5400 Wyandotte Street when she was a little girl. Margaret Ann was looking through what she called "some junk stored up there in boxes" when she found a document showing that sister Carrie had been married to and divorced from a man before she married T. J. Pendergast. "I never got to ask about it," she said, "because Carrie saw what I was doing, snatched the paper out of my hands and bawled me out for meddling in other people's business. She was awful angry. I never saw that paper again. I didn't look for it either. I was afraid to." Several years later, as a high school student, a friend told her that he had overheard someone say that she was really Carrie's daughter. She mentioned this to Carrie "and got a good licking for it."[41]

As a teenager, Margaret Ann, after a quarrel, was sent to live with Carolyn's brother, Luke Dunn. Never to return to the Pendergast household, she eventually married and moved to California. Many decades later, the private investigator hired by Tom Jr. located her. The subsequent investigation left little doubt that Margaret Ann was, in reality, Carolyn's own daughter, father unknown, born prior to her marriage to Tom Pendergast.[42]

PENDERGAST'S BUSINESS EMPIRE

Pendergast's business interests touched just about everyone in Kansas City. He dealt in construction and liquor. With the end of Prohibition, he and his partners restarted the T. J. Pendergast Wholesale Liquor Company. Since the machine controlled the issuing of liquor licenses, the firm soon had a monopoly, and sometimes its trucks simply delivered liquor to drinking establishments, whether ordered or not. There was no choice except to accept the arrangement, and the T. J. Pendergast Wholesale Liquor Company cornered business to the extent that it became one of the largest liquor wholesalers in the United States.[43]

In 1928, Boss Tom established the Ready Mixed Concrete Company with Michael Ross, who controlled Ross Construction. Pendergast made the small Ready Mixed office at 908 West 25th Street his business headquarters, where he spent his working days when not at 1908 Main. Ready Mixed operated a large and well-equipped modern plant for mixing concrete, along with a fleet of twenty-five or more concrete-mixing trucks. In response to charges that the concrete cost too much, Pendergast, citing its superiority and lasting quality, contended that, to the contrary, cost-effectiveness actually held the total cost down. Pendergast claimed that contractors found "that I could give them a better product a hell of a lot cheaper than they could mix it themselves."[44]

Prior to the invention of mixing trucks, crews mixed the concrete at construction sites, thoroughly raking water, sand, and gravel back and forth into a cement mixture. Ready Mixed's trucks saved for an average batch the work of six to eight men, so it usually came in with the lowest bid in competitions for contracts. Matt Devoe, who understood the business, said there "wasn't a fix" because conditions required none.[45] Most of the rigged bidding took place for small jobs, such as sidewalk repairs, where independent contractors needed to have their names on a special approved list to have a chance of receiving a contract. Of course, to avoid trouble with city inspectors, all prudent independent builders used Ready Mixed and other Pendergast business products.

Pendergast denied charges that he had an unfair advantage: "Let me say something: If everybody would hustle for business like I do and others who compete with me do, this would be a livelier town than it is. I am for more and better and bigger business, from Ready Mixed Concrete to ice cream cones. Everything honest and legitimate goes with business or politics."[46] Only the most blindly loyal of his followers agreed with him. After gaining control of Kansas City under the 1925 charter that reorganized the city's leadership, Pendergast moved to expand his business activities, in particular consolidating his already tight hold on the construction industry. The money rolled in, and Pendergast's increasingly lavish manner of living gave an indication of his growing wealth and prosperity.

The names of other concerns in which Pendergast knowingly held stock could have filled a small telephone book. His construction interests included a litany of firms: Centropolis Crusher, Eureka Petroleum, Mid-West Pre-Cote, Public Service Quarries, Midwest Asphalt Material, Kansas City Limeolith, Mid-West Paving, Missouri Asphalt, Kansas City Concrete Pipe, Pen-Jas Oil, Massman Construction, Welch-Sandler Cement, Gidinsky Construction, Missouri Contracting, Dixie Machinery and Equipment, and Boyle-Pryor Construction. Several operated out of the same addresses as Ross Construction and Ready Mixed. Shawhan Distilling and Frazier Distilling supplemented T. J. Pendergast Wholesale Liquor. So did Glendale Sales, Atlas Beverage, and Glendale Beverage. The City Beverage Co., in which Tom Jr. was a partner, distributed all Anheuser-Busch products in the Kansas City area. The Sanitary Service Company, pockmarked with criminal money, had a lucrative garbage-collection contract with the city. Pendergast held the position of vice president in a cigar company owned by political lackey Robert Emmet O'Malley. Commerce Coal and Missouri Carriage were other Pendergast firms, and he had links to the insurance firms United States Fidelity and Guaranty, Maryland Casualty, and Union Indemnity.

As a result of elaborate methods of concealment and deception, such as using the names of others on corporation papers, there was no way of telling the true extent of Pendergast's holdings.[47] His enemies charged that he and criminal elements in classic fashion used the threat of force to horn in on legitimate businesses and that in the construction field honest builders had to use Pendergast products and rent Pendergast machinery or suffer constant harassment from city and county inspectors. Naturally, Pendergast denied the accusations. Noting that the *Star* had used Ready Mixed concrete for a renovation project, he sarcastically commented, "Did I coerce the *Kansas City Star* when they bought cement from my firm?"[48]

Both legitimate and illicit businesses paid the machine regular tribute, a sort of privately collected tax calculated as a normal expense into operating costs, as part of an unorthodox manner of doing business in Kansas City. As a matter of course, many prudent business owners either gave Pendergast blocks of stock or placed him or his surrogates on their boards of directors. On a sliding scale, firms throughout Kansas City contributed 5 to 10 percent of their annual gross to machine collectors.[49] All local police powers—regulating, taxing, and licensing—were under machine control. How much money went directly to T. J. Pendergast can only be conjectured.

THE 1930 CITY ELECTION

In the 1930 city election campaign, Republican leader Raymond G. Barnett excoriated Pendergast and his associates for making a mockery of the party of Thomas Jefferson through open corruption, rigged bidding on city contracts, and kept candidates. Barnett compared the Pendergast machine to a ponderous army of cruel aggressors girding for battle: "Like the grand army of Napoleon supported by the conquered nations of Europe, it sets forth in this campaign, banners waving and bands playing, on its march to another Moscow."[50]

Barnett, getting a little carried away, raved against Pendergast, calling him a "superman" who had started out leading the lowlife of society: "Tom Pendergast once was merely the boss of the First Ward, with its saloons and brothels and barrel houses and herdable vote largely of floaters and gandy dancers and non-taxpaying irresponsibles who could be depended upon to roll up a tremendous ward majority for the Pendergast candidates, offsetting by that one ward the majority of several wards of home owners and taxpayers." Barnett recalled that T. J. Pendergast had owned the "notorious" Jefferson Hotel, rendezvous of "all the typical North End characters, men and women."[51]

In counterarguments, the Democrats called on the Republicans to make specific charges and cited the supposed accomplishments of City Manager

Henry F. McElroy, who had been handpicked by Pendergast. John G. Madden, who became Pendergast's defense lawyer nine years later, loosed an angry attack: "There have been many charges made in this campaign," he said, "and those who make them should have proof of them." He called Barnett a "little whippersnapper" with a "pouter-pigeon air" and the ways of a "peacock."[52]

Bryce Smith, the machine candidate for mayor and a Rabbit, ignored the role of Mayor Beach and gave McElroy credit for a new building for the city-operated General Hospital No. 2 for African Americans, for furthering airport and river harbor expansion, for numerous street improvements, and for putting Kansas City in its best-ever financial condition. Smith tried to stress his own independence: "I entered this campaign unpledged, uncontrolled and without promises aside from the pledge that I made to the people when I accepted the nomination—that I will administer the affairs of Kansas City, so far as falls to my duty and prerogatives as elected mayor, wholly and devotedly as your servant and officer, responsible to the taxpayers as the stockholders in our municipal corporation, and with an eye single to the conduct of the city's affairs from a business standpoint, honestly, efficiently, progressively and economically." Emptier words were never spoken.[53]

The election was a sham, with the results preordained. How effectively the Republicans made their charges stick with the electorate meant nothing. The Pendergast machine dominated both the police and the election machinery. Smith swept to victory and the Democratic organization maintained control of the council. In the fall county, state, and national elections, the machine again elected its candidates, including Shannon for Congress and Truman for a second term as presiding judge, by margins in the 50,000-vote range.

MACHINE TRIUMPHS

On Sunday, December 7, 1930, Asa Hulton, a political analyst for the *St. Louis Globe-Democrat*, assessed the new Democratic unity in Kansas City and its consequences for the people of Missouri: "With an organization capable of bringing to the polls more than 100,000 voters, as was demonstrated November 4, Pendergast in 1932 will be able to throw 60,000 or 75,000 votes to his slate of candidates in the Democratic primary." Hulton concluded that Pendergast held the balance of political power in the Democratic party in Missouri.[54]

In 1931, Boss Tom cooperated with Conrad Mann, the head of the Kansas City Chamber of Commerce and a Pendergast-leaning Republican, to support a $39.5-million bond issue called the Ten-Year Plan for the construction of new public buildings and roads in Kansas City and Jackson County. Enthusiasm for the bond issue came mainly from GOP businessmen banded together in the

"Committee of 1,000," who were campaigning under the banner "Make Kansas City the Greatest Inland City."[55] Such froth was, of course, meaningless in determining the results of the special election because machine workers made sure the proposal passed by a four-to-one margin, far more than the required two-thirds vote. The city used the money for improvements to Brush Creek— a project Pendergast insisted on—and to build, along with other structures, a thirty-two-story city hall, billed as the tallest in the nation. In county affairs, Truman launched a comprehensive rural-road-paving construction program and oversaw the erection in downtown Kansas City of a new county courthouse. The city projects generated abundant business for Pendergast companies, especially Ready Mixed.

In 1938, the leaders of the business community, against a background of recent revelations of vote fraud, played down Pendergast's paramount contribution in the passage of the Ten-Year Plan. A highly laudatory Kansas City Chamber of Commerce publication on the results of the improvements, which listed the names of hundreds of contributing individuals, excluding the boss, blandly stated, "Organized labor had endorsed the program from the start, as had the Pendergast Democratic Organization. Later the Shannon and Welch factions of this party got in line, and various Republican leaders added their endorsement, giving the program a non-partisan setting." What "organized labor" actually thought was hard to say because of Pendergast's influence with labor leaders in Kansas City. Without his help, it was virtually impossible for a union to organize workers. Perrin D. McElroy, the head of the building trades union and a leading American Federation of Labor official for many years, said he considered the boss a great man: "I think he did as much for labor, and for the poor and underprivileged, as any man I have ever known."[56]

Truman went to considerable lengths not to throw contracts to known machine firms, and he received very favorable publicity for this action. He later wrote, "After the issues carried my troubles began. The Boss wanted to give a lot of crooked contractors the inside and I couldn't. He got awful angry at me but decided that my way was best for the public and the party. . . . The Boss tells me that in Kansas City they doctor every bid so that the inside gentlemen get the contract." Truman said he had to compromise by allowing a former saloon keeper and "murderer" friend of the "Big Boss's" to steal $10,000. The future president lamented to himself, "Am I an administrator or not? Or am I just a crook to compromise in order to get the job done? You judge it, I can't."[57] Unsaid is that Truman had no way of knowing whether the companies receiving county road contracts had secret Pendergast ties or paid kickbacks to the machine. Truman took credit for paving more than 230 miles of roads and for building a $500,000 hospital, plus the county courthouse.

In 1932, more or less by accident, Pendergast made a significant stride toward dominating Missouri state politics. In the Democratic primary for governor he backed a longtime acquaintance, Francis M. Wilson, an easy winner. Wilson, who was from the small town of Platte City, thirty miles north of Kansas City, was a former United States Attorney with a reputation for honesty and independence. He was on his way toward a resounding victory in the general election when he died suddenly from a bleeding ulcer less than three weeks before election day. Pendergast, accepting the wishes of the Wilson family, used his influence to persuade the state Democratic committee to name Guy B. Park as the new official party candidate for governor, bypassing a rising and better-known aspirant from eastern Missouri, Lloyd C. Stark. Pendergast knew little about Park, beyond that he was from Platte City and was a close friend of the Wilson family, a circuit judge, and a loyal Democrat. In fact, until the Wilson family brought up his name, Pendergast had probably never heard of him. He reportedly said, "Who the hell is Guy Park?"[58] As it turned out, Park, who triumphed with little campaigning in a general Democratic sweep, proved an inspired choice.

Park was so grateful to Boss Tom for making him governor that he did almost anything he asked, becoming a classic Pendergast lackey. Park shut his eyes to charges of corruption and voting irregularities in Kansas City, refusing to believe the boss could do wrong. In August 1935, Park, speaking to an annual reunion crowd of four thousand in Cassville, Missouri, responded in expected bootlicking fashion to an attack by a St. Louis newspaper on the Pendergast machine: "Mr. Pendergast is a common, humane citizen. . . . The Kansas City organization is successful in turning out the Democratic vote, because it is not only a political organization, but an organization that takes care of the poor, destitute, common men of the city."[59] Pendergast could not have said it better himself.

On the national level, Pendergast influenced and capitalized on the course of events. He wielded his political power at a state convention in St. Louis to gain the leadership of the Missouri delegation to the 1932 Democratic National Convention in Chicago. In both St. Louis and Chicago, Pendergast displayed his violent temper. In St. Louis, he either slugged or slapped, depending on the eyewitness, in the confines of an elevator, a Democratic leader from Springfield. During a meeting at the Chicago convention he threatened another Missouri politician, L. T. Gualdeni, the leader of the St. Louis Italian organization, with bodily harm. "It was a hot fight in that caucus room," Pendergast recalled, "and finally Gualdeni of the St. Louis delegation said something in the heat of argument I didn't like. I started for him. He ran out of the door. Later I saw him in the lobby. As soon as he caught sight of me, he began to plead, 'Don't hit me! Don't hit me!'" Five years afterwards, Pendergast shrugged off the incident: "Now we are warm friends. It's all over now. That's the way it is in politics."[60]

Pendergast, who had gone to Chicago pledged to James Reed as a favorite son, switched, along with several other city bosses, by prearrangement to Franklin D. Roosevelt after the first ballot, helping him to the first of his four Democratic presidential nominations.[61] Beyond political considerations, Pendergast displayed little interest in FDR's views on the Great Depression. But Pendergast felt that a socialist federal government was a distinct possibility, and he had concluded that the economic emergency was more than just an American problem.[62]

On returning to the United States after vacationing in Europe in 1931, Pendergast, who hardly ever mentioned foreign affairs to the press, commented in an off-the-cuff interview about the impact of the world depression. Stressing that he was neither an economist nor versed in European affairs, he observed that the "German people reflected a kindly feeling toward the United States," but that many of the French citizens he talked to feared that the United States and England would help the German economy at the expense of France. He said that even though Germany had five million people unemployed, with the number expected to rise to eight million, Berlin remained a great city boasting the best streets he had ever seen. With that in mind, he predicted, "With all her ills and discouragement I believe Germany is coming back."[63] In retrospect, Pendergast's remarks proved quite perceptive, a demonstration of both his strengths and weaknesses as a practical politician. Just as in considering the American political scene, he discounted ideology in considering that in Germany.

Rolling up huge margins for FDR in the fall 1932 general election, Pendergast compounded his success with the election of all thirteen of his candidates, out of a field of fifty-six, in a court-ordered at-large election for the entire thirteen-member Missouri congressional delegation after Republican governor Harry S. Caulfield vetoed a redistricting bill. Pendergast professed not to consider the results very important for his purposes: "I'm not greatly interested in congressmen. I'd rather have a justice of the peace than a congressman. A justice could do me more good."[64] Of course, that was stretching things a little.

Pendergast was a member of Roosevelt's inaugural committee for Missouri, and machine people, including Harry Truman, soon began to receive important appointments. Truman retained his job as presiding judge when he was appointed as national re-employment director for Missouri. All thirteen Missouri congressmen dutifully wrote separate letters to FDR in support of Truman for the position. Furthermore, Pendergast gained control of a temporary relief agency, the Civil Works Administration, which employed more than 100,000 workers throughout Missouri.[65]

THE BLOCK SYSTEM

Pendergast organized his machine according to what he called the "block system," a term that he never defined and that seemed to characterize only one aspect of his large organization.[66] His absorption of the Rabbits, along with Cas Welch's cooperation as a sub-boss, created a large pool of seasoned political workers for the machine. Every ward had a club and sometimes two, one for Goats and one for Rabbits. In Independence and eastern Jackson County, Truman assembled his own people, handling affairs that had previously occupied a considerable amount of Boss Tom's time. The importance of Truman's expanding role inside the machine is shown by Pendergast's elevating him to a vice presidency of the Jackson Democratic Club, which had about six thousand dues-paying members in the early 1930s. Another important leader, James P. Aylward, a Kansas City lawyer with close ties to Shannon, served Pendergast as a political advisor. Some twenty-five to thirty bankers, attorneys, and businessmen individually and collectively offered counsel on a variety of issues. City Manager McElroy and Pendergast talked on the telephone and met regularly, never at city hall, framing general policy and discussing administrative details. Mayor Smith performed ceremonial duties, and machine members of the city council did as they were told. A weekly machine newspaper, the *Missouri Democrat*, parroted the current party line.

The Missouri Supreme Court had invalidated the state constitutional provision under which the governor appointed two commissioners to run the police department, and under the city charter the city manager appointed one director of police to manage the department. This move made the director of police important in the machine's organizational structure.

The machine counted on the services of a small army of professional politicians, including some African Americans and women. Sixteen ward leaders in Kansas City and eight township leaders in the rest of Jackson County functioned as sub-bosses, some very important in their own right, especially Welch. There were 460 Goat precinct captains, plus 300 Rabbit precinct captains, all amalgamated into a single organization. Almost all the key machine leaders and functionaries, even if they only performed political tasks, held public jobs. During designated campaign periods, they contributed up to 50 percent of their salaries to machine coffers. In addition, they paid annual dues of six dollars to the Jackson Democratic Club and lesser amounts to ward clubs.[67]

All of the Kansas City precincts had one to ten block captains. The machine covered the entire city when campaigning, including Republican sections of town, for practical reasons and to create the illusion of laboring arduously to turn out the vote. The machine claimed that its efforts to court the middle and upper classes had, through hard work and a good record, built a solid base of support in the Country Club District.[68] Vote totals reflected this contention, but no one really knew for sure, given widespread vote fraud. In much the same way, the machine asserted that its candidates received substantial majorities in African American precincts, overcoming the opposition of the Republican *Kansas City Call*, edited by black Republican leader Chester A. Franklin.[69] In the river wards, machine-supported candidates ran up margins all out of proportion with census population totals. It was not unusual for block captains to deliver a precinct by a vote of 250 to 1, or even 251 to 0, in an obviously intentional flaunting of the sanctity of the ballot.

For morale purposes and to make it appear that the Pendergast machine was a legitimate political organization that started at the grassroots and was answerable to the electorate, block captains, precinct captains, ward leaders, and other officials went through an elaborate charade to select candidates and formulate a program. Pendergast orchestrated the whole exercise, deciding the outcome in advance. He warned enemies that a gigantic espionage system kept him on top of affairs: "I expect to have 20,000 to 30,000 volunteer reporters working for me, eager to bring me information. Some of it is misinformation. But experience makes it easy for me to sift it down. . . . I get the viewpoint of every section of the city. I think I know more about how Kansas City people feel than any individual or newspaper." He added ominously, "It is my business to know."[70]

McElroy's job description as city manager required that he be strictly nonpartisan, but he showed what a joke that was when he bragged in 1933 that the machine gained votes the hard way, by providing services:

> They say we steal votes. Sure, we steal. Here's the way—a perfectly legitimate way. You move into a precinct. Before your stuff is unloaded a man calls on you, asking as a neighbor if he can do anything to help you. You're in a lot of trouble. Your telephone isn't connected, your gas and water and electricity aren't turned on. Our man goes down to the corner and makes a few telephone calls, and pretty soon your telephone is O.K. and the gas and water and electricity are running. Before he goes, he finds out where you're from, what you do, and what church you belong to. If you're a Presbyterian, in a day or so a nice Presbyterian lady calls on your wife. Whenever you have any little troubles, the precinct captain takes care of them. Nothing is said about politics until a day or so before election.[71]

This was all very true. Throughout the year, the block captains handled all sorts of individual and neighborhood concerns—everything from expediting garbage collection to the filling of troublesome potholes. Many people felt it especially beneficial to have a block captain living close by in the neighborhood, instead of one who commutes from another part of town. This created a more personal level of service, one that the average citizen could relate to. Shed of its political objectives, the block system was quite similar to that proposed by Progressive Era urban sociologists to solve problems associated with social disintegration in large, closely packed cities.[72] Apparently, Pendergast formulated his plan not from books or from the methods of other urban bosses, but as an outgrowth of his experiences as a ward heeler in the West Bottoms. An innovation of his was to include all sections and economic classes of people, regardless of whether they voted for the machine's candidates or not.

Given the way Boss Tom fixed elections in advance, he was more interested in keeping people reasonably content under his rule than in how they actually cast their ballots. As might have been expected, there was a dark side. Property owners with the audacity to speak out against Pendergast's undemocratic rule could expect to have their property assessed at a higher taxable value—not a pleasant prospect in the middle of a depression. In addition, the Pendergast system had a very high price tag. Large numbers of patronage workers carried on the municipal payroll, especially by the water, parks, fire, and street departments, saw city hall only when stopping by on payday. McElroy admitted as much, bragging, "We're always looking for a bright young man who has a lot of friends in his neighborhood and who can change a precinct from Republican to Democratic. I give him a job in city work. He's the kind of smart young man that we need. It's our duty to the city to get men like that on the payroll."[73]

Without realizing it, McElroy articulated what was wrong with politics in Tom's Town. Political henchmen who actually held city positions were hard to remove. When a director complained to McElroy for reinstating an employee fired for having been drunk on the job, McElroy said, "Now just keep your shirt on young man. That fellow is a fine precinct captain for us, and I don't want to lose him. Do you understand?"[74] The employee stayed.

There was no way of knowing how many city employees actually worked for their paychecks. In early 1933, even before the influx of federal money, the city regularly employed 3,750 people, paying them a total of $450,000 monthly. The city handed out roughly an additional $120,000 weekly to about 5,000 half-time day laborers, each paid $24 weekly. Many labored with picks and shovels, performing duties that could have been done much more quickly and at far less expense by earthmoving equipment. The machine, it might be said, anticipated New Deal make-work programs. Even though no numbers are available, thousands of other Kansas City laborers indirectly received city monies for working on projects funded under the Ten-Year Plan bond program.[75]

Boss Tom pretended to take an evenhanded approach to dispensing jobs. He supposedly told machine officials at city hall, "Give a job to every man who needs one. Don't ask what political party he belongs to. We don't mind making Democrats out of Republicans."[76] Left unsaid was that every day laborer hired under New Deal make-work programs required the endorsement of a machine block captain. A puzzled Pendergast, when asked whether city workers contributed part of their salaries to machine coffers, answered, "Why shouldn't they be? That's how they got their jobs."[77]

Pendergast often hired the department heads and supervisory personnel in the city and county, sometimes bypassing input from McElroy, Truman, and other supervisory personnel. If the job was not an insignificant patronage position, such as reading meters for the water department, he frequently tried to employ the best candidate. When a man whom Pendergast offered an unsolicited appointment as highway engineer for the county said he would not be beholden to anyone, meaning the machine, Boss Tom retorted, "Did I ask you to be beholden to me or anyone else? . . . You fill that bill and that's all I ask of you."[78] The man accepted the job and held it until he died, and Pendergast, whom he had no further contact with, never asked him for a favor directly or indirectly.

When Alex Sachs won election as Jackson County highway engineer for the first of two four-year terms in 1932, Truman was his sponsor. However, a subsequent conversation that Sachs had with Pendergast likely was along the lines of those that Truman himself had with the boss. Although Pendergast products such as road oil probably were often used in highway maintenance, Sachs (like Truman) valued his independence of operation and was never accused of using his office for personal gain. Sachs was interested in a third term in office in 1940, but was subject to the machine's policy of "term limits." On one occasion after the collapse of the machine, when hostile political groups called in civic leaders to conduct investigations of the county departments, one report that amused Alex Sachs was the written comment on an accepted bid, "Why this low price?"[79]

J. Harvey Jennett, M.D., thirty-two years old, had a somewhat similar experience in 1932, when, following a sudden death, Pendergast hired him on short notice to run the General Hospital. Jennett found it unusual when two county officials, Harry Truman and Robert Barr, the eastern judge, neither of whom had any jurisdiction over city health services, picked him up at the hospital in a chauffeur-driven black Cadillac and transported him to 1908 Main, ushering him past a long line of people stretching out around the block, to see the boss.

In a five-minute interview, Pendergast, having obviously checked Jennett out beforehand, hired him and instructed him to handle all personnel and purchasing decisions through city hall and to avoid corruption scandals. "First, run a clean hospital—and I don't mean the floors and windows," Pendergast emphasized. "I mean don't have a scandal. Nothing costs more votes than a scandal at the General Hospital. Don't let that happen." Jennett, just like the highway engineer, never met with Pendergast again. Jennett held the hospital position until 1936, when the city health director abruptly ordered him to resign, explaining that it was nothing personal but the boss had an obligation to fill. Jennett did as ordered and went into private practice, where he worked for the next fifty-three years.[80]

THE RIVERSIDE JOCKEY CLUB

Pendergast, now far removed from his days of living in a modest room in the West Bottoms, as his lavish mansion and grand tours of Europe indicated, adopted regal ways and began to indulge himself like some petty Latin American dictator. He even provided bread and circuses for his loyal and adoring subjects. In 1927, the Missouri Supreme Court reinterpreted a 1905 statute banning betting on horses. Through a loophole, an individual could make a contribution for the improvement of a horse's breed. If the animal helped by that contribution, perhaps twenty minutes later, ran fast enough in competition against other equines, say, running first on an oval track with starting and finishing lines, the person became eligible for an appropriate "refund." Hence, the racetracks had sets of windows labeled "Contributions" and "Refunds." In response to criticism, Pendergast once said, "Only slanderers would attribute a bad name to a town because people lay bets on horse races."[81]

In 1928, Pendergast organized the Riverside Jockey Club and converted a former dog track in suburban Riverside, north of the Missouri River in Clay County, into a large and efficient thoroughbred racecourse known as "Pendergast's track." He hired a topflight manager, William Kyne, who later ran Bay Meadows in California. Kyne's high-quality Riverside operation attracted leading owners, trainers, and jockeys from across the country. Very efficient tabulators at Riverside, ciphering by hand in the days before computers, acquired a reputation for quickly posting results. The track surface of packed loess soil provided good footing, and thoroughbreds seldom broke down on what was admittedly a rather slow course.[82]

A typical meet lasted thirty-two days, attracting daily crowds upwards of seventeen thousand people. Pendergast raised and trained his own thoroughbreds on a farm south of Kansas City. For many years, he raced a string of horses, usually numbering around fourteen at any given time, at Riverside and other tracks. He dearly loved them all, but few of his beasts, with the notable exception of King Saxon, ran fast enough to win major races. Another of his horses, Bo McMillin, was an also-ran in the 1928 Kentucky Derby. At Riverside, Boss Tom, in regal style and with his son at his side, preferred a box in the grandstand at the finish line, disdaining the comfort of the enclosed clubhouse. Just about anybody who counted in the Kansas City area attended the track at one time or another. Once, sitting beside the race announcer, Judge Truman, probably looking back toward the turn after the win, place, and show horses had crossed the finish line, was heard to say over an open microphone, "Where's that sonofabitch I bet on?"[83]

High Society and the Pendergasts

Boss Curley and his family never really gained acceptance socially in Boston, and Tom and Carolyn Pendergast faced a similar situation in Kansas City. Despite a small and pretentious coterie of sons and daughters of Kansas City pioneers, a "catfish aristocracy," Kansas City was young and far more egalitarian in outlook than the old New England hub. Kansas City did have a semblance of high society, though, the "old money" folk listed in the *Social Register*. They rarely permitted their names or businesses to be publicized in the dailies and, of course, were the least likely to rub elbows with anyone as boorish and crass as the Pendergasts. They were also the least likely to be intimidated by Tom's power. The newspapers regularly ran gushy stories about prominent Kansas Citians. These were, however, the "new money" people: the Kempers, the Nicholses, and even the Pendergasts. J. C. Nichols, after all, consciously created Mission Hills as an enclave for a new-money upper class. Only a city block and State Line Road separated 5650 Ward Parkway from Mission Hills.

Pendergast belonged to the Elk, Eagle, and Moose lodges and even the socially correct Kansas City Club. The wealthy came out in droves to the lavish society weddings of his two oldest children, treating these events more like sideshows than solemn occasions. Still, an invisible barrier remained. Pendergast had to exert pressure to get himself invited to join the Kansas City Club and some other organizations. He claimed that he did not care about joining, but did it for his family. He once said that he was never happier than when he lived at 200 West 54th and never as unhappy as when he lived at 5650 Ward Parkway.

There was no way a former saloon bouncer and suspected bawdy-house owner and his West Bottoms woman were ever going to gain complete social acceptance in Kansas City. They were generally tolerated in person and disdained behind their backs, with few, if any, close friends outside the family. Truman caught the hypocrisy in a private memorandum: "Who is to blame for

Tom and Carolyn Pendergast, ca. 1935. (*Photograph by Jack Wally, courtesy the Western Historical Manuscript Collection, Kansas City, Mo.*)

present conditions but sniveling church members who weep on Sunday, play with whores on Monday, drink on Tuesday, sell out to the Boss on Wednesday, repent about Friday and start over on Sunday." He added, "I think maybe the Boss is nearer heaven than the snivelers."[84]

Tom and Carolyn traveled extensively. In addition to going to Europe in 1927, they went again in 1931, in 1935—in a trip curtailed when Carolyn fell ill with an infected gland, and in 1936. Tom liked ocean travel and once said he slept best when he heard water lapping against the side of a ship.[85] Certainly, under the cloud of economic distress in the 1930s, the overseas expeditions of Tom and Carolyn set them apart from all except a few Kansas Citians, rich and poor. The Pendergasts also took frequent family excursions to New Orleans and New York City. In the Empire City, Tom rented a large suite of rooms at the Waldorf-Astoria. Carolyn, Marceline, and Aileen shopped in the best Park Avenue stores, spending huge sums of money on fine clothes and jewelry. In season, the family went to Saratoga Springs, New York, and other fashionable resorts, mingling with the highest levels of society. They seldom missed the spring racing meet at Churchill Downs, watching the Kentucky Derby from a private box. The Kansas City papers, including the *Star*, published stories about the trips, almost treating the Pendergasts like legitimate social lions. Outwardly, Tom and Carolyn lived a comfortable life, their own version of the American Dream. But the marriage was in reality somewhat strained, for Tom's political duties always beckoned, as did his growing insatiable avidity, drawing him back to 1908 Main Street.

With surprising swiftness, Pendergast consolidated his rule over Kansas City, firmly establishing his invisible government. Seldom if ever had a person so completely dominated life in a large city in the United States. As the Great Depression deepened, bossism seemed part of an ominous national trend. From the maverick governor William Langer in North Dakota to the flamboyant Huey Long in Louisiana, rising petty dictators defied the federal government by threatening its ultimate authority.[86] Clearly, at some juncture, even as the New Deal worked to effect an economic recovery, Roosevelt was going to have to take steps to reestablish federal control throughout the land. Until then, men like Thomas J. Pendergast would continue to ride high.

FIVE

Debacle

1933–1938

Between the two world wars, Tom's Town arguably ranked as the most wide open city in the United States. Edward R. Murrow, during a visit, compared Kansas City to such notorious world sin centers as Singapore and Port Said, which may have been stretching matters, but not by very much. Prohibition did not stop the carnival of vice. Hundreds of speakeasies operated with impunity, popular ones around the clock. The end of Prohibition simply afforded legitimacy to a continuing process. The cleaning up of Omaha, where authorities closed sixteen hundred illegal saloons and a large red-light district, presented Kansas City with close to a monopoly on large-scale iniquity west of Chicago. Orland K. Armstrong, writing in the fall of 1934 for a New York audience, observed, "If you want excitement with roulette, cards, dice, the races or a dozen other forms of chance ask a patrolman on the Kansas City streets. He'll guide you. It's perfectly open. You just walk in."[1]

It goes without saying that illegal vice in the 1920s and 1930s was not confined to Kansas City. Just about every place of any size in the United States had a red-light district. Hurley, Wisconsin, for example, an old mining town on the border with Michigan, was notorious for its bawdy houses. Chicago had a well-deserved reputation as a vice center, with everything from "B-girls," who enticed customers into bars, to "call girls," who were available for a price. In Prohibition days, the head of the vice division in the Chicago Police Department estimated that the city had at least thirty thousand rooms that were used for immoral purposes.

John Torrio, the predecessor of Al Capone in Chicago, grossed more than $2 million a year from prostitution and $3 million from gambling. Capone certainly did much better, bringing in possibly as much as $100 million yearly from his criminal empire. While New York was, in terms of sheer size, volume, and money transacted, the vice capital of America, various groups fought to gain monopolies over components of the industry. What Capone did was to create a monopoly, a sort of model for big-time criminals, consolidating through ruthless methods a variety of illegal vice businesses into a single all-powerful crime syndicate. In Kansas City Pendergast's take reportedly was $20 million annually from gambling, with another $12 million from prostitution and narcotics,[2] placing him below Capone but by any stretch of the imagination in the major league of American civic corruption.

In 1938, estimates held that more than half of all adult Americans placed bets. Hundreds of country clubs offered gambling. Slot machines were commonplace, even sitting in service stations in some states. In Nevada, which had legalized games of chance, Reno had several profitable small casinos, but Las Vegas was still essentially a railroad division point at that time. Resorts in Hallandale, Florida, and "lake houses" in Saratoga Springs, New York, catered to wealthy wagerers. Gambling boats operated outside the legal coastal limits off south Florida and southern California. Millions of people played numbers games and placed small bets in football pools. On paper, outside of Nevada, gambling was against the law almost everywhere in the United States, and Kansas City was no exception. What set Tom's Town apart was the unabashedly open promotion of gambling in all forms and for all classes. Pendergast, in the name of helping commerce, took the lead in fostering an environment that drew the dregs of society from all across the nation.[3]

Gambling constituted a big business in Kansas City, employing, depending on the source of the estimate, anywhere from 2,000 to 3,500 bookmakers, dice throwers, stick men, card dealers, and other gamesters. Several downtown dens did a roaring business. The Turf, the biggest of a hundred-odd bookmaking parlors, had craps rooms, plus betting centers for football and baseball. Baltimore Recreation had a $1 million yearly take from blackjack. Crapshooting was the specialty of 12th Street Recreation. The Fortune Club in midtown netted $480,000 a year and offered prizes ranging from $5 to $50 for 10-cent bingo games. Floating craps games operated all over town, and many drugstores and various small shops had at least one slot machine.[4]

Multipurpose Kansas City nightclubs offered a variety of different kinds of wine, women, song, and gambling. The better-known ones, generally called "Pendergast sin places," included such popular cabarets as the Blue Goose, the Winnie Winkle, the Bowery, the Oriental, the Jubilesta, and the Stork. More than 250 bawdy houses operated openly. Houses of ill fame lined the sides of 14th Street just east of downtown for four blocks.[5]

The notorious Chesterfield Club was a famous Pendergast sin place. Located only one block from the federal courthouse downtown, it served as a daily reminder of who actually ran Kansas City to judges and lawmen of the United States; it seemed a deliberate affront to conventional morality. Even though common practice for appearance' sake called for confining gambling to back rooms, at the Chesterfield Club roulette wheels and dice tables greeted patrons the moment they walked through the front door. The establishment pretended to operate as a swank supper club, offering a menu of "soup and striptease." Madams brought the female performers, some of whom doubled as unclothed waitresses, from nearby houses of ill fame. Not infrequently, the women went considerably further than city ordinances allowed. Once in a great while, the police would stage mock raids. On one occasion they apprehended a madam using the generic name Gladys for leading her charges in an indecent dance.[6]

A memorable experience for many of the male customers was watching the beautiful waitresses who wore only shoes and a change belt. "These gals would come out completely nude and give the boys a kick," a male diner recalled in vivid detail decades later. "These gals would come around to your table and display themselves—*close.*" A young musician who performed at the Chesterfield found the scantily clad young women very distracting, making it hard to concentrate on the music. On Friday afternoons, the Pendergast machine held regularly scheduled ribald sex parties featuring nude dancing and backroom sex at the Chesterfield as a reward for male precinct workers and others. Few saw the sinister side of the Chesterfield. The club's gang of rough enforcers routinely rolled drunks and beat up disruptive customers. One night they killed a Texas cattleman who tried to defend a waitress, took the body over to Kansas City, Kansas, dumped it in a street, and reported the crime as a hit-and-run accident.[7]

According to Commissioner Harry J. Anslinger of the Federal Bureau of Narcotics, Kansas City was the drug distribution center of the Midwest. Anslinger directed the nation's war on drugs during the Great Depression. His agents broke the Affronte drug syndicate in Kansas City in 1933. Six years later, a series of coordinated raids in Kansas City netted forty-six street dealers and higher-ups, including the four-hundred-and-fifty-pound James Abbott, described as "the biggest drug peddler in the world." Unfortunately, the Bureau of Narcotics had neither the resources nor the enforcement powers needed to make a major intervention in Kansas City. Anslinger concentrated on spreading information on the dangers of drugs, trying to prove that the Mafia existed, and pushing anti-marijuana legislation.[8]

Pendergast justified charges that Kansas City was a "wide-open" town in which protected gambling and prostitution flourished by stating, "Well, the rich men have their clubs where they can gamble and have a good time. Would you deny the poor man an equal right?" In keeping with this sentiment, one police official said that patrol wagons were for "vagabonds and drunks" and not for Kansas Citians who liked to play "poker and bridge."[9]

In a class by themselves were a cluster of "black-and-tans" in the vicinity of 18th and Vine streets, east of downtown in a large African American district. Fabulous black jazz musicians performing there perfected a distinctive and lasting Kansas City sound. There was an unfortunate aspect to their great achievement, however. A number of the musicians involved in the creation of Kansas City jazz polished their style playing together in late-night jam sessions, sometimes because their regular gigs paid so poorly that they needed the extra work to make ends meet.[10]

THE AFRICAN AMERICAN COMMUNITY

The jazz musicians received more acclaim from whites than from their fellow blacks. Only a small coterie of African Americans ever ventured inside any of the 18th and Vine establishments. Most of the musicians were from out of town, and they played in clubs operating illegally after closing hours and rumored to have unsavory proprietors with criminal connections. Far more popular and accepted in the black community were players for the baseball team the Kansas City Monarchs, a perennial power in the Negro American League.[11] The Monarchs were the "angels of the day" and the jazz men the "devils of the night."

The Kansas City African American community had roots extending back to Reconstruction, with the arrival of former slaves from rural Missouri. In 1890, the census reported 13,700 black people in the city. The number increased to 23,566 in 1910 and rose moderately over the next three decades. Between 1930 and 1940 the population grew from 30,893 to 38,574.

While about a third of the African Americans in Kansas City at any given time were rooming-house floaters and temporary laborers, the rest built a stable society in wards controlled by Cas Welch east of downtown, bounded west to east by Charlotte and Cleveland streets and by East 10th Street on the north and East 29th Street on the south. They often aspired to home ownership, which somewhat unsettled the white population of Kansas City. The general educational level was high school. Except for a small number of professionals and businessmen, few black people in Kansas City had much money. Most were employed in postal, transportation, and factory work, plus a large number in domestic service. All but a few jobs were low paying and offered little hope of significant advancement. Social life centered around church, fraternal, and voluntary activities.[12]

Kansas City, by custom and by law, still was largely segregated in the 1930s and for decades after that. Missouri had been a border state very divided over the slavery question, and it still reflected all the antagonisms and divisions of the Civil War. Even though it remained in the Union, Missouri experienced more than ten thousand armed clashes during the war, the vast number of which were small-force actions, but statistically more than in any other state. The war left a legacy of distrust, bitterness, and hatred in Missouri that lasted far into the twentieth century. So Kansas City had both a northern and southern heritage, with a taste of the western frontier thrown in for good measure.

No public accommodation legislation or city ordinance ensured African Americans equal access with whites to hotels, restaurants, theaters, and other public places.[13] The city and county hospitals and correctional facilities were rigidly segregated. State law mandated separate public schools. Because of restrictive covenants pioneered by J. C. Nichols, it was impossible for black people to buy property in many residential neighborhoods. Still, certain inconsistencies prevailed. The city operated all-white golf courses and swimming pools, but there was no forced segregation in the Municipal Auditorium. The county courthouse, built when Truman was presiding judge, had common rest rooms for blacks and whites, unlike the situation at the Clay County Courthouse, just north of the Missouri River in the old town of Liberty. African Americans could shop in downtown Kansas City department stores, but could not eat in the lunchrooms. The greater number of white Kansas Citians saw blacks only on the job, and after work black people went home to what social scientists called a "separate city," replete with its own commercial section and range of professional services.

Cas Welch's "Little Tammany" ultimately controlled thirty-six predominantly African American precincts, twenty-seven in a redrawn small Second Ward. The ward, considered the poorest in the city, had many rooming houses and a large transient population. Welch's precinct captains and enforcers worked hard to make inroads into the traditionally Republican black vote. Until Welch switched from Shannon to Pendergast, the black precincts voted Rabbit in city Democratic primaries, so they hardly figured into Pendergast's calculations. In the 1925 mayoral election, the Democratic candidate received 62.8 percent of 3,338 votes cast in the Second Ward, for a plurality of 856, not enough to change the outcome of the election, which was won by Republican Albert Beach by only 523 out of a total of 113,563 ballots tallied.

The impact of the Second Ward on Kansas City elections changed with the inauguration of massive ghost voting. Without a significant population increase, the number of voters in the ward more than doubled to 8,128 in 1930 and rose to 15,940 in 1934, when the machine mayoral candidate carried the ward by 13,721 votes. In 1936, Franklin D. Roosevelt received 88 percent of 21,242 recorded votes in the ward. This represented a very significant swing of African Americans to the Democratic column, but the problem was that many of the "voters" did not exist. Basically, what Pendergast did was to subcontract the black vote to the Welch faction, and Welch did his part by providing in excess of 15,000 fraudulent votes. Because machine officials destroyed the registration rolls, it is impossible to determine the actual number of real people registered to vote or what number of them voted. After the Pendergast machine collapsed, the Second Ward voting totals dropped sharply. In the 1944 election, the reform candidate for mayor won by 901 out of 4,067 ballots, the number of voters more proportionate to the Second Ward's population.[14]

Given his cynical methodology in dealing with the African American electorate, Pendergast never placed himself in a position where he needed to express his actual views on racial questions. About as close as he came in public was automatically endorsing the platform of the national Democratic party, so routine an action that it meant nothing. He was under no pressure to change social conditions in Kansas City and he acted accordingly, keeping the status quo. He did include black people in his machine, and, from all accounts, he distributed welfare in color-blind fashion, even before the implementation of New Deal relief programs. Pendergast did attempt to seek the support and advice of Kansas City's African American religious, political, and business leaders, and he financed a pro-Pendergast, mainly black-read newspaper, the *American*, and worked with African American criminal elements. But by no stretch of the imagination was he a social reformer.

OPEN DISCUSSIONS OF CORRUPTION

Pendergast machine officials discounted concerns over criminality and gambling in Kansas City. When the *Star* and a parent-teacher association launched a crusade against slot machines, citing their bad influence on the youth, City Manager Henry McElroy announced he would order their removal only if widespread "agitation" surfaced against them. Even then, McElroy said he would refuse to tamper with slots in small stores, asserting that they made the difference for the owners between solvency and bankruptcy. He ridiculed claims that slot machines corrupted little children.[15]

Such a loose policy begged larger questions, which crusading rabbi Samuel Mayerberg, addressing the reform Government Study Club, raised in a May 1932 speech that made headlines in the *Star*. Mayerberg, age forty, had since 1928 been the senior rabbi of Temple B'nai Jehudah, which numbered among its membership many prominent Kansas City business and professional leaders. Mayerberg, a slim, courtly, outspoken man with a strong intellectual bent, believed that as a religious leader he had an obligation to speak out on pressing public and social questions. "Fighting is my nature," he once told an interviewer. "I would like to think I am a man of peace. That, above all, is what I have worked for."[16]

Mayerberg lived up to his creed of standing up for what he believed in when he spoke to the Government Study Club, bluntly telling the members, "You've turned your city over to a gang and given it into hands of crooks and racketeers because you are asleep. The time has come for action. The time for study has passed." The city council gave Mayerberg a polite public hearing on the issue of removing McElroy over technical charter violations, and, as expected, took no further action. However, a botched attempt by parties unknown on Mayerberg's life, coupled with threats against state and federal grand jury members investigating vice, lent enough credence to Mayerberg's accusations to unexpectedly place the machine on the defensive.[17] McElroy's rash comments about slot machines only exacerbated criticism.

Thomas J. Pendergast increasingly cultivated the impression that he was above mere newspaper-generated controversies. A sort of combination chairman of the board and constitutional monarch, he felt compelled to reassure his subjects. He granted an interview to a *Star* reporter and, with unusual solemnity, reversed McElroy, calling for the removal of all slot machines. Furthermore, with the impending end of Prohibition, he pledged his support to preventing the return of the old-time saloon.

Pendergast dismissed as exaggerated all reports of rampant gambling and racketeering in Kansas City, basing his comments on his long experience as a political observer and on recent visits to New York, Philadelphia, Chicago, and other cities. "I say there is more gambling in these cities in comparison than there is in Kansas City," he asserted, "except as may have existed there thirty years ago down on the state line in the Bottoms." In particular, he praised the police for keeping Kansas City freer from racketeering than any city its size in the country, stating, "Outside of the gambling and slot-machine complaints, I say that Kansas City is the standout city of the country as far as the protection of its city by the police is concerned." Of course, slot machines did not go away, although a police officer actually testified under oath in 1934 that he had never seen one in Kansas City.[18]

Presiding Judge Harry S. Truman disagreed with his political mentor, whom he called the Big Boss, on conditions in Kansas City. In private, Truman called Cas Welch "a thug and a crook of the worst water," speculated that Miles Bulger stole half a million dollars as a county judge, and condemned other fixers and corrupters. On reflection, Truman attributed the situation to larger ills of society rather than to the policies of the machine that he

Tom Pendergast (front) and associates in 1934. *(Photograph from the Kansas City Museum Archives)*

served and helped to lead. "We teach our boys to worship the dollar and to get it how they can," he lamented. "And we have an extraordinarily clean local government. Chicago, Pittsburgh, San Francisco, Los Angeles make us look like suckers."[19] Despite any reservations, Truman, whose political future depended on machine support, remained an officer of the Jackson Democratic Club, continuing to demonstrate faith and trust in T. J. Pendergast.

Johnny Lazia and the Underworld

The greatest cloud on Pendergast's horizon was the concern of direct criminal infiltration of his organization. In fact, what appeared to be progress was a hostile takeover attempt by sinister forces. One could say that, even though it had been a long time coming, what happened was a natural consequence of the Pendergasts' old gambling ties and the use of criminal enforcers. In some ways, Pendergast, probably without design, contributed to the formation of a home-grown crime syndicate in Kansas City. Despite isolated Black Hand extortion plots in the 1910s, no known organized criminal group with ties to the Mafia existed. However, the North Side's heavily Italian community produced a coterie of young criminal types influenced by Pendergast ruffians.

Albert L. Reeves, who through his position as federal judge was privy to reliable inside information about machine criminality and recruitment practices, deplored the role of Pendergast's North Side henchmen. He said they were, of course, a bad influence for the younger generation of foreign-born parents and led many promising youths along doubtful paths. "Since they found easy money in their operations and immunity from prosecution, they quickly submitted themselves to a state of complete servility to the orders of the political boss," Reeves asserted. "In many instances these young Italians, and others, came of good families and were young men of infinite promise."[20]

Many candidates for a life of crime, feeling discriminated against for honest jobs in keeping with what they considered to be their talents, found the prospect of easy money too tempting to pass up. Pendergast ward captains gave illegal concessions to selected leaders, including limited local monopolies over the selling of narcotics. Other promising Italian youths worked for the Pendergast machine in the numbers racket, collected protection money from bawdy houses and gamblers, and performed enforcement duties at the polls. In the 1920s, these home-grown criminals coalesced into a gang headed by Johnny Lazia.[21]

Born in the United States in 1897, Lazia belonged to a hard-working, respectable, and fairly prosperous Italian immigrant family. He graduated at an early age into a life of crime. In 1916, he served time on a state charge of highway robbery, gaining an early release from a Pendergast-connected lieutenant governor after Pendergast business associate Phil McCrory testified as a character witness for him. Lazia, a criminally talented young man, moved up very quickly in the Pendergast machine under the tutelage of the ward captain in "Little Italy," Michael Ross, a Pendergast associate. When Lazia was married in 1924, he was masquerading as an honest citizen, the owner of a soft drink distributorship that marketed a rather distasteful and unappealing bottled brew, Golden Mist, which his henchmen forced stores to carry. As a rising politician, Lazia claimed to control 7,500 Italian votes. He undertook some enforcement duties for the machine, allegedly working through lawyer James Aylward.[22]

In May 1928, using a special city bond election as a cover, Lazia carried out a coup d'état against Ross. Lazia's hoodlums slugged and roughed up a number of Ross's poll workers, kidnapping his chief Italian American lieutenants, the so-called Big Five. Lazia issued what amounted to a proclamation of justification, claiming to fight for home rule for all North Side Italians. He emphasized that Ross, who was Irish, had moved away from the North Side several years earlier.

A confidant sent an unsigned letter to Senator James A. Reed in Washington, placing the takeover in the broader context of the cold war between the two local superpowers, the waning Rabbits and the victorious Goats. The correspondent saw in the actions the fine hand of justice of the peace and Pendergast ward boss Cas Welch, who wanted an expanded role in Kansas City machine politics: "Judge Welch no longer regards himself as a lieutenant, and has strong ambitions to be on an equality with Pendergast and Shannon. So far Pendergast has been able to prevent such a situation . . . and, as I view it, Pendergast is not any too sure of Welch."

The observer went on to give inside information on the Lazia coup, which he said had served to "frighten Mr. Pendergast":

> A new situation developed on the day of the Bond Election. A rebellion, apparently successful, was launched against the leadership of Judge Ross in the old Fifth Ward. All of Ross's lieutenants were kidnapped, and other smaller fry were driven away from the polls at the point of guns. This rebellion was led by an Italian by the name of Lazia. Lazia is a henchman of Jim Aylward, who in turn is Judge Welch's very close political friend. The opinion in some quarters is that this Italian rebellion was instigated by Welch. This seems plausible.[23]

Lazia organized the new North Side Democratic Club and signed up 2,500 members. At first, Pendergast indicated he would never desert Ross, but he changed his mind after Lazia, probably at gunpoint, persuaded the Big Five to join his North Side Democratic Club. Pendergast bought Welch off with patronage appointments and negotiated a pact with Lazia. Afterwards, Pendergast became quite serious about carrying a revolver.[24] This more influential role of gangsters in the machine suggested a continuity—not a worsening—from earlier periods in the development of the Pendergast faction.[25]

The stylish and well-groomed Lazia, frequently wearing spats and carrying a walking stick, displayed a flashy and conspicuous presence. His Cuban Gardens, a popular nightclub adjacent to Pendergast's Riverside racetrack, took in as much as $8,000 from gambling on a good night. As one of his more lucrative rackets, the Cuban Gardens netted over $2 million a year. A government informant said Lazia sold his interest in a dog track for between $12 million and $15 million. Lazia held court on a downtown street corner, increasing his popularity by giving dollar bills to passersby. He was a smooth talker; he was slightly built, chewed gum constantly, and wore thick rimless glasses. He suffered from glaucoma and underwent several operations performed by the internationally prominent ophthalmologist E. J. Curran, M.D., of the University of Kansas's Bell Memorial Hospital.[26]

An important turn in Lazia's career came in October 1930, with the killing of Solomon "Cutcher-Head-Off" or "Big Solly" Weissman by the owner of a downtown horse-betting service. Weissman, a violent and fanatical three-hundred-pound bootlegger, a career gangster, and a Pendergast election enforcer, was until 1929 a partner of Lazia's in a dog track. Weissman had formed ties with mobsters in other cities—Chicago, Cincinnati, and Baltimore—ties that Lazia exploited after his murder, hastening his elevation to the leadership of Kansas City's underworld. In solidifying his control, Lazia divided Kansas City into five racketeering districts, each operated by a different gang of his organization. As part of a grand design, Lazia took steps to work out an informal, mutually beneficial alliance with Al Capone of Chicago, who wanted to use Kansas City as a bootlegging distribution hub.[27]

Pendergast handed over to Lazia broad powers in the municipal police department, especially after the city officially took over jurisdiction from the state in 1932. The criminal leader recruited new officers, in a short period hiring seventy recently released convicts from Leavenworth for second careers in law enforcement. At one time an estimated 10 percent of the police officers had criminal records.[28] Several sensational kidnappings resulting in large ransom payments successfully delivered to gain the release of the victims further tarnished the image of the department. Police officers were paid low wages intentionally, to encourage them to take bribes. The director of police, Eugene Ruppert, a former used-car salesman, and a number of officers were close friends of Lazia's. Therefore, it was little wonder that many Kansas Citians feared the police.

Lazia established a policy under which, for a high price, the police would grant protection to fugitives who wanted to hide out in Tom's Town. Hoodlums from Chicago, skilled in the use of shotguns and displaying no compunction about using their fists, were contracted to help on election days.[29] They stayed at the 101-room Monroe Hotel adjacent to 1908 Main and owned by Pendergast since 1924. On occasion, Lazia allowed criminals from outside to come into Kansas City to commit specific crimes, sometimes of a very sensational nature.

On the morning of June 17, 1933, an extraordinary criminal action in Kansas City made national headlines. The night before, Lazia reputedly was formally introduced to the perpetrators, commonly identified as Charles "Pretty Boy" Floyd, Adam "Machine Gun" Richetti, and Vernon C. Miller. Wielding submachine guns, three men attempted in broad daylight to free a criminal colleague, Frank "Jelly" Nash, from police custody in the parking lot in front of Union Station, one of the most conspicuous places in town. Nash, a convicted bank robber, had been recaptured in Arkansas after escaping from Leavenworth penitentiary and was in transit back to prison under the escort of several law enforcement officers. The officers had Nash in an automobile and were preparing to drive away when the gunmen appeared and, after someone yelled "Let 'em have it," opened fire. In a fusillade of bullets, four peace officers and Nash died. During the gun battle, a federal agent may have shot Nash in the back of the head. The killers escaped and drove several miles through busy traffic to their hiding place in the Country Club District, where one of them received medical attention for a shoulder wound.[30]

Upon hearing about the shootings, Lazia rushed to the station and acted as an unofficial crime investigator, supervising the search for evidence. He later arranged for the killers to leave town, providing them with a car and an escort. Later in the day, one of the criminals went back to the station, where he told Lazia, "I'm sorry about this, but the officers started shooting." Lazia answered, "You've put a lot of heat on us." Of those shot, one who died and two who were wounded were federal agents, enabling J. Edgar Hoover to dramatize the implications of the "Union Station massacre" as part of a general drive to obtain more power from Congress for his agency.[31]

Pendergast kept a low profile after the massacre, and machine apologists attributed it to a national epidemic of crime. In other words, it could have happened anywhere. Nevertheless, as an unexpected consequence, the incident focused attention throughout the country on the breakdown of law and order in Kansas City.[32]

THE 1934 CITY ELECTION

Reformers mounted a challenge to the Pendergast machine in the March 1934 city election. Unreconstructed Rabbits, the *Kansas City Star*, the Jackson County Republican Committee, and many young college-educated people belonging to an organization called the National Youth Movement combined forces into a temporary fusion organization. After Rabbi Mayerberg, citing a religious conflict of interest, declined to run for mayor, the reformers, dominated by the NYM and flaunting their collegiate ties, ran A. Ross Hill, a former president of the University of Missouri, on a citizens' ticket against incumbent Bryce Smith. Machine spokesmen sarcastically wrote the NYM off as a group of Country Club District silk-stocking college students and boy scouts. Boss Tom labeled the leaders a "bunch of nice boys and girls misled by GOP soreheads." Congressman Joseph Shannon called the fusionists "a Jekyll and Hyde Republican opposition now masquerading under various titles."[33]

Notwithstanding that Hill had no chance of winning, the machine mobilized 6,000 campaign workers and exhorted them to produce a 50,000-vote or more victory for Mayor Smith. The Hill forces, citing street fighting and voting irregularities in the primary, asked Governor Guy Park to call

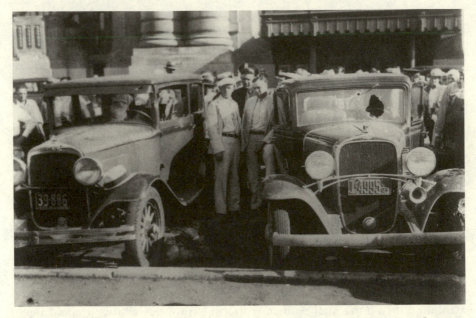

This official FBI photograph was taken at the Union Station massacre site on June 17, 1933, the day of the killing of four peace officers and an escaped convict, who was being transported back to the Leavenworth penitentiary. (*Photograph courtesy the National Archives– Central Plains Region*)

out the Missouri National Guard to ensure a peaceful election. Park rejected the request out of hand, praising Tom Pendergast's fairness and promising an honest election. However, on election day, March 27, someone—who remains unknown—decided to send a very clear message.[34]

An unusually large number of hoodlums transported in from out of town were out in force on election day. The tone for the day was set early. Hardened men handling the polling books in a midtown precinct cursed at a voter who arrived just after the polls opened, "Why you son of a bitch, you voted here an hour ago." He prudently nodded and left.[35] During the day, toughs killed four people and injured dozens of others, eleven seriously. Armed enforcers chased through downtown and fired on a *Star* reporter who had witnessed a vote fraud. Governor Guy Park rejected urgent requests to call out the Missouri National Guard, and the police looked the other way. The NYM actually elected two councilmen in South Side districts somewhat free of ballot-box corruption. The machine, through a combination of calculated violence, honest support, and illegal voting, swept to victory in the other seven council races. Mayor Bryce Smith won 63.5 percent of the total vote.[36]

The bloody election, coming less than a year after the Union Station massacre, was a front-page story throughout the country, and it further blackened Kansas City's image. Boss Tom ignored a barrage of criticism by newspapers throughout Missouri, pointed out that the Democrats as a party had nothing to do with the disorders in the nonpartisan election, and sat back to enjoy the victory. The *Star*, discounting claims that North Side Italian thugs had taken advantage of the election to go on a crime rampage, placed the blame squarely at the door of the machine: "This sort of thing cannot go on. It is horrifying to all decent people, regardless of how they voted yesterday. Kansas City must be cleaned up."[37]

The *Missouri Democrat*, presenting what might be called an official machine view, blamed the violence on the "Ku-Klux *Star*" for stirring up bigotry against Democrats and made the fantastic charge that the reformers had tried to take Kansas City over at gunpoint: "In numbers of cases especially deputized policemen were set upon by hoodlums in the service of the secret NYM and the fusion movement." Much of the election violence was passed off as part of the electoral process in Kansas City: "For the most part, the fights were such as normally occur on election day." The paper also claimed that "the youth racketeers" had mounted "the most dastardly campaign ever mounted by political knaves."[38] A Hitler paper in Nazi Germany could hardly have said it better in attacking Jews for causing Crystal Night.

A month later, Mayor Smith called Cas Welch over a tapped line at his political headquarters. Who placed the tap is unknown; one wonders about Hoover's FBI. Welch asked Smith if the reformers were still giving him "hell," and he replied, "Oh, I'm getting all kinds of hell. I hardly know what to do about the damn thing." Welch, thinking ahead to the general election, observed, "We can't do in November like we did in March. . . . We'd have been elected this time without those votes. You'd have been elected—I figured it out—by 10 or 15 thousand votes." Smith, officially reelected by a margin of 59,000 votes, said, "I don't doubt it."[39]

Pendergast responded to the election violence by ordering McElroy to dismiss Eugene Ruppert as the director of police. According to rumors, Welch, always unhappy about his share of patronage, had talked about cutting a deal with the reformers. In return for handing over to them his two kept councilmen, they would, under the table, allow him to name the new police director.[40]

The Big Boss responded to that kind of overt blackmail with a telephone call to Welch, picked up on tape after the start of the conversation:

Welch: That's always been my attitude . . .
Pendergast: No, it hasn't been always. And if you start in on that, I'm not going to do it at all. I know how things are done. Now if you want to talk sense, if you want to get along with me, I'm perfectly willing. But if you don't, there's no use.

Welch: I'll do anything you want me to do.
Pendergast: That's all right then. And that's the way it makes some sense. I'm willing to be your friend, but by God you have got to be mine. That's all that's necessary. Do what I ask you to do and don't be raising hell all the time . . . and we'll get along.
Welch: You won't have no trouble with me from now on.[41]

Welch, thoroughly chastised, gave up his challenge, and Pendergast named his own man, Otto P. Higgins, as director of police. Pendergast, with his deep, gravelly voice, could sound very menacing on the telephone. He once snarled at a Welch henchman, sounding for all the world like a gangster instead of a political leader and friend of the poor, "Why don't you open up your goddamn ears!"[42]

Welch reverted to his traditional subservient role as a ward leader. In keeping with his flamboyant nature, he bought and piloted his own airplane. A marriage to a young woman, Pawnee Brown, ended in tragedy when she and a baby daughter fell ill and died within a couple of months of each other. On April 17, 1936, Welch, who had a history of heart trouble, died suddenly at age sixty-three while conducting routine business in the chambers of his justice-of-the-peace court. An hour earlier, Welch had responded to an inquiry concerning his health with the reply "I never felt better; everything is fine."[43]

LAZIA'S MURDER

Johnny Lazia's illicit activities continued to raise questions. Convicted of federal income tax evasion on February 14, 1934, ordered to pay a $5,000 fine, and sentenced to a year in jail, he remained free on appeal in the summer of 1934. Pendergast wrote Postmaster General James Farley a pleading letter on May 12, 1934, claiming that Lazia was "being jobbed because of his Democratic activities" and that "my interest in him is greater than anything that might come up in the future."[44] Pendergast wanted Farley, who handled political problems involving city bosses for Roosevelt, to secure executive clemency for Lazia. Unfortunately for Lazia, Farley was not in a position to influence federal judicial decisions in western Missouri.

The issue became moot in the early morning hours of July 10, 1934, when Lazia and his wife, Marie, returned to their fashionable midtown apartment near the busy intersection of Armour Boulevard and Gillham Road in an automobile driven by business associate Charles Carrolla. Assailants with a submachine gun and a shotgun fired on Lazia as he stepped out of the car, hitting him eight times with bullets and slugs. His wife and driver were unhurt. An ambulance rushed Lazia to St. Joseph's Hospital. Word of the shooting spread quickly, and small clusters of Lazia's henchmen soon milled around the hospital entrance. Pendergast arrived and exhorted his personal physicians to save Lazia, but all efforts failed and he died at dawn. As the end neared, Lazia supposedly said, "If anything happens, notify Tom Pendergast, my best friend, and tell him I love him."[45]

Johnny Lazia's funeral was the largest within memory in Kansas City. Thousands of people filed by his casket at the South Side home of a sister at 55th and Tracy Avenue. The funeral procession to a final resting place in the southwest corner of Mount St. Mary's Cemetery contained hundreds of automobiles, one of them carrying T. J. Pendergast.[46]

An extravagant obituary in the *Missouri Democrat*, doubtless approved by the boss, described the departed underworld leader as "one of the most lovable men imaginable—a lovable character" who could easily have passed for a college professor or a man of God. He was "a poor man's friend" who had overcome a youthful mistake to devote his life to encouraging the children of Italian immigrants to "walk in the straight and narrow path," to feed the hungry, clothe the naked, and help the jobless. Perhaps his greatest attribute, the obituary said, was the tenderness in his heart for his ultimate leader: "Lazia loved Mr. Pendergast with dog-like devotion, and there has never been a time during the past six years when he would not have died for him."[47]

Who killed Johnny Lazia? The murder, one of the most infamous in Kansas City history, went unsolved and no one claimed responsibility. Federal authorities unsuccessfully interviewed three hundred suspects on a list of known criminals. The Kansas City police made no progress questioning several dozen men, almost all with Italian-sounding surnames. Over the years, a number of possible perpetrators died violently. A few may have held personal vendettas against Lazia, unrelated to his broader activities as crime boss. A theory that the murder was a way of changing chief operating officers in the underworld failed to hold up. Charles Carrolla succeeded Lazia, smoothly assuming among other things his collection duties for the machine. No gang war or other untoward events followed the murder. As for Carrolla, he died in bed. The Kansas City police tried to turn their unofficial leader into a hero, advancing the supposition that Oklahoma and Minnesota gangsters killed Lazia because they were enraged that he had kept them out of Kansas City.[48]

Inevitably, conspiracy buffs said that Pendergast, concerned about Lazia's rising visibility and appalled at the March 1934 election violence as a deliberate attempt to embarrass him, engineered the "hit." Boss Tom may have had a motive, but so did many others. If Pendergast had tagged Lazia for elimination, why would he have written the letter to Farley to try to keep him out of jail? Moreover, affairs were going very well for Pendergast in July 1934, so why would he have wanted to rock the boat and risk retaliation? Finally, Pendergast, through both implied threats and overt verbal intimidation, did

Johnny Lazia, second from left, on the move. *(Photograph from the Kansas City Museum Archives)*

not need to assassinate his minions to control them, as his telephone call to Cas Welch indicates. However, Lazia was far more powerful than Welch.

Did Tom Pendergast have Johnny Lazia murdered? Such a vendetta against Lazia is possible, but unlikely. Pendergast, over and above his image, was basically a political operator and white-collar criminal. Despite his quick temper, there was little in his makeup or methods that equated him with an Al Capone, running around like a loose cannon crushing perceived and real foes in sustained pathological rages. Of course, questions will always remain, as will conspiracy scenarios.

Senator Truman

On the day of Lazia's splendid burial, Judge Truman was away from Kansas City campaigning for the August Democratic primary for the United States Senate. Pendergast decided to send Truman to Washington after his apparent first choice, James Aylward, whom he groomed for the job, unexpectedly declined to run. Cas Welch had the task of making key telephone calls to Governor Park and other Democratic leaders to sound out attitudes toward a Truman candidacy. Park, at first sounding independent, asserted, "If it's not Jim, I think it ought to be somebody not right in Kansas City, see what I mean?" Asked about Truman, Park, possibly realizing Welch represented the boss, quickly reverted to his expected servility. "Well," he said, pausing, "I don't know. . . . He's a nice fellow . . . nice fellow." When Welch asked a St. Louis Democratic leader what he thought about Truman, he replied, "I don't know nothing about Truman."[49] This made little difference, because all Truman needed to win was Pendergast's backing.

In announcing his support of Truman, Pendergast said, "He has been a most efficient and trustworthy public official in Jackson County, and has rendered splendid service as director of re-employment, and enjoys the confidence of state and national administrations. We will put forth our best efforts in his be-half." The *Missouri Democrat* called Judge Truman and the boss "close friends."[50]

Truman's easy victory in the general election soon paid dividends for Pendergast. Matthew S. Murray, a Pendergast stooge, received an appointment as Works Progress Administration director in Missouri, handing the boss vast power over all relief jobs and recovery projects in the state. At the time of his appointment in 1935, Murray, a former Missouri state highway commissioner, was director of public works in Kansas City. He owed his job to Truman and the boss. Harry Hopkins, the head of the WPA, appointed state directors on the advice of the state's two senators. Bennett Champ Clark, Missouri's other senator and a Democrat, convinced he needed Pendergast machine support in advance of what proved his bid for a second term in 1938, acquiesced to Murray's appointment.[51]

All evidence to the contrary, Pendergast tried to foster the fiction that he was just another Missouri Democratic politician. On July 9, 1935, accosted by a New York reporter upon his return from Europe on the liner *Normandie*, Pendergast modestly played down his own importance: "I am not a national figure, never want to be and never will be and I can't see what this fuss is about." He admitted running a "great machine," claimed that Missouri was "75 percent" behind Roosevelt, contended that the people of the state had "faith and respect in the Supreme Court," and predicted FDR's reelection. He added, "I am a Democrat and I am going to support the Democratic ticket and platform. That goes, right or wrong, and I hope to God they're right. I am interested in the welfare of the Democratic party, but especially in Kansas City and Missouri."[52]

TALES OF THE MACHINE

Stories about the greatest days of the Pendergast machine, sometimes true and occasionally embellished, abounded, helping to create enduring images.

Lawyers handling many kinds of cases, such as divorce, needed to either be or retain an attorney on an approved list to improve their chances before Pendergast-elected judges. Special jury pools for the cases of people with machine ties consisted of city and county patronage employees, friends and relatives of the accused, barkeepers, WPA relief workers, and others allied with the Pendergast organization. One Jackson County judge, charged in an apparently airtight case of misappropriating public funds, received an acquittal in only eighteen minutes.

The head custodian of a public building turned a tidy profit selling the building's zinc roof, which was supposedly worn out. Officials contracted with a Pendergast firm to tear down the Convention Hall, sold the site to themselves at a low price, and then arranged for the city to buy it back at an inflated price for a parking lot. The city paid a Pendergast company, using municipal trucks and crews, by the ton to collect garbage, watering it thoroughly before weighing it to increase the weight.[53] Ranking machine officials routinely purchased their personal automobiles on city warrants. The head of purchasing for the city purchased supplies from "approved lists" without bothering about the cost or taking required bids. No one in authority ever considered independent audits.

City Manager McElroy, once the owner of a country store in Iowa, solved the problem of city debts simply by wiping them off the books, pretending to use what he referred to as "country bookkeeping." He boasted of keeping the city free of debts and scandals, once explaining, "Tom and I are partners. He takes care of politics and I take care of business. Every Sunday morning at Tom's house or at mine, we meet and talk over what's best for the city."[54]

Numerous excesses of the machine involved construction projects. Independent sidewalk contractors needed to have their names on specially approved lists to bid successfully for even the very small jobs. While federal authorities took great pains to ensure honest practices in the construction, with some New Deal money, of a large and impressive Municipal Auditorium, the same careful scrutiny did not apply to certain other projects. Enough Ready Mixed concrete went into the laying of a runway at the municipal airport to pave twenty-four miles of standard highway. Crossover points at the airport were reportedly as much as thirty-six feet thick. Answering charges that he used his political power to gain contracts on public construction projects, Pendergast said, "Yes. Why not? Aren't my products as good as any?"[55]

In one notorious example of Pendergast make-work, hundreds of workers paved the bed of Brush Creek, an open sewer and drainage ditch that ran through Jesse Nichols's Country Club Plaza. Nichols felt the paving ruined the natural beauty of the stream. His son Miller Nichols recalled, "I remember his feelings about it. I can almost hear him talking about it at our family dinners,"

Machine workers distribute food baskets to depression victims in the Fifth Ward, ca. 1930.
(*Photograph from the Kansas City Museum Archives*)

because he "didn't think it was aesthetic and he was 100 percent right." The
Brush Creek project, held up for ridicule as an example of blatant corruption,
proved worthwhile as a flood-control improvement. The concrete lasted many
decades until it was torn up in the 1990s by the Corps of Engineers for a much
larger scale and vastly more costly flood-control program. All rumors to the
contrary, the old concrete was of no unusual thickness.[56]

Pendergast's lust for money became insatiable. The influx of federal money,
in particular for relief projects, lessened Pendergast's need to use the tribute
paid to the machine for his welfare distributions; this should have made the
boss wealthy enough to build a fabulous fortune and retire in style. Carrolla
later admitted in federal court to collecting $20 million in one year alone in
payoffs to the machine from gambling interests. But with the great new sums
available, Pendergast's gambling on horses, always heavy, escalated from tens
of thousands of dollars a week to hundreds of thousands. He once wagered
$20,000 on a single race, losing money like water down a drain. To make it
easier for him, a wire service installed teletype equipment in the basement at
5650 Ward Parkway, enabling him to communicate directly with bookmakers.

He used an elaborate system of fictitious names to cover his transactions. In response to pressure from his family, he would promise to stop, only to resume his addiction. Late in life Tom Pendergast Jr. wrote, "He was like a man on dope. He needed a fix. A fix for him was each race."[57]

PENDERGAST'S ENDORSEMENT OF STARK

People who knew Tom Pendergast wondered about his health and its impact on his decision making. He endorsed Lloyd Stark for governor in October 1935, a year before the presidential election, which turned out to be a Democratic sweep. "The organization here will support Stark," Pendergast's statement read. "I am of the opinion he has more independent strength than any other candidate. I think he will make a splendid governor." Stark, a wealthy apple grower from Louisiana, Missouri, had been both a naval and an army officer.[58] Many Pendergast associates considered Stark too rigid, too unpredictable, and, especially, too honest. Stark had strong support, however, outside Kansas City, and Pendergast could hardly expect another Park to fall into his lap. In backing Stark, the boss followed an established pattern of favoring candidates at the state level who appeared sure winners so he could take credit for their victories.[59]

The truth of the matter was that Pendergast did not care that much about who was governor, as long as a Democrat held the position. Of course, he took a calculated risk that in return for an endorsement, Stark, if elected, would remain loyal enough to stay out of Kansas City politics. "Ten people spoke for Major Stark throughout the State where one spoke for all the rest of the candidates put together," Pendergast later explained. "My organization could have beaten him with any decent man. But the people wanted him. It was up to us to satisfy them." Furthermore, he claimed that Stark had put great pressure on him, as if their positions as boss and candidate were reversed: "When he was a candidate for the nomination he had at least 500 people in Missouri and Kansas City seeing me from day to day asking for my support, and there were fifty outstanding Democrats of Kansas City whom I could mention except that time does not permit."[60] Stark, demonstrating that he was no Guy Park almost from his first days in office, stopped his predecessor's practice of consulting with Pendergast over routine appointments.

PENDERGAST'S HEALTH

William Reddig, who covered the machine for the *Star*, wrote in his book *Tom's Town* about disquieting changes in T. J. Pendergast about 1935: "He was heavier and grayer, and his eyes carried a sick look. His two hundred and forty pounds made him look shorter than the five feet nine that he measured. When he sat at his desk at 1908 Main Street, giving orders and answering questions, he was still the powerful Boss whose eyes and voice intimidated all others in the room, but the marks of age were painfully visible on him, and within him was a great tension."[61]

In March 1936, Tom and Carolyn escaped the anxieties of Kansas City. As was their custom, they attended the racing season at Saratoga Springs; after that, they went to London and took another European trip. They returned to New York on June 2, crossing on the first Atlantic voyage of the *Queen Mary*. In preparation for the Democratic National Convention in Philadelphia, Pendergast rented a suite on the twenty-ninth floor of the Waldorf-Astoria. Holding court there, he received a steady stream of visitors, mainly Missouri politicians. On June 23, he took a short train ride to the City of Brotherly Love for the opening of the convention. In wire-service photographs taken there with Truman and Aylward, Boss Tom, puffy in the face and with a very red nose, looked like a heavy drinker, even though he seldom touched alcohol. He snacked on something that did not agree with him and returned immediately to New York. During the night, he fell deathly ill at the Waldorf-Astoria, suffering a severe coronary thrombosis. Until his condition stabilized, emergency physicians feared for his life.[62]

His attending physicians in New York recommended as much as six months of rest, removed from stressful situations. Given that Pendergast had already been away from Kansas City for several months, that seemed a difficult prescription to follow if he wanted to remain in charge of the machine. The lead physician hedged a little: "Although Mr. Pendergast is a stranger to me, I can see that he is a man of great energy and forcefulness, physically and mentally."[63]

A year earlier, Percy B. Sovey, a machine propagandist, writing in a Pendergast publication, *Democracy*, had already produced what amounted to a eulogy. Doubtless, Pendergast, who was never averse to planting complimentary celebrations of himself, had given approval. Using words usually reserved for the likes of Washington, Jefferson, and Lincoln, Sovey called Pendergast honest, alert, and intelligent, extolling his unwavering loyalty to his friends and unfailing respect for the spoken word. Sovey explained, "It is this combination of personal characteristics which has won for him political standing that has never been challenged within the party." He called Pendergast an arbiter more than a boss, a man whose love for the Democratic party had religious overtones. Through sheer ability, Pendergast had reached the state of perfection expected of an ultimate leader: "It is not easy to deceive him; he has the logician's mind and what is said to him must make sense. . . . Being perfectly truthful, he expects others to be so. . . . If he had not been truthful and wise, he could not have retained his leadership. He remains the boss because the party needs and wants a boss upon whom it may depend. He has never failed."[64] Even in life, Thomas J. Pendergast belonged to the ages.

By August 1936, Tom had been moved from the hospital to a New York hotel. He had lost thirty-five pounds, and he remained a very sick man. Then, just as he started to take renewed interest in Kansas City and Missouri politics, he suffered a severe setback: an intestinal blockage required emergency surgery. Until he rallied, his life hung in the balance. He accomplished only a partial recovery, but his physicians decided that he was strong enough to return home. In mid-September, he made the trip to Kansas City in a private railroad car, arriving quietly. He entered Menorah Hospital, had a second serious operation in which a colostomy was performed, and spent the rest of the year recovering.[65]

THE MASSIVE 1936 VOTE FRAUD

With the Big Boss away, the 1936 voter-registration drive came off so obviously fraudulent that it brought the machine under fire by a grand jury. This is surprising, considering that by this time the machine had for many years had the entire voting process, cradle to grave, down to a science: Voter registration took place only on specified days, with Pendergast minions running the machinery. Pendergast judges made up laws to validate the method. Tens of thousands of registered voters either did not exist or had died years earlier. Pendergast had added 60,000 "pads" between 1920 and 1928 to counter a Republican growth trend, starting a practice that continued into the next decade.[66] On election day, pimps, whores, crooks, derelicts, and other nonconformists, given lists of names, hurried from precinct to precinct casting ballots, receiving twenty-five cents per vote. One woman set a dubious record by voting forty times in a 1932 contest. Lying, stealing, herding, and other forms of chicanery occurred in every canvass. Standard methods saw the switching of ballot boxes, the quick certification and destruction of ballots within minutes after the closing of the polls, the deployment of police to help ruffians intimidate citizens, and the use of pre-prepared ballots. Vote-fixing purists favored marking ballots in advance on the grounds of cost-effectiveness. Not too subtly, some fixers gave the impression that they could tell how voters cast their ballots. Precinct captains who increased their registration totals received praise, promotions, and sometimes their own small rackets, giving them incentives to look as good and efficient as possible at 1908 Main, despite the fact that their huge vote totals looked suspicious elsewhere.[67]

Pendergast had little to say about his own election methodology, but he did describe his impressions of a Sunday election that he observed on his 1931 European trip in Barcelona, Spain, where voters, following the abdication of King Alfonso, elected members of a lawmaking body: "I watched that with a lot of interest, even though I did not understand everything that was being said. You know they were just as intense as we get in Kansas City, although I did not see any fights. But how they hustled out the vote. They went to the polling places in motor cars, buggies, and on the backs of donkeys." He became so interested that he visited several precincts. "There were two groups, just like you find in our country and they certainly worked at it," he explained. "A Sunday election was a new one on me, but I will say that holding it that way gave everybody a chance to vote."[68]

In Kansas City, Republican poll watchers were either ignored, bought off, or threatened. An honest Republican election official recalled his experience on the 1936 registration day in a letter written a couple of years later to Governor Stark: "The presence of the police of this city is no protection. When I served as Republican judge of election on registration day last I was insulted, cursed many times, my official papers grasped from my hands and torn up in the presence of the other officials and prospective voters, threatened to be taken for a ride and finally the next morning was refused admittance behind the counter on which the registration books were lying."[69]

At least 70,000 and possibly as many as 80,000 "ghosts" voted in both the 1936 August primary and the November general election. In the Second Ward, a Pendergast candidate won a primary contest in a state race by a vote of 19,201 to 13 over a man who ran very well outside of Kansas City.[70] Such an obviously fraudulent total distressed even machine officials and associates. Congressman Shannon called the primary "so corrupt it was a disgrace to American civilization." Tom Pendergast Jr. years later admitted that the precinct captains "got carried away and voted the sick, the dying and the dead." Things had gone so badly that even Boss Tom felt compelled to deny responsibility: "I was ill throughout the primary registration and election period and know nothing of the conditions referred to." A few days before the Democratic sweep in the general election, the *Star*, following its own investigation of the voting rolls, stated in a front-page article, "An honest election here Tuesday is an utter impossibility."[71]

United States District Judge Albert L. Reeves believed that Pendergast knew exactly what was going on. "It was apparently his thought," the judge speculated, "that with increased majorities in Kansas City and Jackson County he could command the intercession of state and national officials if his tax returns were challenged."[72]

REEVES, OTIS, AND MILLIGAN

The judge was the same Albert L. Reeves who believed he had lost a 1918 congressional election to a Pendergast candidate because of voting irregularities. Warren Harding appointed Reeves to the federal bench of the Western District of Missouri in 1923. Born in 1873 in the Ozarks, he had taught country school, read for the law, and passed a bar examination in 1911. Before becoming a federal judge, Reeves served a term in the General Assembly and held appointed offices, notably in an appellate judicial position as a commissioner of the Missouri Supreme Court. Reeves was a rock-ribbed conservative Republican and Baptist Sunday school teacher. His zealous enforcement of the Prohibition laws helped define him as a jurist. A stern, austere man and rigid moralist, he deplored the actions of the Pendergast machine. As a believer in suffrage as fundamental to a democratic system, he found the election practices of the machine reprehensible.[73]

Reeves was one of two federal judges in the Western District. His colleague, Merrill E. Otis, born on a northwestern Missouri farm in 1884 and a 1910 graduate of the law department of the University of Missouri, was an assistant to the solicitor general of the United States when Calvin Coolidge made him a federal judge in 1925. Like Reeves, Otis strictly enforced Prohibition. Very much a partisan Republican, he strongly opposed Franklin Roosevelt and his New Deal. Otis, known for his popular after-dinner speeches and learned opinions that made many references to the classics and the Bible, deplored the Pendergast machine as a matter of course.[74]

Otis expressed his feelings, devoid of his usual rhetoric, about the criminality in the machine in summing up Lazia's character at the time of his sentencing for tax evasion: "His general reputation was unsavory. . . . Even the testimony of the defendant himself described in part the basis for his reputation. He was a gambler, a backer and promoter of gambling enterprises. . . . His reputation was such that not one witness was brought forward to testify that he had a good reputation."[75] Otis signaled that the federal court understood the situation in Kansas City and stood ready, if the opportunity presented itself, to take steps to resolve it.

In October 1936, less than a month before the general election, a delegation composed of prominent Kansas City Democrats and Republicans asked Judge Reeves to immediately call a grand jury to look into the question of voting irregularities. This delegation argued that bogus votes for president and Congress violated the Constitution and various federal statutes. Reeves declined, deciding to wait until after the election and for further documented proof. He informed U.S. Attorney Maurice Milligan, "It is my opinion that a grand jury should be called to investigate those claimed violations of law."[76]

Milligan, a country lawyer and minor Democratic politician from Richmond, a small town near Kansas City, had received his four-year federal appointment in February 1934. A favorable newspaper feature story by Spencer McCulloch in the *St. Louis Post-Dispatch* in 1939 described him as an intensely "individualistic" and "human" man with "personal foibles" and "idiosyncrasies," who dressed well and assiduously performed his duties: "As a lawyer he is not subtle. He couches his questions in plain language. Once embarked upon a course of action he sticks to it, 'despite hell and high water.' His final arguments are tinged with such familiar rhetoric as 'from early morn until dewy eve,' but also contain cold logic and cogent reasoning."[77]

According to Milligan, Attorney General Homer Cummings handpicked him for the job, explaining that Kansas City, along with Chicago and Minneapolis, qualified as a "hot spot" that needed cleaning up. On behalf of the Roosevelt administration, Cummings had launched a well-publicized war on crime in the United States. Even though there may have been a bit of truth in Milligan's assertion that Cummings had sought him out in Richmond to help clean up Kansas City, his nomination for the position had been sponsored by his own brother, Congressman Jacob L. "Tuck" Milligan, and by Senator Bennett Champ Clark, both Missouri Democrats. Friends considered Milligan an above-average and somewhat egotistical person with minimal political skills but much interest in politics since his university days. Machine detractors contended that he loathed Tom Pendergast and wanted revenge for Truman's defeat of Tuck Milligan in the 1934 primary. Whatever the motives or manner of his appointment, Milligan, even though he had been warned by Judge Reeves that he would come under immediate and prolonged personal attack, was more than ready to take on the Pendergast organization.[78]

THE VOTE-FRAUD TRIALS

The grand jury convened on December 14, 1936, and Reeves gave the body a ringing charge intended to make headlines: "The election rolls of Kansas City and Jackson County are padded with thousands of fraudulent names. The last election and the preceding elections over a long period of years, have been controlled by plug-uglies, villains and ruffians. The election machinery has been used by them. These vote thieves have had the aid and support of men in high places." He said conditions had reached the state where he could no longer sit quietly by and witness the open and brazen flaunting of the election laws. The judge raised his right hand with a clenched fist and implored, "The time has come when you should move on them, and reach for all, even if they be found in high places."[79]

Ultimately, four federal grand juries brought in scores of indictments. A letter on behalf of state authorities in Missouri and leaders of the Kansas City business community energized the FBI, which only reluctantly intervened in local affairs, to help orchestrate the hunt for corrupt election workers, called by Judge Otis "two-by-four criminals who had robbed citizens of the priceless right to vote."[80] Indictments started to come down in the spring of 1937. As predicted, the machine employed its favored defensive methods of ridicule and intimidation, designed to discredit and frighten opponents. Milligan kept a revolver on his nightstand and developed the habit of searching his automobile and garage for explosive devices. Otis and Reeves received a constant stream of threatening telephone calls. A machine representative told Reeves that the Big Boss was having trouble restraining his trigger men, but this failed to stop the judge, who said the prosecutions would continue. The machine planted stories mocking the way Otis and Reeves had zealously enforced the Prohibition laws, implying they were Carry Nation–type social activists, classic narrow-minded bluenoses. Hoodlums threatened grand jury members, forcing Reeves to replace a number of jurors.[81]

In 1937 and on into 1938, federal petit juries brought in 259 guilty verdicts for conspiring to interfere with the right of citizens to vote in Kansas City. Out of 278 persons indicted, 19 received dismissals; no one was acquitted. Two hundred of those convicted went to jail. Some had functioned as criminal enforcers, but most were essentially honest men and women who were following orders, engaging in standard election practices. Judge Reeves, sentencing a batch of 52 defendants who he said were "minions and puppets," called on "persons in high places"—obviously meaning Pendergast and key machine members—to show "some gallantry and chivalry" and "surrender," instead of hiding behind "poor people" being "humiliated and punished for doing their bidding."[82]

The machine responded by paying all fines and placing those incarcerated on salaries during their prison terms, the money coming from a special surtax on gamblers. Milligan concluded that the trials exposed the "fraud and chicanery" practiced in Kansas City elections: "Each revealed a new and startling method of defrauding voters. The most incriminating factor in all these trials was the display before the eyes of the jurors of the corrupted ballots themselves. These mute witnesses spoke more eloquently than words."[83] In frauds during the 1936 general election, one precinct judge carefully filled out 110 ballots and another filled out the tally sheets as soon as the polls closed. Roosevelt carried the latter precinct 815 to 23, for an improbable 97.3 percent of the vote.[84]

PENDERGAST'S RETURN TO 1908 MAIN

Pendergast returned to 1908 Main and broke his long silence by granting an interview to St. Louis journalist Ralph Coghlan on November 30, 1936. Pendergast called himself a realist, emphasized the idea of politics as a business, stressed the importance of delivering votes, and bragged that he always kept his word. None of this said anything new, nor did Pendergast want it to. The transparent purpose of his statements was to show him in charge again, in good health, and in fighting trim. Coghlan wrote, "He is dressed sedately. His hat is on. He seems to be about to spring. It is not the tautness of strained nerves, merely the barely repressed energy of a person whose physical movements are of tigerish speed." Despite the image of Pendergast that Coghlan presented to the public, he prophetically concluded, "He is back at the old stand. Again the worn stairs of the Jackson Democratic Club sag under the weight of governors and senators and bankers and bums. Napoleon is now at Austeritz. But the epilogue remains to be written. Even now the forces of retribution are gathering."[85]

Even though he gave a brave show of vim and vigor, Pendergast continued to have serious problems with his health. He was unable to climb stairs, so to reach his 1908 Main office he had to take an elevator to the second floor of the Monroe Hotel next door and enter through a newly cut passageway between the two buildings. He no longer went regularly to his headquarters to meet the public. Jim Pendergast, his nephew, filled in for him, handing out most of the patronage. Increasingly, the notes to city department heads dictating the hiring and promotion of employees came from Jim rather than Tom.[86]

Judge Reeves believed that, "like all oppressors," Boss Tom understood the problems created by his continual need for more money and the growing independence of his criminal associates: "He was entirely familiar with the growing revolt and endeavored to checkmate his henchmen, minions, and representatives as against their open and too bold methods. So many of these, however, were criminals and ex-convicts that they were not satisfied with anything less than complete license to operate as their wild and reckless judgment might dictate to them. In other words, his machine was getting out of hand."[87]

TRUMAN'S OPPOSITION TO MILLIGAN

On November 19, 1937, Truman learned from James Farley that Roosevelt intended to nominate Milligan to a second term.[88] At Christmas, Senator Truman returned to Jackson County and found time to meet with the Big Boss. On January 28, 1938, Truman announced his intention to oppose the nomination of Maurice Milligan to a second term as U.S. Attorney in the Western District. This required a vote of the Senate, which Truman intended to use senatorial privilege to block.[89]

On February 15, Truman delivered a hard-hitting speech on the Senate floor attacking Milligan for unethical practices and, for good measure, making bitter remarks about Otis and Reeves, neither of whom were before the Senate. Truman denounced the two judges as the most "violently partisan" judges since the Federalist party appointees that vexed Thomas Jefferson. Truman said Reeves and Otis wanted "convictions of Democrats," and he sneered at their appointments by Harding and Coolidge. Truman said, "A Jackson County Democrat has as much chance of a fair trial in the Federal District Court as a Jew would have in a Hitler court or a Trotsky follower before Stalin." Only under pressure from the White House did Truman abandon formal opposition to Milligan, allowing for his confirmation by a voice vote. Remaining adamant, Truman asserted, "Since the president wants this, I shall not oppose the confirmation, although politically and personally I am opposed to Mr. Milligan because I do not think and never have thought he was fit for the place."[90]

Judge Reeves, astounded that Truman upheld the conduct and the practices of the Pendergast machine in the face of massive revelations of vote fraud, publicly described his diatribe as a speech by "a man who had been nominated by ghost votes, who had been elected with ghost votes, and, if the truth were known, a ghost writer" had written.[91] Truman was one of the few remaining upright supporters of the machine, continuing to claim that the fraud prosecutions were simply an exercise in dirty politics.

The Milligan speech did not necessarily mean that Truman was, in all except name, the senator from Pendergast. Most of the Big Boss's recorded dealings with Truman involved practical political considerations, patronage matters, and constituency relations. The two men occasionally discussed Missouri politics, as when they concluded after a two-hour conversation in 1935 that they liked none of the possible Democratic candidates for governor. In an unusual move, Pendergast asked Truman to support a resolution directed against the Mexican government that, as it turned out, he had already decided to vote for. Pendergast letters to Truman sometimes concerned appointments, including to Annapolis and to middle-level federal jobs. In one of the few preserved items of correspondence between the two men, Pendergast sent a red-penciled note seeking help in expediting the escape from Germany of some Jewish refugees with a relative in Kansas City. In late 1936, Pendergast brokered the selection of John Caskie Collet as a United States district judge in Missouri in a meeting at 1908 Main with Truman and Missouri's other Democratic senator, Bennett Champ Clark.[92]

Aside from the expected demand of loyalty, Pendergast left Truman free to chart an independent course, gambling that he would act prudently in affairs relating to the well-being of Pendergastism. Asked about the Big Boss's influence on how he voted on questions before the Senate, Truman replied, "I don't follow his advice on legislation, I vote the way I believe Missourians as a whole would want me to vote."[93]

By 1938 and 1939, the Pendergast machine appeared in the process of crumbling. The intolerable alliance with criminals had progressed far beyond the use of thugs at the polls and support of wide-open gambling. The Union Station massacre focused unfavorable attention on Kansas City, leaving an enduring impression of the city as a Dante's inferno of vice and crime, a far different image than local boosters wanted to convey. An atmosphere of mistrust and fear pervaded the community. As in a police state, people never knew whether comments they made might come to the attention of machine enforcers. Lazia's elimination raised questions about who actually controlled the underworld. Both legal and illegal interests resented paying increased tribute, amounting to an increase in taxes without representation. Then came the vote-fraud prosecutions. The boss's excesses threatened to destroy the House of Pendergast and his carefully crafted invisible government. Attacks on the machine failed to take Pendergast down, but he was soon to face a personal attack that was more effective.

SIX

Downfall

1935–1939

T. J. Pendergast's arrogance gave him a false sense of invincibility. Not infrequently, he required quick cash over and above his normal income from his business ventures and machine activities—usually to pay off gambling debts. Pendergast's heavy wagering and losses on horse racing inevitably came under the scrutiny of Elmer Lincoln Irey, the head of the elite Intelligence Unit of the Bureau of Internal Revenue. Informants claimed that Pendergast sometimes lost more than $100,000 in one week to big New Jersey and New York bookmakers, who code-named him "Sucker." Pendergast told a friend that he needed to "slow down" because "bookies from the Atlantic to the Pacific began to think I was their biggest sucker."[1] However, he could not stop.

Given his pressing needs and the fact that he was accustomed to dishonest methods, Pendergast quickly accepted an opportunity in 1935 to receive a very large sum of tainted money. As is typical of such transactions, the affair was complex and murky. It showed Pendergast's dishonesty and cynical attitude toward the people of Missouri. It differed from such regular and time-honored Pendergast practices as exacting kickbacks from honest businessmen, rigging bidding on construction projects, and shaking down gambling dens. What appeared most unusual in the affair was that Pendergast extended his dealings far beyond Kansas City but exhibited no concern about any trouble with the federal government. Despite the high stakes involved in the much-publicized and highly suspicious deal, Pendergast treated the matter as so routine as to suggest that it represented a not unusual way—indeed, a normal one—for him to carry on business.

In 1930, insurance companies operating in Missouri went to federal court, arguing that a 10 percent rollback on fire-insurance rates by the Insurance Department of Missouri was a confiscatory act that infringed on their constitutional rights. A three-judge panel, temporarily enjoining enforcement of the rollback, allowed the companies to collect the higher rates, placing the money in escrow until a final judgment. Next, the insurance companies actually *raised* rates by 16⅔ percent. The federal court ruled against the increase, stipulating that the money collected be added to the escrow account, which eventually totaled more than $10 million.[2]

In greatly involved litigation, a federal master, Paul V. Barnett of Kansas City, issued a report generally favorable to the insurance companies. In May 1935, one day before the court had scheduled arguments on the report, Robert Emmet O'Malley, the superintendent of insurance in Missouri, signed a so-called compromise agreement with the authorized agent for the insurance companies, Charles R. Street of Chicago. Under the settlement, the policyholders received 20 percent of the impounded funds and the companies 80 percent. Street was the vice president of the Great American Insurance Company and chairman of the Subscribers Actuarial Committee of the 137 associated insurance companies involved in the litigation. Except for legal counsel, Street, described as a dominating personality, virtually acted alone, having the power to make decisions for the companies. O'Malley, a Kansas City cigar manufacturer and political hack associated for years with the machine, had been appointed to his post in 1933 by Governor Guy Park at Pendergast's insistence.[3]

In early January 1935, O'Malley twice met at the Coronado Hotel in St. Louis with Street and A. L. McCormick, a St. Louis insurance executive and president of the Missouri Insurance Agents Association. McCormick knew both Street and Pendergast, and O'Malley explained to the two men that the rate controversy could be settled through an agreement between them.[4]

On January 22, 1935, Street and Pendergast met in Chicago in McCormick's room at the Palmer House. After a lengthy conversation, Street got down to business, suggesting that O'Malley sign a settlement agreement as soon as possible. Pendergast indicated that such an arrangement was feasible if he received money to influence O'Malley. Pendergast then asked Street to make an offer. Street first proposed $200,000, which Pendergast rejected out of hand. After more discussion, Street raised the amount to $500,000, a sum Pendergast found acceptable. Before the three men separated, Pendergast agreed that as soon as he returned to Missouri he would put pressure on O'Malley.[5]

When little happened over the next several weeks, an apprehensive Street decided that he had not offered Pendergast enough money. The result was another Chicago gathering of the conspirators, this time in McCormick's room at the Stevens Hotel. Pendergast, ostensibly in town on unrelated business, walked over from his quarters next door in the Congress Hotel. At the brief conference, Street indicated that he wanted prompt action and without further ado raised the original offer to $750,000. With very little reflection, Pendergast accepted the $250,000 increase.[6]

The next step was to pay off the money. Six weeks later, Street summoned McCormick to Chicago. McCormick stayed overnight at the Palmer House and on the morning of May 1, 1935, kept an appointment with Street at his office. There, Street counted out $50,000 in cash, instructing McCormick to take the money to Pendergast. McCormick, somewhat nervous about hauling that much money around the Chicago Loop, took it back to the Palmer House, checked out, rushed to Midway Airport, and caught a two-hour commercial airplane flight to Kansas City. He delivered the money to 1908 Main, where Pendergast immediately placed the loot in his office safe.[7]

On May 14, stage-managed negotiations opened at the Muehlebach Hotel in Kansas City between O'Malley, on one side, and Street and McCormick on the other, with both sides flanked by their assistants and lawyers. Governor Guy Park arrived to give his blessing prior to a signing ceremony on May 18. O'Malley then boarded a plane for New York to make a show of clearing the settlement with Pendergast, who was preparing to sail within a few days for Europe.[8]

On June 22, McCormick again traveled from St. Louis to Chicago. He did not even bother to register at a hotel. Instead, he went directly to Street's office, picked up another $50,000, took a train to Kansas City, and, in a morning meeting, presented the money to Pendergast at his headquarters. This time, Pendergast only pocketed $5,000. He returned the remaining $45,000 to McCormick, giving him orders, which he followed, to give $22,500 to O'Malley and to keep the rest. Before boarding a train home to St. Louis, McCormick accompanied the pleased boss to the races at Riverside Park.[9]

This set the stage for a much larger installment, with events set in motion by a court order of February 1, 1936, authorizing the distribution of the impounded premiums. During the latter part of March, Street, who needed time to gather the necessary funds from the insurance companies, asked McCormick to come to Chicago for an April 1 conference. McCormick, on arrival, checked into the Palmer House and walked to Street's office, where Street handed over another Pendergast installment, this one amounting to a staggering $330,000 in cash. McCormick, by now accustomed to his duties, had come prepared with a Gladstone bag. With obvious resolution and considerable courage, he returned to the Palmer House, checked out, hailed a cab to Dearborn Street Station in a grimy part of Chicago, and boarded the

Santa Fe Chief for Kansas City, arriving at the Union Station in early evening. He lugged the Gladstone a block through the station, which was notorious for its petty thieves, and took a six-mile cab ride to Pendergast's Ward Parkway mansion.[10]

The boss, despite his prohibition of private or political business in the sanctity of his mansion, made an exception in this case. Fingering the cash, he carefully counted it out on the dining room table. Next, he said he would only keep $250,000, giving the remaining $80,000 back to McCormick, ordering him to split it with O'Malley. McCormick, readily agreeing, left the Pendergast residence in time to make a midnight train home to St. Louis. Later, following instructions to the letter, he gave $40,000 to O'Malley.[11]

On October 23, 1936, Pendergast requested and obtained from Street an emergency payment of $10,000. McCormick presented the money to Pendergast as he lay in a hospital bed in Menorah Hospital in Kansas City. As it turned out, Pendergast never collected the remaining $310,000 of the $750,000 agreed upon. Street, if he ever had the intention, failed to raise the remaining money prior to his death from natural causes on February 2, 1938. In all, Pendergast received a grand total of $440,000, keeping $315,000 and giving McCormick $125,000 for an equal division between himself and O'Malley.[12]

Technically, under federal law, Pendergast had perhaps not taken a bribe. Rather, he had engaged in a rather classic form of influence peddling. If he had paid federal taxes on the money he might have avoided the penitentiary. But he apparently used the entire amount to settle pressing outstanding debts owed to bookmakers. As Maurice Milligan stated in court, "Of course, the defendant did not report to the government that he had received these payments from Street for procuring the settlement, or offer to pay income taxes on them."[13]

THE SEARCH FOR EVIDENCE

From the start, there was an unsavory ring to the insurance settlement. The companies had a good defense, as shown by the report of the master, but few people expected the state to concede to such a one-sided agreement without a fight. Rumors of impropriety circulated, as rumors will, although no one came forward to offer any proof. The first break came in April of 1936, the same month Pendergast received the $330,000 payment, when treasury agents questioned Street about a possible tax liability involving 114 checks from various insurance companies. The checks, which Street appeared to have cashed, amounted to $100,500. Advised that he should pay taxes on the amount, Street insisted to the revenue men that all he had done was to act as a disbursing agent. He refused for reasons of confidentiality to tell who got the money, beyond explaining that it was someone high in Missouri politics but not holding public office.[14]

When pressured to be more explicit, Street wrote a letter on May 4, 1937, in which he said, "Leaving for South Dakota. On my return next week will take a run to Mo. on business anyway—and see what they have to say. Don't think can do anything at least before the Queen Mary comes in."[15] Of course, Thomas J. Pendergast was among the passengers on that maiden voyage of the *Queen Mary*. Street failed to provide the promised further information. Elmer Irey, aware of the potential political implications, informed his superior, Secretary of the Treasury Henry Morgenthau Jr., who supposedly said, "You have carte blanche on this and any other case involving law violations."[16]

Street filed an amended return on March 8, 1937, paying taxes of $47,048.08 on the money. The Bureau of Internal Revenue responded by assessing a 50 percent penalty that Street contested, with the matter dragging on when he died. In light of the possible Pendergast link, revenue investigators shifted their investigation to an alleged slush fund that Street kept in connection with the Missouri rate settlement. The bureau suspended all routine work on examining Pendergast family tax returns, consolidating them in Washington for a possible detailed investigation.[17]

THE WAR AGAINST THE MACHINE

The insurance settlement became a factor in the escalating war against the machine. At some point in 1937, rumors of Pendergast's involvement in the insurance settlement had come to the attention of U.S. Attorney Maurice Milligan and Governor Lloyd Stark. In 1939, for transparent political purposes, Stark claimed credit, out of whole cloth, for starting the investigation during his 1936 campaign for governor, confiding to a pliant reporter in a "now it can be told" account that he had "tipped" off President Roosevelt about Pendergast's role in the insurance scandal.[18] Milligan opened an independent investigation of Pendergast's banking transactions in Kansas City.

In August 1937, Pendergast, vacationing at the Broadmoor Hotel in Colorado Springs, tried to soften his image by discussing his public career over several days of lengthy interviews with *St. Louis Post-Dispatch* writer Spencer McCulloch. "At times he would display an assumed gruffness," McCulloch wrote. "At other times he would laughingly recall highlights of his long career. The only times he would become indignant were when he mentioned someone who didn't keep his word." During the interviews Pendergast drank lemonade, modestly depreciated his personal attributes, expressed concern that he might say something that would offend someone, and emphasized how over the previous three decades he seldom spent a night away from his wife. He stressed his honesty, claiming he had once turned down a $20,000 bribe. He defended wide-open gambling in Kansas City as better than having separate laws for the rich and the poor, reiterating a long-stated theme that the wealthy gambled unmolested at private clubs. He admitted getting a "certain satisfaction out of being an influence on anything," insisting, "Besides, I like to help people."[19]

Pendergast, justifying his great power, said in true totalitarian mode that all except a small number of citizens cared about politics only at election time and that political machines run by bosses helped keep the system going: "We must face things as they are. An efficient political organization, run intelligently, performs a service to the State. The fewer people you have running anything the better it is for the public. Then you can place responsibility." He professed to favor "social reform," which he did not define, for Missouri, but lamented that in the General Assembly he could only block legislation and lacked the power to keep rural legislators from opposing measures. He resented the implication that he was "a Mussolini," asserting that friends considered him an "easy boss," one who followed the advice of associates. Possibly with the vote-fraud prosecutions in mind, he said that any organization as large as his had some bad actors.[20]

As for his own life, he emphasized, "Every human being, including myself, has to live with his own conscience. There comes a day when he has to account for himself. There's no one there but himself. It's a fearsome time when a man faces his own conscience. But I'm willing to live with mine. I haven't an elastic one either. I'm living with my conscience today in peace and contentment."[21]

Before Pendergast returned from Colorado to Kansas City near the end of the summer, Governor Stark, on his way back to Missouri from an Alaskan trip, stopped by the Broadmoor to see him, initiating a rare two-hour summit meeting to discuss their growing differences. Outwardly, matters appeared to go well, but behind the scenes it was a disaster, with the two men in disagreement over appointments to the four-member Kansas City election board and other issues. In October, when O'Malley, in a speech doubtless approved by Pendergast, called Stark a "polecat" for questioning the insurance deal, Stark summarily fired him and kept a campaign promise by appointing a new insurance commissioner with no ties to the machine. The boss acted with equal dispatch, arranging for O'Malley to become Kansas City water commissioner. With the divisions sharpening, an open split threatened to disrupt the Democratic party in Missouri. The boss warned, "I ask no quarter and will give no quarter."[22]

Late in 1937, Stark made a special trip to Washington and returned to Jefferson City believing that he had convinced Franklin Roosevelt to throw the full weight of the federal government against Pendergast. It became an article

This rare photograph of a downtown Kansas City business selling gaming equipment was taken with a hidden camera by news photographer Jack Wally in 1938. *(Photograph by Jack Wally, courtesy the Western Historical Manuscript Collection, Kansas City, Mo.)*

of faith among both foes and supporters of Pendergast that Stark and Roosevelt orchestrated his downfall. Many people, including Stark, would have been surprised if they had seen a memorandum sent by the director of the Bureau of Internal Revenue to Henry Morgenthau on April 10, 1939, reviewing the course of the Pendergast investigation: "Special Agent Rudolph Hartmann, who is in charge of the present investigation, states that Governor Stark says that he visited Washington in December 1937, and requested the President to direct an income tax investigation into the Missouri insurance cases. Governor Stark says also that he was given assurances that this would be done. So far as I can ascertain, however, no instructions were given to the Bureau of Internal Revenue as the result of any such request by Governor Stark."[23]

Perhaps the president, under the heavy press of his duties, forgot his promise. More likely, of course, is that Roosevelt realized it would have made little political sense for him to contribute to a split in the Democratic party in Missouri, in the process possibly destroying one of the most influential Democratic political organizations in the United States.[24] Roosevelt did, over Senator Truman's vehement objections, nominate Milligan to a second term, but he apparently did nothing to stop certain FBI harassment investigations against Milligan, Reeves, and Otis.

In his unpublished memoirs, Judge Reeves, obviously feeling that the unsavory methods of Pendergastism required a clearly stated response, revealed how the boss's tentacles of power reached to the highest levels of the federal government. Reeves said that Pendergast, becoming "desperate" with his "henchmen and minions being convicted wholesale," had "resorted to his influence at Washington" to pressure Attorney General Frank Murphy to order the FBI to investigate Milligan and the judges in the Western District of Missouri. Reeves noted that a man he called an "authority" told him, "Judge, at the insistence of Attorney General Murphy you are being investigated right now." The judge sent Murphy a protest letter to the effect that his conduct was interfering with the administration of justice and that any investigation "ought to be expeditiously made openly and aboveboard." Reeves wrote, "A reply from Attorney General Murphy was that the investigation was for the purpose of vindicating the author, and a short time later he sent word that when he discovered an investigation was being made, he ordered it stopped." Reeves, far from feeling vindicated, commented in stark terms, "The purpose was terrorism and intimidation." Reeves never made a public statement. Doubtless, if he had there would have been a great national uproar, at a time when the FBI had on paper much more limited power than in later days. But, as Reeves recognized, Pendergast knew he faced serious trouble and was frantically calling in his chips to save himself and his machine.[25]

The Pendergast machine demonstrated that it was still powerful, and very much alive, by winning a surprising election victory over disorganized reformers in the relatively clean spring 1938 city election. A new state permanent registration law in 1937 eliminated tens of thousands of ghost voters; machine officials' wholesale destruction of voting lists made it impossible to tell exactly how many. Through the efforts of the election board appointed by Stark, voter registration was slashed to 215,000 voters. Even so, the machine, running on a program that emphasized "planned city progress" and safe streets, reelected Mayor Bryce Smith by a margin of 44,000 votes, plus six of its eight council candidates.[26]

Pendergast said in a rare interview, "We won fair and squarely. It was a vote of confidence." Speaking of Stark, the boss, jabbing a finger in the air, thundered, "I have never done a thing in my life except support Democratic officeholders to the best of my ability. I have not received that kind of consideration from Governor Stark. . . . If his conscience is clear—I know mine is. I now say, let the river take its course."[27]

In a test of wills, a candidate that Stark supported for the Missouri Supreme Court, James M. Douglas, won an impressive statewide primary victory in August 1938 over James V. Billings, who had Pendergast's support. Before the election, a determined Governor Stark told the people of Missouri, "The political boss can be licked. He and the corrupt machine are in the main responsible for organized crime in our cities. I propose to lead the fight

Three men socialize while a table of gamblers play blackjack in this unique Jack Wally photograph taken inside Baltimore Recreation, downtown Kansas City, in 1938. *(Photograph
by Jack Wally, courtesy the Western Historical Manuscript Collection, Kansas City, Mo.)*

against Boss Tom Pendergast and keep at it until Kansas City is cleaned up."
Pendergast, accustomed to a world of favors and obligations, hated turncoats,
and he considered Governor Stark one. Calling him an "ingrate," Pendergast
said, "I am perfectly willing to let the Democrats and all the people of Missouri
be the judge of my honesty and integrity, my actions, and my democracy."[28]

A young reformer and future federal judge, John W. Oliver, recalled,
"I served as secretary of the Douglas committee in Kansas City in that
election and learned, or at least I thought I learned, that the reformers could
be brought into a single campaign organization that would have sufficient
volunteer rank and file workers to meet those of the machine in every ward and
precinct in Kansas City. . . . On the national level, Stark became convinced
and convinced the national administration that corruption was the name of
the game as far as Pendergast and his machine was concerned." Considering
the importance of the election, Oliver concluded, "Pendergast's defeat in the
Billings-Douglas race convinced a lot of hesitant people that the time to attack

the machine was at hand."[29] Milligan soon received additional help from the FBI and the Bureau of Internal Revenue in bringing down the boss.

The increasingly beleaguered Pendergast showed a natural interest in his pursuers. He wrote Stark off as "an apple knocking son-of-a-bitch,"[30] but became curious about the activities of William H. Becker, a young attorney from Columbia and, like Oliver, a future federal judge. Becker was officially Stark's lawyer, but he acted as the liaison between the governor and Milligan. Becker made frequent trips to Kansas City. Asked in an oral history interview in 1989 whether machine officials knew his actual role, he exclaimed, "Hell yes, they knew!" One day in 1938, O'Malley invited him to lunch at the prestigious Kansas City Club. Decades later, Becker vividly recalled what transpired: "Pendergast was with O'Malley at the Kansas City Club. . . . We had Kansas City steak, which the doctors would rule out nowadays. They had heard that I was up there representing the governor. . . . They were just trying to see what I was like, and I was just listening to them and answering their questions. Pendergast asked me if I really lived in Columbia and if I practiced law there. It was mostly small talk."[31]

The feared boss did not impress Becker: "I thought he was a fat slob. He had a voice that was not free and clear; it was a gravel voice. He wasn't responsive. He wasn't interesting. O'Malley was nicer looking and acting than Pendergast, but it was obvious that Pendergast was the boss." Speculating on what specific knowledge Pendergast and O'Malley had of his activities, Becker said, "They knew that I had been investigating things, and I think I had gotten into some of the insurance business by then. You know, they would just declare an insurance company to be bankrupt, and O'Malley would take it over. It was depression times, and things were tough."[32]

THE INVESTIGATION

The Bureau of Internal Revenue launched a formal investigation of Thomas J. Pendergast on May 9, 1938. In June, a number of bureau officials conferred in Washington with Stark and Milligan. According to a bureau report, neither man provided any new information. No swarm of armed federal agents advanced on the House of Pendergast. The federal government simply did not have actual proof or even strong evidence of wrongdoing. Rather, a decision to go after Pendergast meant, more than anything else, finding help in opening new avenues of inquiry. Milligan, his small staff, and a special revenue agent who performed a considerable amount of legwork began tracking Pendergast's daily withdrawals and deposits at a large Kansas City bank. They did such a thorough job that after his conviction Pendergast admitted that Milligan had a better grasp of the transactions than he did. Of course, they were unable to follow the majority of Pendergast's financial transactions because he not only often dealt in cash but also kept sums in his head.[33]

Milligan explained in open court the lengths of Pendergast's attempts to keep his financial affairs as difficult to trace as possible. He kept "negligible" records, rarely used a bank account, almost always accepted only cash payments, made virtually all expenditures in cash, and sent large amounts by wire under assumed names. "Even when sojourning in another city, and having money sent to him there from Kansas City, the defendant went to the extremity of using an assumed name," Milligan emphasized. "Always he attempted to conceal." As one of the American turf's biggest players, Pendergast frequently needed to move large amounts of money in a hurry. Milligan said that "reliable information" in the "possession" of the government indicated that he wagered $2 million on horse races in 1936, actually losing $600,000. In 1938, he lost $75,000 in November and won back $43,000 the following month.[34]

In the continuing investigation, still in progress when he pleaded guilty, government agents discovered that in the period from 1927 through 1937, Pendergast failed to report as income the "staggering figure" of $1,240,746.55. He had defrauded the American people of $551,078.75 in taxes. Pendergast's discovered unreported income was $206,135.26 for 1935 and $393,044.69 for 1936, reflecting the insurance deal. Tracing all the money he had received proved impossible, given his use of hidden dividends, falsified books, fictitious loans, and imaginary salaries paid to nonexistent people. For example, of eight corporations in which he openly had large or controlling interests, he paid taxes on income from only three, Ready Mixed Concrete Co., T. J. Pendergast Wholesale Liquor Co., and W. A. Ross Construction Co. In addition, he obviously had secret stakes in numerous other enterprises and gained money from various additional legal and illegal sources. Even so, early in 1939, Milligan told Stark that a tax case had started to fall into place.[35]

On January 23, 1939, at Milligan's request, Judge Reeves convened a grand jury to consider both routine matters, such as the transportation of stolen vehicles across state lines, and, more importantly, tax evasions of illegal and illicit incomes. Over the next nine months the grand jury brought in tax evasion indictments against a number of key Pendergast machine personalities, including Pendergast and O'Malley. Residents of Kansas City and Jackson County were deliberately excluded from the blue ribbon panel. The method used, unusual in 1939 and unacceptable in later times when everyone became more aware of civil liberties, may have been the only way to gain the indictments. The twenty-one members, selected from an eighty-man pool, came from farms, villages, and small towns across western Missouri. One fairly typical member was Daniel C. Harmon of Neosho, the former sheriff of Newton County—hardly the kind of person expected to show sympathy for suspected corrupt Kansas City politicians. In long sessions, the jurors considered evidence from state and federal sources and heard testimony from machine lieutenants, minor officeholders, professional gamblers, and racketeers, plus hardened male and female dregs of the underworld.[36]

After the jurors finished their work, Spencer McCulloch exalted them in the St. Louis Post-Dispatch. He called the jurors meritorious "soldiers" who questioned witnesses in "homespun fashion," seeing through the "suave politician, tailored executive, or evasive machine politician." Judge Reeves made similar laudatory comments in discharging the grand jurors: "It is one of the heartening experiences, to know that good citizens brought together from different parts of a great judicial district, largely strangers to each other, will so readily unite in a common enterprise of preserving the country from crime by searching out and bringing to the bar of justice those who transgress the law. Nothing argues so strongly for the perpetuity of our institutions. It illustrates that there is a vast predominance of upright and patriotic men who are ready at all times to answer their country's call."[37]

When the grand jurors had commenced their work, Reeves had charged them to go after the "big man," believing that conditions in Kansas City were "astounding." He claimed that the "machine leader" promoted Kansas City as a wide-open town because the more vice there was, the bigger his income from graft: "The result was that huge incomes had been derived from crime in its various phases, not only by the machine leader, but by a multitude of his cohorts. The levies upon gambling and other places of vice were so heavy that it was natural for operators to complain bitterly of the exactions." Reeves called Kansas City "a seething cauldron of crime" in which "terrorism continued." Under the circumstances, "It was only a matter of marshaling the facts before a grand jury to justify indictments against the leader and his lieutenants."[38]

The biggest break in the insurance case came when McCormick confessed. In July 1938, treasury agents discovered the transfer of funds from Street to McCormick. After lying for several months about his role in the insurance settlement, on March 17, 1939, McCormick, placed under pressure, broke and admitted he had been the "payoff man." He testified in the afternoon before the grand jury and in the evening answered questions posed by Milligan and officials of the Intelligence Unit. Milligan said, "McCormick paused a moment in his story as though sensing that what he had said was of supreme interest to me. It was. I was getting a true picture of the shrewd, calculating boss gambling for big stakes."[39]

On March 18, the special Intelligence Unit agent in Kansas City in charge of the investigation wrote his superior in Washington about McCormick's revelations: "It is believed that this testimony virtually assures the successful culmination of the Pendergast investigation, especially since the amounts of

Horse-race bettors study their racing forms and mark their choices in this rare 1938 photograph taken inside The Turf, a downtown Kansas City club. *(Photograph by Jack Wally, courtesy the Western Historical Manuscript Collection, Kansas City, Mo.)*

the payments and the dates of payment coincide with the possession shortly after those dates of currency by the alleged recipients, as had already been disclosed by the investigation."[40]

The grand jury indicted Pendergast on two counts of tax evasion. On Good Friday, April 7, 1939, he appeared in court to be fingerprinted and to give bond. The boss, in a surly moment, compared himself to Jesus Christ of Nazareth, snarling at reporters, "There's nothing the matter with me. They persecuted Christ on Good Friday and nailed him to the Cross." Judge Reeves commented, "Coincidentally with the return of the indictment against the underworld leader the crooks who had supported him so faithfully during the long years of his unscrupulous reign began to scatter abroad and to run."[41]

In Washington, Senator Truman, continuing to see Pendergast's problems in a political, rather than criminal, context, said to a journalist from the *St. Louis Post-Dispatch*, "My opinion is that the District Attorney at Kansas City is behind this, because of political animus. I am sorry it happened. My connection with

Pendergast was, of course, purely political. He has been a friend to me when I needed it. I am not one to desert a ship when it starts to go down."[42] A few weeks later, Truman wrote a letter to a Kansas City friend, Jackson County Highway Engineer Alex Sachs, agreeing with him concerning events back home, that "'Hellzapoppin' is about the only way to describe the situation back there."[43]

George K. Wallace, the state correspondent for the *Kansas City Star*, predicted, "Idols may be smashed. Organizations may be torn apart and rebuilt. There is no telling for certain what the outcome will be." Before the end of April, Water Commissioner O'Malley, Director of Police Higgins, and, more importantly to the machine, City Manager McElroy had all resigned under fire. In pronouncing an end to McElroy's long tenure, the *Missouri Democrat* commented, "He passes from public life; but he will not pass from the memories of those who appreciate fine and patriotic effort."[44] Three months later, broken in spirit and facing a federal trial for tax evasion, McElroy died following a massive heart attack.

On April 24, 1939, *Life* magazine ran a feature article about Stark under the headline "The Governor of Missouri Helps Indict the Boss of Kansas City and Becomes a Presidential Possibility." The article inaccurately claimed, "A few months ago, Governor Lloyd C. Stark of Missouri gave President Roosevelt a tip that Tom Pendergast, boss of Kansas City, had failed to report a huge amount of his 1935 and 1936 income. The President told the Treasury and the Attorney General." *Life*, which supported the Republican party, speculated that Roosevelt wanted to make Stark a Democratic version of the crusading New York "Crime Fighter" and special prosecutor, Thomas E. Dewey. "It was clearly a New Deal effort to dim some of Tom Dewey's crusading glory by destroying a political boss even more powerful than New York's Jimmy Hines," the article asserted. "It seemed, moreover, an effort on the President's part to build up a 1940 Democratic presidential candidate." Pendergast, despite an operating agreement with the underworld, was said to run Kansas City on a "reasonable basis" and not to "unduly burden" honest citizens with taxes.

Pendergast was released on $10,000 bond, and he gave every outward indication of planning to fight the indictments. His able and seasoned lawyers were John Madden, James Burke, and J. J. Brewster. Madden, who had given speeches defending the machine during the 1930 city-election campaign, was a long-standing acquaintance of the boss's, a Rhodes scholar, and the chairman of the Jackson County Democratic Committee, which was inseparable from Pendergast's Jackson Democratic Club. Burke was one of Madden's associates. Brewster, a Republican party leader in Kansas City and a friend of Reeves's and Otis's, had strongly supported the two judges' nominations to the federal district bench. Brewster received a retainer from Pendergast of $100,000, then an unheard-of fee in Kansas City. His presence brought a cynical reaction among young Kansas City lawyers, some of whom speculated that his role on the legal team was to gain a light sentence in case a jury found the boss guilty, a case of lawful influence peddling.[45]

On May 1, Pendergast pleaded not guilty before Judge Otis. Otis set a June 12 trial date, but the innocent plea may have been only part of a legal strategy. On April 27, Milligan had brought a superseding indictment against Pendergast that included additional unreported income for 1935 and 1936. This raised the obvious possibility of what a more thorough examination of Pendergast's sources of income for other years might reveal. For instance, the government charged him with only $15,655 in unreported income in 1931, when Johnny Lazia's gambling operations alone netted tens of thousands of dollars every week.[46]

With considerable resolution, the federal grand jury, the Intelligence Unit, and Milligan pressed on with their work. Treasury agents interviewed Thomas J. Pendergast Jr. on April 18, 1939, finding out little beyond that he paid taxes and that his father owed him $7,500.[47] The questioning of Edward L. Schneider, an officer of several Pendergast-connected companies, proved another matter. Following three weeks of intensive interrogation, Schneider, fearing a perjury indictment, confessed on April 28, admitting that large blocks of stock held in his name actually belonged to Tom Pendergast. Schneider explained that Pendergast had granted him permission to tell the truth. Whether that was the case remains a mystery. On May 2, 1939, a few days after Schneider had testified before the grand jury about Pendergast's manifold financial dealings, police found his empty car parked in the middle of the Fairfax Bridge over the Missouri River. He left two notes, one to his wife and one to his daughter. Authorities recovered his body from the river a few days later, and while the coroner ruled his death a suicide, suspicions remained. Reeves wrote that Schneider was "forced" to jump off that bridge. Five hundred friends and associates, among them Thomas J. Pendergast Jr., attended funeral services at a Kansas City mortuary. T. J. Pendergast, conspicuous by his absence, sent a wreath of roses, snapdragons, and sweet peas.[48]

Another close Pendergast business associate, Lester Jordan, felt himself under terrible pressure both from the government and from the machine, with little room between. Indeed, Jordan, president of the Pendergast-dominated Sanitary Service Co., suffered a heart attack after narrowly avoiding a perjury indictment on May 18. Like Schneider, Jordan admitted that Pendergast owned and received dividends on shares in his name. Jordan said that Pendergast, in light of what had happened to Schneider, had authorized him to be truthful.[49] By then, Pendergast had decided to change his plea, which was completely out of character for him.

THE GUILTY PLEA

On May 19, 1939, Madden and Brewster visited Milligan at his office and announced Pendergast's intention to plead guilty on two counts of attempted evasion of income taxes due the United States for the years 1935 and 1936. Given the government's airtight case, the plea change made a great deal of sense. An admission of responsibility usually meant a lighter sentence than that imposed following a jury conviction. Judge Otis, informed of the change of plea, reset the case for just three days later. Milligan obliquely admitted surprise: "This information was a severe blow to those who had worshiped and believed in the boss. His friends could not believe the news when they heard it. His followers were not the only ones who could not believe this to be the fact." Milligan, like many others, recognized that Pendergast had averted public disclosure of the whole sordid story of his machine: "The boss and his attorney were fairly aware of this. The only smart thing to do was to trust the leniency of the court. Whatever the verdict, it could not be as humiliating as a long-drawn-out trial."[50]

In a dramatic court session that Judge Otis called to order at 9:00 A.M. on May 22, 1939, Pendergast publicly admitted his guilt. The court met in a building normally used for storage and as a federal printing plant, located directly behind the construction site of the new courthouse. Judge Otis, professional in his demeanor, ignored the large crowd that spilled from the temporary courtroom out into the corridors. Throughout the proceedings, sounds could be heard of people milling about, of clattering telegraph keys carrying the news throughout the nation, and of the muffled voices of radio commentators. The portly and subdued boss, wearing a dark business suit, sat at a front table flanked by Tom Jr. and nephew Jim Pendergast, the heir apparent to the organization.[51]

Madden quickly set the tone. "Stripped of all its drama, ignoring all things extrinsic to the case, the issue is simple," he emphasized. "The charge is tax evasion." Seeking clemency on medical grounds, Madden called to the stand Abraham Sophian, M.D., Pendergast's personal physician. Dr. Sophian, using notes, gave a litany of Pendergast's health problems, detailing the extent that his patient suffered from the effects of coronary thrombosis, an enlarged aorta, and an obstruction of the bowels that necessitated a drain on his right side above the thigh. Dr. Sophian said that Pendergast had to take as many as half a dozen doses of nitroglycerin a day and cautioned that excessive stress could bring on another heart attack. He contended that Pendergast had, according to insurance statistics, an average life expectancy of seven years.[52]

After Dr. Sophian finished testifying, Milligan put on his eyeglasses and, without oratory or dramatics, read a twenty-page statement. He publicly disclosed the promised $750,000 as part of the insurance deal for the first time and laid out, step by step, the government's findings of fraud and tax evasion. Some Pendergast supporters considered the presentation unnecessary posturing, but Milligan followed instructions from Judge Otis, who wanted the full extent of Pendergast's avarice made known. In summation, Milligan said that during the investigation Pendergast had "obstructed justice and suborned perjury."[53]

Milligan emphasized that the government could establish "beyond doubt" that Pendergast had tried to defeat the income tax in other years than the two specified in the indictment, but he went on to state, "Believing that the court will consider these additional offenses in assessing the defendant's punishment for the offenses which he admits committing, as we understand the rule to be, we desire now to state that there will be no further criminal prosecution against the defendant for these additional offenses, and, of course, this is just, since they are here to be taken into account by the court in assessing the defendant's punishment, and, in practice, should not be presented against him again." If this convoluted eighty-word sentence, in sharp contrast to the rest of the clearly presented statement, related to a deal, few caught it. A reporter for the *Kansas City Star* praised Milligan for giving "a cold, merciless recital."[54]

After Milligan finished, Brewster made brief remarks blaming Pendergast's need for tremendous amounts of money, which compelled him to accept the insurance "payoff," on his "mania" for gambling. Brewster graphically described how the addiction of horse-race gambling affected the boss: "He told me that when the afternoon was here, 2:30, 3 o'clock, he would go into a little room, and there he would take the form sheet, and with the advice of a friend of his would handicap horses, and then he would sit with the telephone at his ear and he would hear the call, 'They're at the post.' Later, 'They're off,' and so over that telephone, by ear and not by eye, he watched those horses run to the finish line—all the thrill that can come to any man, for which possesses him and which he cannot down." Brewster quoted a remorseful Pendergast as saying, "I don't know what it is, but it has been with me all my life since I came from St. Joseph to here."[55]

Brewster's presentation of the boss's addictions, dovetailing with the expert medical testimony of Pendergast as a sick and troubled individual not entirely responsible for his actions, probably had little impact. Few people in 1939 considered compulsive gambling an illness, and general perceptions of Pendergast's ruthlessness made it difficult to evoke even a small measure of compassion.

Judge Reeves later wrote, "Although Mr. Pendergast had not known the words mercy or leniency, yet, at the bar of justice, he whimpered and whined because of claimed physical ailments and begged for that leniency and mercy

Several women can be seen among the gamblers in Kansas City's Fortune Club, 2 West 39th Street, in 1938. *(Photograph by Jack Wally, courtesy the Western Historical Manuscript Collection, Kansas City, Mo.)*

he had never shown. He even sought mercy at the hands of the very judge whom he had so grossly and grievously maligned."[56] Reeves had a reputation for meting out harsher sentences than Otis, so one might wonder what kind of sentence Reeves, if he had handled the case, would have imposed on Pendergast.

THE SENTENCING

Judge Otis concluded the May 22 session by sentencing Pendergast. Otis, in a statement he called "The Applicable Principles," brushed aside any contention that Pendergast's sentence should reflect the excesses of his whole career: "If the crime charged is, as here, attempted tax evasion, the punishment should be for attempted tax evasion. Not a job or title should be added to the punishment because it is judicially noticed that the defendant has been a political 'boss,' nor because it is judicially noticed that the city and county which he has dominated have been governed with indescribable corruption and dishonesty. There are those, I know, who think such matters should affect the sentence imposed for attempted tax evasion. They who think so err."[57]

Otis also felt compelled to recognize Pendergast's health problems: "The true reason for considering ill health is that the quantum of punishment is not determined by the single factor of length of imprisonment. The effect of imprisonment is another factor. The effect on a sick man may be double the effect on a well and strong man. This defendant is physically afflicted. Some consideration must be given to that fact." Otis stressed that although Pendergast was a man of intelligence totally responsible for his actions, he felt it reasonable to take his health into consideration in determining a penalty.[58]

Judge Otis sentenced Pendergast on the first count to fifteen months in the penitentiary. On the second count, Otis handed down a three-year prison term and imposed a fine of $10,000. He then suspended the sentence on the second charge and substituted five years' probation, following the serving of the fifteen months on the first count. In addition to the usual conditions, Otis imposed a number of stipulations on Pendergast's conduct during the five years of probation. He would have to pay his fine, plus more than $430,000 in delinquent taxes and penalties. In addition, Otis ordered, "He will not be permitted to bet on the races or gamble in any form. He will not be permitted, directly or indirectly, to take part in any sort of political activity unless his full civil rights shall be restored by Presidential pardon. He will not be permitted to visit 1908 Main Street during his probation." Earle Frost, a Republican precinct captain present in the courtroom, heard an elderly woman exclaim, "Oh, my poor leader! Oh, my poor leader!"[59]

On May 27, Otis followed up his Pendergast decision by sentencing O'Malley, humiliatingly described in a newspaper account as "Pendergast's stooge," to a year in jail. In sentencing O'Malley on the tax evasion charge, Judge Otis commented on the former insurance commissioner's role in the insurance settlement: "For thirty thousand pieces of silver, it may be, he betrayed Missouri. It is likely that the tax he attempted to evade was on the bribe money he had received." Like his leader, O'Malley changed a not guilty plea to guilty. In another action, a court decision disallowed the insurance settlement, leading to new rounds of prolonged litigation.[60]

O'Malley's length of imprisonment received little notice, but newspapers across Missouri excoriated Judge Otis for giving Pendergast what they considered too light a sentence. Under prevailing federal rules, the fallen boss had the option of applying for parole after only five months behind bars. The *Kansas City Star* set the tone with a front-page editorial headlined "Inequality Before The Law!" expressing "profound amazement and disappointment" at the "light" sentence for the leader of the "ruthless and corrupt Pendergast dynasty." Noting that Otis had conferred on Pendergast associates in the vote-fraud cases longer prison terms than the boss himself received, the editorial maintained, "Pendergast was not an underling acting on orders from someone higher up of whom he stood in fear. He himself was the man higher up, setting the amount of loot from the insurance companies, supervising its distribution and evading the revenue act."[61]

Other commentaries were just as scathing. According to the *St. Louis Globe-Democrat*, "extenuating circumstances" did not apply in Pendergast's case because of "the circumstances out of which the crime itself grew—shameless spoilation of government and corruption of officials." With considerable sarcasm, the *St. Louis Star-Times* noted, "*Fifteen months*, and the man will be eligible to apply for parole in five. . . . *Fifteen months*, under circumstances that make it highly probable that good old Boss Tom will be back in Kansas City in time to give the boys a little advice before the August, 1940, primary. Judge Merrill E. Otis merits no vote of thanks from the people of Missouri." The editorial called Pendergast's punishment "shocking," a victory for "the discredited, corrupt and corrupting Kansas City boss." The *St. Joseph Gazette* protested, "Pendergast has been let off lightly," describing him as a "stripped and shivering figure that only a little while ago was a state above the state." The *St. Louis Post-Dispatch*, after denouncing Pendergast's "super-criminal" career, said, "The evil he has done, within the area of so-called business, cannot be measured by the moneys that flowed into his possession through tortuous channels." Putting the best face possible on the guilty plea, the editor of the *Missouri Democrat* on May 26, 1939, wrote, "We are inclined to believe that if only those persons who have always filed an absolutely honest assessment of personal taxes alone could cast the first stone at Pendergast, he would be in little danger of being stoned to death."[62]

Pendergast's evasion of taxes became in the minds of many only a small aspect of his illegal activities—the tip of the iceberg. No one appeared swayed by the argument that his physical condition should have precluded subjection to the stress of a lengthy stay behind bars.

The storm of protest took Judge Otis aback, unexpectedly placing him on the defensive. When he sentenced O'Malley, he read a telegram from James W. Morris, the assistant U.S. attorney general, stating, "All things considered, Pendergast sentence quite in line with comparable cases." On August 20, 1939, a memorandum Otis authored for the *Federal Supplement* sought to further silence his critics: "The criticism certainly was sincere, but hasty, unanalytical, spoken and written apparently in complete blindness to the particular crimes for which sentences had been imposed and to the solemn obligations of the judicial oath." He stressed that much of the criticism entirely ignored substantial parts of the sentence, overlooking altogether the large civil penalty—in excess of $170,000.

Commenting on why the grand jurors in the vote-fraud cases had failed to indict Pendergast, Otis emphasized, "*There just was no evidence and the federal grand juries would not indict a man against whom they could find no evidence.*" He called the tax evasion indictment a near thing, hanging on the testimony of McCormick. Otis praised Milligan and others who helped him break Pendergast: "He set out upon a dogged pursuit of what first was a mere phantom. . . . When the real nature of his purpose began to be understood, powerful individuals did what they could to obstruct him. But others, more powerful, who deserve great credit, came to his assistance—the Governor of Missouri, the Secretary of the Treasury, the Attorney General, perhaps even the Chief Magistrate."[63] Of course, that ignored the issue of the length of the sentence. Actually, there was no easy answer to that question, and the sentence remained a bone of controversy decades later.

Otis pleased Kansas City political reformers by including in his memorandum a colorful statement on how Pendergast exercised influence from his "monastic-like" 1908 Main "throne room," the "local Mecca of the faithful," where "came alike great and little," craving favors. "Each who came, it is said, awaited, hat in hand, his turn, humbly presented his petition, listened to the mandate of Caesar, and backed away from the Presence," Otis wrote. "And those who did not actually go in person to bend the pregnant hinges of the knee, even the mightiest, telephoned respectful inquiries, as they passed through the city, asking concerning 'Tom's health.'" The judge observed that Pendergast's portrait adorned the offices of eminent public servants both in Jefferson City and in Washington, "along with that of the Father of His Country and that of the Sage of Monticello, between these other portraits, on a somewhat higher level."

Otis recognized that Pendergast had no real rival and brooked no real competition. He made it clear that until the insurance deal the boss had never been convicted or even charged on indictment for any specific state or federal crime. Hence, he was a first offender with no prior criminal record. This did not mean that Pendergast had a good reputation or had committed no other crimes than failing to pay his taxes: "It was believed that the tentacles of his octopus-like power reached into every nook and cranny of the city and into every enterprise, legitimate and illegitimate, good and evil. Over and over again for a score of years it was whispered that he must be *particeps criminis* in a hundred different offenses against the laws of state and nation."[64]

Otis tried to explain, without stating the obvious, that he had not only sent Pendergast to jail, but through the terms of his probation effectively ended his career in politics: "Pendergast was sentenced to wear the badge of 'Convict' for one year and three months behind penitentiary walls, in the seclusion of a prison, and then to wear it for five years longer before the eyes of his fellow men."[65] Otis never entirely lived down the charge that he had given Pendergast special treatment. In an unusual twist of fate, the man who sent Pendergast to prison felt compelled to defend himself before the boss's legions of enemies. Anything that involved Pendergast generated controversy. He seemed bigger than life to all; to most, he seemed an ogre who personified evil in America.

WHO CAUGHT PENDERGAST

Otis was correct when he concluded that catching Pendergast, even in such a blatant crime, was surprising. Harry Truman, an astute observer of matters Pendergast, wrote his wife, Bess, that he thought the Big Boss would never be indicted for anything because he was always under investigation and always beating unproved charges. The same thing could have happened in the insurance case. If Street had not been questioned about the $100,500, Pendergast could have been home free, despite the rumors and bad taste left by the insurance settlement. What if Street, when initially interviewed by agents, had immediately paid taxes on the money? And what if investigators had decided that the business about the involvement of an important Missourian and the docking of the *Queen Mary* was just a subterfuge by Street to hide an embezzlement? After all, fingering Pendergast seemed almost too obvious. Finally, what if McCormick, when cornered, had held out for another month? If Pendergast had been able to buy more time to exert pressure in high places, he might have succeeded in stopping the investigation.

Several individuals, some gratuitously, took credit for smashing Pendergast. Milligan and Stark both aggrandized their roles for political purposes. J. Edgar Hoover, days before the indictment, along with Attorney General Frank Murphy, made a hurried trip to Kansas City to promote the contribution of the FBI.[66] Elmer Irey of the Intelligence Unit gave himself a great deal of credit. Otis and Reeves had their say. The fine hand of Franklin D. Roosevelt was another possibility. And what about Secretary of the Treasury Morgenthau, who gave a green light to the tax investigation?

Actually, while many people participated in the pursuit of Pendergast, the larger context was inescapable. Pendergast, through insatiable greed and arrogance, brought himself down.[67] As is clear from his past practices, Pendergast unquestionably believed that he was above the law, that he could steal from the public with impunity. Yet, as his excesses became ever more obvious, he broke the law once too often, got caught in the act, and paid the price.

SEVEN

Prison

1939–1940

On May 29, 1939, the gates of Leavenworth penitentiary slammed behind Thomas J. Pendergast, a sick and defeated man, a mere shadow of his former self. Dr. Abraham Sophian's foreboding testimony had actually painted a brighter medical picture than existed for Pendergast. The chance of his dying in prison loomed as a genuine possibility.

On June 1, Justin K. Fuller, M.D., the medical director for the Bureau of Prisons, sent a memorandum to the director of the prison system, James V. Bennett. Dr. Fuller, reacting to information relayed from Leavenworth, offered a grim prognosis of the condition of the fallen boss: "He has attacks of severe pain in the region of the heart. A heart such as this is a very serious thing indeed. It is difficult, if not impossible, to give any opinion as to when such a heart may stop working: it may go on for years or it may stop at almost any time."[1]

On receiving Dr. Fuller's information, Bennett immediately passed the bleak news on to Attorney General Frank Murphy; it was probably the last thing he wanted to hear, given all the public relations problems involved for the Bureau of Prisons. Bennett reported that Pendergast suffered from chronic heart trouble and was in "very bad" physical condition. He indicated that "ordinarily" Pendergast would have been given a special diet and committed directly to the prison hospital for treatment of his physical disabilities, but that nothing could be done until the warden received specific recommendations from the medical officers. In the meantime, Pendergast remained in a main cell block set aside for newly imprisoned felons. With a sense of alarm, Bennett confided, "I understand that yesterday he nearly collapsed when being taken from the cell block to the hospital." In bureaucratic language, Bennett said that, while the prisoner had not yet been hospitalized, any improvement in Pendergast's health was "not now anticipated."[2]

Bennett's warning proved justified. On the evening of June 2, at 8:30, guards found Pendergast in his cell looking extremely pale; bluish, especially around the lips; and complaining of severe chest pain radiating to the shoulder and arm. His pulse appeared weak, rapid, and irregular. Administering nitroglycerin "somewhat relieved" him, but at 9:30 P.M. guards rushed him on a stretcher to the prison hospital, where he received further medication, spending a restless and sleepless night. At 9:15 A.M. the next day, his blood pressure stood at 102/76, compared to 116/76 when he entered prison.[3]

Leavenworth's chief medical officer, C. H. Waring, M.D., of the U.S. Public Health Service, examined Pendergast and reported in a detailed letter to Dr. Fuller on June 3, "Our opinion is that the patient is having an acute coronary occlusion which is a possible recurrence of previous attacks and in our opinion is considered to be in serious condition." Dr. Waring diagnosed Pendergast as having a history of syphilis for more than twenty-three years, of acute coronary thrombosis for three years, of many anginal attacks for the past two years, and of chronic disease of the bowel. Further complications related to his colostomy and his suprapubic prostatomy operations, both performed in 1936. In addition to other treatment, Dr. Waring ordered "absolute rest in bed." Dr. Sophian and the prison's consulting physician, Lawrence Engle, M.D., of Kansas City, both examined Pendergast, confirming the diagnosis.[4]

On June 5, prison officials waived visiting restrictions for new prisoners and allowed Carolyn Pendergast to see her husband.[5] On the same day, the Bureau of Prisons finally informed the media of Pendergast's condition. An "official news bulletin" announced that Pendergast had suffered a "rather serious heart attack" and was "not yet out of danger."[6] For the next several weeks, Dr. Waring received regular reports on Pendergast's condition, detailing his blood pressure, pulse rate, ankle swelling, lung congestion, coughing spells, and sleeping habits.[7] Pendergast's physical condition, except for a persistent swelling of the ankles, gradually improved to the extent that prison social workers interviewed him, completing his prison "Admission Summary."

At the beginning of the medical process, on June 1, for the first and only time, an intelligence test was administered to Pendergast. Standardized instruments to supposedly test comparable levels of knowledge, or I.Q., had not been used when he attended school. Indeed, he was probably the only important old-style city boss ever subjected to such an exercise. Pendergast scored 107 on the test, well within the normal range but lower than expected, given his reputation for great cunning and his accomplishments in life. He became confused on a subtest designed to measure abstract reasoning, professing that he could not "seem to get the idea." The test giver observed, "On this and other tests he showed evidence of emotional upset, and it is probable that his test performance was lowered on this account. He was slow in his reactions, probably in part because of his physical condition, and this also tended to lower his score. Performance on several of the subtests was excellent, however, cooperation was very good. There is little doubt that the subject has been a person of superior intelligence. Although there has probably been some slowing up of his mental abilities there is no evidence of significant mental deterioration."[8]

A psychiatric examination evaluated him as a "very pleasant, courteous, cooperative old man, whose physical condition suggests that he may be approaching his dotage, although he is more alert mentally than would be expected from his apparent poor physical health." An "apparent cheerfulness and carefree attitude" was attributed to a special effort to conceal "deep-seated feelings of depression and despair." Nothing indicated that he had a hostile attitude, held grudges against society, or had symptoms of any mental disorder. The conclusion was that Pendergast needed no psychiatric treatment, that his disciplinary prognosis appeared good, that he required a single cell if not hospitalized, and that his work assignments should take physical factors into account. It would certainly have confounded and surprised many of the boss's enemies to hear him described as a "very pleasant, courteous, cooperative old man" with a "cheerful and carefree attitude."[9]

Inevitable charges were leveled about the mollycoddling of a wealthy and influential criminal and the faking of illness to secure preferential treatment or an early release. Judge Merrill Otis had considered health and age in determining Pendergast's sentence. Not a single editorial writer suggested that physical disabilities should have kept him out of the penitentiary. The whole subject was a touchy one for Pendergast's jailers. Even before he passed out of immediate danger following his heart seizure, Dr. Fuller wrote from Washington advising Dr. Waring that Pendergast's hospital residence should not be unduly prolonged "beyond the time he can safely be returned to the cell block."[10] Inexplicably, authorities never considered transferring him to the federal medical center for prisoners in Springfield, Missouri, where he could have received more aggressive care for his immediate medical problems. Hard-line advocates of harsh punishment for criminals considered that facility a glorified country club.

A Medical Diagnosis

Various possibilities, some plausible and some not, contribute to blurred images concerning Pendergast's actual medical condition. Accusing notables

Members of the federal grand jury that indicted Pendergast on charges of tax evasion line up for a photograph. *(Photograph by Jack Wally, courtesy the Western Historical Manuscript Collection, Kansas City, Mo.)*

of having syphilis has a venerable, if not honorable, history. Were the dire reports on Pendergast's heart troubles part of a carefully orchestrated plot, involving large bribes, to gain Pendergast an early release? Such a ploy might have worked. Pendergast himself had first raised the health issue, citing illness in disclaiming responsibility for the 1936 vote fraud. Among others, Tom Pendergast Jr. thought that his father's declining health contributed to the demise of the Pendergast machine, that he was never again the same strong leader after his 1936 heart attack.

In 1993, Robert Hudson, M.D., of the University of Kansas Medical Center, examined the medical records of Thomas J. Pendergast in the Notorious Offender Case Files. Dr. Hudson, who achieved professor emeritus status in 1995, was for many years chair of the Department of History and Philosophy of Medicine at the University of Kansas Medical Center. He is an authority on clinical diagnosis, and has lectured and written extensively, most notably on the medical histories of presidents, including Franklin D. Roosevelt and John F. Kennedy. Clearly recognizing all the pitfalls of retrospective diagnosis, Dr. Hudson considered Pendergast's records with three basic questions in mind: Did he have syphilis? Did he instead have common arteriosclerotic heart disease? Did he also have aortic insufficiency?

Prefacing his statements with the caveat that "retrospective diagnosis is always a treacherous business" and that "it would help immediately in Pendergast's case to have the medical records from his private physicians over the years," Dr. Hudson concluded that "Pendergast had syphilis in his earlier years, but that this was adequately treated, and that he died of arteriosclerotic heart disease, myocardial infarctions, and eventual congestive heart failure." He noted that "Pendergast was a prime candidate for arteriosclerotic heart disease," being "overweight and a smoker, and apparently not given to exercise." Among other reasons, the fact that "Pendergast survived almost a decade after his first heart attack in New York" is "more in keeping with a diagnosis of coronary arteriosclerosis than syphilitic involvement of the coronary artery openings, where a fatal outcome often occurred within three years at the time."[11]

On the question of aortic insufficiency, Dr. Hudson explained that Pendergast's blood pressure readings taken in prison and the absence of mention of a heart murmur in his records "[lead] me to doubt that Pendergast had significant aortic insufficiency."[12]

Another factor in Pendergast's health that cannot be ignored is the reality that both of his parents and several of his siblings died of heart disease. Consequently, genetics, more than any other factor, may have determined the declining years of his life.

PRISON LIFE

Although Pendergast recovered from his prison heart attack to the extent that he could move around in a limited way, he did not gain enough strength to climb a flight of stairs, and during the rest of his Leavenworth experience he remained in the prison infirmary. On July 10, 1939, a penitentiary physician described him as "feeling fairly well of late," having an "irregular but forceful" pulse, and continuing to experience persistent ankle swelling. His general condition was considered fair.[13]

As best he could, Pendergast settled into life behind bars. He opened an account at the prison bank for $100, but participated in no educational programs and checked no books out of the library. He had indicated shortly after admission that he desired to correspond only with members of his immediate family, plus James Pendergast and two machine insiders, Bernard Gnefkow and Phil McCrory. Pendergast was visited by his attorneys on legal and financial affairs. When able, he performed duties as a clerk in the hospital, transcribing x-ray results, patient records, and medical notes. One newspaper story erroneously claimed that his duties included the demeaning task of picking up scraps of paper in the prison yard with a pointed broomstick. A confidential prison work report rated his work level as "good," calling him "trustworthy," "friendly," and "pleasant." On August 18, 1939, a high-ranking Leavenworth official, commenting on Pendergast's attitude, informed the United States Board of Parole, "Conduct excellent to date."[14]

ATTEMPTS AT EARLY RELEASE

Quite naturally, Pendergast wanted to gain an early release. On June 28, 1939, from a hospital bed, he signed a parole application, proposing James Kemper, the president of the Commerce Trust Co. of Kansas City, as his parole officer, and Robert P. Lyons, the vice president of Ready Mixed, as his parole employer. Pendergast, in stating his version of his "present offense," stated, "I plead guilty, I will pay the fine." He clearly indicted his future plans: "I will return to 5650 Ward Parkway, Kansas City, Missouri, to reside with my wife and family. Kansas City has been my home for forty-six years. I will resume my duties as President of the Ready Mixed Concrete Company."[15]

Both Milligan and Judge Otis, as was usual practice, wrote letters indicating that Pendergast should complete his full term.[16] In a footnote, however, to his August memorandum designed to answer his critics, Otis implied that Pendergast had suffered enough: "Rarely in history has any criminal been branded as a 'convict' with such pitiless publicity. Within a week some of the greatest newspapers in the land published photographs of Pendergast and O'Malley, his fellow prisoner, *in convict garb*. . . . Literally millions of copies of the pictures were printed and circulated, for members of the families of the prisoners and for the whole world to see, that the world might know how a man is punished who attempts to evade a tax." Otis, in biblical language, claimed that Pendergast had lost his strength: "So did the eyeless and broken Samson, chained, a prisoner, toil in Gaza at the mill with the slaves."[17]

Pendergast's subordinates, working hard in his behalf, sought favors in the highest places and renewed their attacks on Reeves and Otis—attacks that had temporarily stopped following the indictment. Along with Milligan, the two judges again received intimidating and vicious telephone calls. Reeves, in his unpublished memoirs, claimed that Attorney General Murphy "authorized" the FBI and other "individuals" to "investigate the judges, and, if possible, to secure something that might be twisted or tortured into a just criticism." Reeves said Murphy enlisted the aid of ex-convicts that he and Otis had sent to prison, with a resulting "interference with the administration of justice in the Western District of Missouri." Reeves wrote to Murphy to request that he "cease and desist from such interference," receiving what he called a "pathetically evasive" response: "He pretended that the investigation was ordered in the interest of the judges, and not to harm them or to interfere (as was the actual fact) with the administration of justice."[18]

T. J. Pendergast's April 7, 1939, arraignment. (*Photograph by Jack Wally, courtesy the Western Historical Manuscript Collection, Kansas City, Mo.*)

In any event, attempts to persuade President Roosevelt through Postmaster General James Farley, who continued to handle relations between the key urban bosses and the national Democratic party, to grant executive clemency to Pendergast ended in naught. Consequently, Pendergast had to take his chances with the parole board.

Pendergast was one of 370 prisoners scheduled to appear before the United States Board of Parole during its regularly scheduled early November meeting at Leavenworth penitentiary. Commissioner Arthur Wood, the board's chairman since 1930, presided at the Leavenworth session. Wood, a former county juvenile judge in Michigan, from 1908 to 1927, had been state commissioner of pardons and paroles from 1927 to 1930. Under federal rules, the only persons present during a hearing besides one commissioner of the board and the prisoner were a secretary and the institution's parole officer. Wood had to confer with two other members of the parole board before making a decision. The action of the board was final and no appeal was possible. Even though the prosecutor and the judge in a criminal case had no official role, the board usually took their recommendations into consideration. Wood, when pressed by reporters about whether he had been placed under pressure by the attorney general or by Director Bennett to give Pendergast special consideration, gave a careful reply: "I have served under two Presidents, three attorney generals, and two bureau of prisons directors, and never as yet has a suggestion been made by any of them regarding the disposition of an applicant for parole."[19]

As it turned out, Pendergast got an unexpected form of special consideration. Dr. Waring had explained to his superiors that Pendergast had a "severe" coronary attack on October 11, followed by several "mild episodes." According to Dr. Waring, "either mental or physical exertion" on Pendergast's part could precipitate a fatal seizure, and his colostomy required special attention and interfered with his "normal ambulation."[20]

In a memorandum marked "Personal," Director Bennett forwarded to the attorney general a report received from Leavenworth concerning Pendergast: "Possibly due to his knowledge of news flashes and general publicity being given in the newspapers, the condition of the above named inmate has again become aggravated. His blood pressure is 136 over 60; pulse rate 65—very irregular; and he will require increased care."[21] Bowing to the reality of the situation, Wood interviewed Pendergast in a hospital ward on November 4, 1939.

According to the transcript, Pendergast, very contrite, politely answered all the questions asked him in the short proceeding. He emphasized his poor health, his desire to go home, and the fact that he had admitted his guilt. Unexpectedly requested to make a statement on why he should receive parole, he first said he did not know what to say, before hurriedly putting some words together: "Well, the only thing that I can say is that I am not a very well man and I suppose you have those conditions there. I have a bad heart and I have a colostomy here and of course I think that I would like to have a parole; I just don't know what to say to you. I am 67 years old, and I have never been charged with any offense before."

Wood asked, "Well, how did you happen to go wrong this time?" Pendergast, after first calling the jurist by the wrong last name, replied: "Oh, pardon me, Mr. Wood, I don't know, I evaded the income tax as I am charged with and I am guilty and that is about all I can say about it. How I come to go wrong I don't know. I have lived 66 years out there and didn't go wrong, at least I don't think I did, and I couldn't tell you how I happened to go wrong. There are a lot of other things about it." These hardly sound like the words of a feared and ruthless leader. Instead, they sound like those of a docile and sick old man with all the fight taken out of him.

When Wood inquired in conclusion whether he had anything further to add, Pendergast again returned to the theme of family life: "Well, I don't know any other thing that I could say that would be of any benefit to me except my

James Pendergast, Tom Pendergast Jr., and Tom Pendergast Sr. confer at the sentencing on May 22, 1939. *(Photograph by Jack Wally, courtesy the Western Historical Manuscript Collection, Kansas City, Mo.)*

health and my condition, and I suppose you have some record of that there. I don't know anything else to say except that I would like to be home with my wife and children."

A short exchange followed between the two men. Wood, commenting on Pendergast's desire to go home, said, "Well, that is true with every other married man in this institution." Pendergast, by now relatively at ease, agreed, "It certainly is. I don't know what I could tell you, I could tell you a lot of things I suppose, but I don't know whether they would have much bearing on the case, they would be personal. There are a lot of things I could say but they wouldn't have any particular bearing; my health is the biggest thing and wanting to get home to my family; I have had several attacks in here and I suppose those are recorded, some records made of them, and I am liable to have an attack at any time."[22]

In lengthy remarks attached to a transcript of his interview with Pendergast, Wood suggested that the parole board in Washington, D.C., issue an order denying Pendergast parole. Wood acknowledged Pendergast's severe health problems; he also said that he recognized that Pendergast had a wife, children, and the promise of a job. He then touched on the nature of Pendergast's crime, drawing on Milligan's statement at the trial and a report by a revenue agent. Wood went on to stress that Pendergast had committed many other misdeeds as a "political czar" who ruled with a "ruthless hand," negating the "no prior criminal history" factor. It was not unusual to take a convict's entire career into account in considering parole. Pendergast, according to Wood, "had gradually built up a political machine which corrupted public officials and debauched the franchise of the free voters of the city. When the law-abiding citizenry of Kansas City would attempt to overthrow the tentacles of his political octopus, citizens were way-laid, brutally beaten and murdered at the ballot boxes."[23]

On November 21, 1939, the board officially rejected Pendergast's application. A scathing press release condemning the boss declared that, in light of Pendergast's crime and his record of corruption in Kansas City, parole "would be unjustifiable and incompatible with the public interest." The release said, "Kansas City became a haven of refuge and a rendezvous for some of the most notorious criminals and underworld figures in the land." It described the Otis sentence as "moderate." Pendergast, the release noted, had not presented any evidence to show that confinement aggravated his chronic disabilities. The Division of Press Intelligence of the Bureau of Prisons collected newspaper commentaries from around the nation universally praising the denial.[24] As for the disheartened Pendergast, he gave up any further efforts to gain a parole.

PENDERGAST'S PURPORTED ACTIVITIES

Early in 1940, the *Kansas City Star* published a feature story purporting to illustrate Pendergast's prison life, claiming that he had experienced no further medical "setbacks" and was "adjusted" to his lot. The article depicted him as rising before dawn from a spring bed rather than the prison-issued kind used by the other three thousand inmates, and washing and dressing by 6:00 A.M. He then waited in his tiny isolated ground-floor room for the *Kansas City Times*, which reached him uncensored, just as it did other prison subscribers. Pendergast ate breakfast sparingly off a tray, carefully reading the entire paper. Aside from the morning *Times* and the afternoon *Star*, he read little except the *Reader's Digest*. At work in the hospital, he took dictation from physicians in "firm, clear, rather rotund handwriting."[25] Matt Devoe, who was then serving time in Leavenworth for vote fraud, talked to Pendergast from time to time in the dispensary. "He was doing all right," Devoe recalled, "but he had a family and it was embarrassing. He looked in good spirits, but he didn't laugh about it."[26]

Inevitably, rumors began to circulate that Pendergast, in violation of his sentence, was surreptitiously continuing to carry on political business. On January 9, 1940, during a private meeting at the governor's mansion in Jefferson City, Governor Stark informed Special Agent W. Harold Lane of the Intelligence Unit of the treasury department that he had received word that Pendergast might still be deeply involved in Kansas City political manipulations. This confirmed Lane's own suspicions. Lane told Stark that an agent had accidentally overheard a conversation between Pendergast machine officials at a funeral, in which they talked about getting the organization out of state politics and concentrating on Kansas City and Jackson County. Lane suspected that Carolyn Pendergast passed a message from her husband detailing the strategy for the move.[27]

Governor Stark used Lane's comment as the basis for a speech, asserting that federal authorities suspected Pendergast of conducting political business. Because Stark had a reputation for carefully checking out information before going public, his comments received considerable publicity. In this instance, he may have acted prematurely.[28]

Lane, after checking and rechecking sources, decided that the rumors about Pendergast were unfounded and, after talking with Warden Robert Hudspeth, concluded that nothing was amiss at the penitentiary. Lane wrote in a letter, "Warden Hudspeth informed me that the only visitors had been attorneys for Mr. Pendergast and members of his immediate family; that on each occasion the warden's office was informed in advance of the purpose of the visit; and that a guard was present during the interview with the prisoner to ascertain that the conversation with Mr. Pendergast did not pertain to subjects other than those of which the warden had been advised." Prison records listed all of Pendergast's approved visitors. Warden Hudspeth, with some heat, later expressed dismay to Bennett that the Intelligence Unit "gave considerable credence to the ridiculous rumor that Pendergast was permitted by the management of the institution to continue his political administration from his prison cell."[29] Whatever the reason, Governor Stark decided to drop the matter. While it is doubtful that federal officials would condone continuance of Pendergast's administration of his machine from prison, it is also unrealistic to assume that he did not try, or even succeed at some level. He was incarcerated and ill, but he was still the boss.

Whether or not Pendergast was able to continue his political administration from prison, there is some evidence that he was able to circumvent

Tom Pendergast sits in the courtroom and waits to hear Judge Merrill Otis's sentence. *(Photograph by Jack Wally, courtesy the Western Historical Manuscript Collection, Kansas City, Mo.)*

the prison security system to further his gambling habit. On June 13, 1940, J. Edgar Hoover furnished information to Bennett suggesting that Pendergast wired what a bureau informer called "considerable money" out of Leavenworth to "big Jersey horse books."[30] Because Pendergast had already been released by that time, the Bureau of Prisons made no effort to follow up on Hoover's intelligence.

PENDERGAST'S RELEASE

The process that led to Pendergast's leaving Leavenworth began in the spring of 1940. A "Medical Release Report" underscored his poor physical condition throughout his incarceration, but said he had shown "no evidence of psychosis, depression or maladjustment." The report observed, "We still consider him to be a gravely ill patient as he had a coronary disease and is likely to have a fatal attack at any time."[31] Against that grim assessment, Pendergast spent his last days in Leavenworth. He paid his $10,000 fine, closed out his prison account, presented proof that he had a position at $2,500 a month waiting at Ready Mixed, and promised to fulfill the terms of his probation.[32]

Of the more than $430,000 in delinquent taxes and penalties that Otis had determined Pendergast should pay in addition to the $10,000 fine, Pendergast's lawyers negotiated a compromise tax bill of $350,000 with the government; he paid $140,000 of this when he left prison. Under the agreement, Pendergast had until April 15, 1941, to pay the remaining $210,000. The government called the deal a good one, contending that otherwise it would have had to foreclose on some of Pendergast's properties and in effect lose money, selling them at rock-bottom prices at forced sales. Sources said Pendergast intended to raise the funds to clear the rest of his debt by soliciting friends and associates. A sarcastic comment in the *Kansas City Star* suggested that "contractors and others who in the 'good old days' were recipients of machine largess, may expect to be asked to contribute toward the amount with which Pendergast will wipe out his tax debt to Uncle Sam."[33]

Given three months off for good behavior, Pendergast spent a total of twelve months in jail. At 9:00 A.M. on May 30, 1940, Memorial Day, a parole officer took Pendergast into custody and drove him to the new United States Courthouse in Kansas City.[34] A crowd of about two hundred watched his arrival, and about fifty people followed him in the public elevator up to the parole office on the fourth floor. There, Pendergast received a memorandum setting out the provisions of his probation. He left by a freight elevator and went directly to the county courthouse for a quick arraignment on a state bribery charge. Subsequently, accompanied by family members, he went home to 5650 Ward Parkway.

Pendergast required extraordinary treatment throughout his confinement. This would have been the case even if he had enjoyed excellent health. When he first entered Leavenworth, the associate warden had written that he would require segregation from the general inmate population to shield him from the demands of inmates who believed he could bestow favors on them. As it was, the medical evidence seems to indicate that Judge Otis, far from being too lenient, may actually, given the circumstances, have handed out too harsh a sentence. Once Pendergast entered Leavenworth, parole after only five months was out of the question for political reasons. The board would have been widely denounced if it had paroled Pendergast. Perhaps the most devastating circumstance of his imprisonment was that out of the general citizenry in the whole of Jackson County, only one woman in Kansas City, calling him a "good man," requested that he be paroled.[35] No matter how long it was or the terms of his sentence, Pendergast entered and left prison in complete disgrace.

EIGHT

Final Days
1940–1945

The Pendergast machine did not fold in May of 1939. Although it was clearly a grievous blow, Tom Pendergast's departure for Leavenworth seemed far from fatal. The machine remained on paper one of the most powerful political organizations in America, and it continued to control Kansas City from top to bottom. Jackson County was machine territory. Without the direct guidance of the boss, however, things quickly began to unravel. Statewide, despite efforts by Governor Lloyd Stark, who was barred by the Missouri constitution from running for reelection, the machine exercised great influence, dominating the judiciary and numerous elected and appointed officials. Machine subordinates continued to direct federal relief efforts throughout Missouri.

In a large impressive reception room in the capitol building in Jefferson City, legislators, surrounded on all sides by a Thomas Hart Benton mural, deliberated over financial issues. The mural illustrates the social, political, and economic history of Missouri, and on the east wall of the room, Benton painted a glowering, very much in command, bigger-than-life Thomas J. Pendergast.[1]

At the time of his sentencing, Pendergast clearly indicated that his nephew, James Michael Pendergast, would take over as head of the organization. Whether or not Tom Pendergast intended the arrangement to be permanent remains problematic. Jim Pendergast had routinely served as caretaker when Tom made trips abroad and during his 1936 illness. The media had long considered Jim the heir apparent. A question in many quarters was whether he could handle the job. Jim, with a reputation as a friendly and decent man who would rather be home with his family than contriving political deals in a smoke-filled room, believed in goodwill and pursued compromise to the extent that he favored the harmonious handing out of patronage. Even his enemies professed to admire him, a dubious qualification for the ruthless pre-election tactics and cold-blooded planning deemed necessary to succeed in even the most legal and honest machine politics.[2]

Tom Pendergast Jr. sincerely believed that Jim had plotted for years to take over the machine, ingratiating himself and playing on Pendergast's sentimental side and family ties. Under such a scenario, Jim and Harry S. Truman, a much more partisan and hard-boiled politician, worked together. The assumption was that Truman would spend only one term in the Senate and then would return to Jackson County politics.[3] Even if Tom Jr. was completely incorrect, the possibility of a Jim Pendergast and Harry Truman alliance raises intriguing questions. No one, however, could have predicted in 1939 the abrupt way that Jim advanced to power or that Truman, then a man of little national stature, would go on to become president of the United States and a world leader.

When Jim assumed direction of the machine, it was facing trouble on several fronts. Governor Stark was maneuvering against the machine's patronage power outside of Kansas City, aiming to destroy the semblance of a pro-Pendergast rural base. Inside Kansas City hundreds of city employees who did little more than run political errands lost their jobs; the more conspicuous gambling dens and sin places, including the Chesterfield Club, closed, either on their own or by state order; many racketeers went into hiding. The federal government took steps to overhaul its relief operations in Missouri, placing control of all WPA jobs under Governor Stark. Key machine personalities followed the boss to the federal penitentiary. Matthew S. Murray, who had earlier headed WPA activities in Missouri, and Otto P. Higgins, Pendergast's director of police from 1934 to 1939, entered Leavenworth for tax evasion. Charles Carrolla, underworld kingpin and successor to Johnny Lazia, drew eight years in the federal prison for mail fraud, tax evasion, and perjury. In June 1939, a special act of the General Assembly placed control of the Kansas City police department back in state hands.[4]

REFORM EFFORTS

On July 11, 1939, just six weeks after Pendergast entered prison, a new state-appointed police board named Lear B. Reed as Kansas City's new chief of police. He said the new state legislation "rescued the police department from the talons of the venal political vultures, who, with their many associates of the underworld, wept with chagrin, wondered and waited." Reed, a former FBI special agent and an avid J. Edgar Hoover devotee, found his experience as the head of the Kansas City police department somewhat disturbing. In step with the legacy of Johnny Lazia, the department, in a shambles, continued

Tom Pendergast and his nephew Jim Pendergast pose in happier days at 1908 Main Street. *(Photograph by Jack Wally, courtesy the Western Historical Manuscript Collection, Kansas City, Mo.)*

to have direct underworld ties. As soon as Reed moved into his new office, a multitude of bribe offers descended upon him.[5]

Prostitution and corruption were still widespread, and Kansas City remained a clearing center for narcotics. Reed angrily noted, "Even if we could overlook all the crookedness, ghost voting, job selling, fixing, framing, lugging, country bookkeeping, numbskull prosecutors, 'piano player' management, wholesale grand larceny in high places, and all the other phases of the fiasco of the Heart of America, no man or woman with a spark of decency or conscience could condone a political outfit that not only permitted but aided and abetted the narcotic traffic."[6]

Appalled at the widespread corruption and racketeering in Kansas City, Reed declared, "Kansas City tax money, emergency funds and other cash, all out of the property owners' pockets, kept the underworld riding the gravy train."[7] During his two-year battle to clean up the department and rid the area of what he called the "human wolves," Reed often found himself physically threatened. "Finding daggers on my automobile seat," he later recalled, "poisoned candy on my desk, prostitutes sitting in my car, the ace of spades with a bullet hole through it stuck under the door, samples of tar and rope in neat little packages delivered in several different ways, threatening notes and black-hand letters by the hundreds, little coffin-shaped bichloride of mercury tablets placed in convenient locations, whiskey planted in my car, and other threats to scare me off got to be monotonous and inconsequential after so long a time."[8]

The rehabilitation of the Kansas City police took some doing. According to Reed, the department had to be "cleaned, bathed, soaked, disinfected, deloused, and aired in the sun." No inventory of supplies existed, and arrest records of prominent citizens and infamous criminals had been purged from the police files. Reed related, "The wholesale theft and sale of criminal records from the department during the machine rule was a fact almost beyond belief."[9] Unfortunately, the problems in the police department were not unique. Echoes surrounding the gradual disintegration of the Pendergast machine rumbled throughout all the agencies of the Kansas City government.

State grand jurors, in spite of the machine's usual tactic of sending unmarked black automobiles filled with gangsters to drive by their homes, indicted dozens of people in connection with machine excesses. Rumors persisted of citizens seeing smoke from burning city hall records and trucks rushing through the night full of documents for dumping into the Missouri River.

Following the jailing of the boss, the generally ineffectual Mayor Bryce Smith, a Rabbit turned Pendergast man, actually tried to administer the city and to lead a reform effort. An article in a national magazine shamed Smith by stating that he had been a "powerless dummy." Smith's opening of books and ledgers that revealed to the public that Kansas City had a staggering $20 million debt thanks to the machine, followed by the firing of 748 out of a listed 5,049 city employees, failed to achieve the desired impact of making him appear in charge.[10] His term as the last true Pendergast mayor would soon come to an ignominious end.

On June 12, 1939, former mayor Henry Jost caught the essence of matters in a letter to his friend and associate, old Rabbit leader Congressman Joseph Shannon: "This local political situation is explosive. . . . Smith—who never had any backbone of his own as you and I long since found out—has completely surrendered to and is being managed by the Star. Of that there cannot be the possible shadow of a doubt."[11]

A broadly based coalition of Rabbits, reform Goats, Republicans, businessmen, and reformers came together in the Forward Kansas City Committee. Shannon came from Washington in time to ensure a considerable Rabbit hue to the movement, despite *Star* editorials and cartoons that called for a clean sweep of Pendergastism. Shannon wanted primarily to win reelection, and he also felt an obligation to help Rabbits keep their patronage jobs. Some supporters hoped Shannon would come back to Kansas City to take over the tattered remains of the machine. That was wishful thinking, as few active identifiable loyal Rabbits remained. In addition, since his nervous breakdown in 1935, Shannon increasingly lived in the past, deeply shaken by the deaths of old friends.[12]

In a 1937 letter to Jost, Shannon faced reality and candidly admitted that the fortunes of what was left of the Rabbit faction depended directly on Boss Tom: "The patronage, so far as our friends are concerned, has been constantly diminishing, and would be to a large extent wiped out if it were not for the interception of T. J. Pendergast. So you can see things are not all a bed of roses for me."[13]

Smith first tried to work with the Forward Kansas City Committee, but he broke with it in the fall of 1939, partly over the issue of his possible recall. The release of an auditor's report showing widespread waste and inefficiency in the city water department, coupled with disclosures by a state grand jury of corruption in Jackson County and Kansas City, exacerbated affairs. Few people took Smith seriously when he whined, "I am a Democrat—not a 'Pendergast man.' I am a servant of every citizen of Kansas City, the humble and the great—and the others." Much acrimony followed, culminating in Smith's resignation on January 5, 1940. The city council replaced him with coal dealer Charles S. Keith, and reform forces challenged this action as a violation of the city charter.[14] Pendergast must have read about this from inside Leavenworth with consternation—even a sense of amazement. His enemies were winning, and his great machine was disintegrating before his very eyes.

In February 1940, the Forward Kansas City Committee, which evolved into the more broadly based United Campaign Committee, won a charter-amendment election by a vote of 95,683 to 17,316. The amendment was a technical change necessitating another election in April for a new mayor and council. The reform candidate for mayor was John B. Gage, a lawyer, reformer, and member of a prominent old Kansas City family. A nominal Rabbit, Gage won by 94,192 to 76,033 over a Pendergast candidate in what proved to be his first of three election victories. Eight out of nine candidates on the United Campaign's slate for the city council triumphed.[15] About all a machine propagandist could do was to lamely claim that 99 percent of its officials were honest and that it should not be punished for the "betrayal" of some leaders.[16]

The defeat was the first significant loss by the Pendergast forces in a local contest since 1924. In that context, the 1940 election represented a failure by

Jim Pendergast to hold the machine's traditional coalition together—perhaps, under the circumstances, an impossible task. In the wake of the victory, Kenneth Midgley, a lawyer and interim city manager handpicked for the task, fired virtually all the old Pendergast department heads at city hall. "Why sure I enjoyed doing that," Midgley recalled in 1988 of his role as a hatchet man. "These (department heads) had been doing the wrong types of things for years. I fired them. I didn't give a darn." The new permanent city manager, L. Perry Cookingham, had previously managed Saginaw, Michigan. During the Great Depression, he had undertaken important relief responsibilities in the Detroit area. He was nonpartisan and the founder of a national association for city managers.[17]

Cookingham's appointment fulfilled a cherished *Star* dream of bringing in an out-of-towner to administer Kansas City, an objective that Henry Jost believed had sinister overtones. He thought the *Star* wanted a man who could be boosted by praise as long as he followed the bidding of the newspaper, or else be driven from town by repeated condemnation if he failed to obey marching orders. In a letter to friend and reformer Charles Keith written at the end of 1939 before Mayor Smith's resignation and the charter amendment election, Jost denounced the city charter: "There will never be any peace and quiet in this town, and never any kind of decent government until this present city charter is abolished and eradicated, root and branch. The *Star* used Mr. Pendergast and his machine to get it adopted, and then Mr. Pendergast used it for his own purposes."[18]

WORLD WAR II

The reverberations of the boss's downfall continued to sweep through Missouri, much to the detriment of the Pendergast machine. In the fall 1940 general election, Missouri voters approved by an impressive 90,000-vote majority a constitutional amendment that abolished direct partisan election of many state court judges, including circuit judges in metropolitan Kansas City and St. Louis.[19] In a mild upset, a Republican candidate, Forest Donnell, won the gubernatorial election, ensuring further patronage losses. One of the few bright spots for the machine was the reelection of Senator Harry S. Truman, who ran on his public record as a New Deal Democrat. He won a bitterly fought primary over Governor Stark and Maurice Milligan, who divided the reform vote, canceling each other out. Both men, whose closest friends thought they had poor political judgment in this matter, underestimated Truman's strength in rural Missouri. They could have used advice from Tom Pendergast, who, after all, had made Stark governor in 1936.

The entry of the United States into World War II brought with it a temporary suspension of politics as usual in Kansas City. The global war took precedence over almost everything else. The local economy surged ahead, and the population, stagnant throughout the Great Depression, rose in only a few years from 400,000 to 450,000.

The city's centrality and remoteness from any military action, plus the agricultural advances in Kansas and on the Great Plains in general, assured Kansas City an important role in the hostilities. The packing plants experienced a great expansion. Large defense plants moved into town, adding an impressive manufacturing component to the economic mix. The city became a wartime staging point and junction, with a dramatic increase in passenger and freight rail traffic. Overall, the stockyards continued to define Kansas City, still very much blue collar despite its white collar Country Club District, as the largest cow town in America.

Kansas Citians enthusiastically supported the war effort. The city oversubscribed in war-bond drives and strongly backed wartime controls on everything from rationing to blackouts. More than forty thousand Kansas Citians entered the Armed Forces. Although Kansas City lost some of its attributes as a wide-open town, with closing laws generally enforced and with prostitution and gambling less noticeable, the city retained its reputation as an entertainment center, sadly with one of the highest venereal-disease rates in the nation, particularly among teenage girls. Some scholars thought that a dedication to winning the war held Kansas City together, preventing serious social fragmentation. City Manager Cookingham successfully marshaled war endeavors, establishing a central authority to coordinate programs and to organize the city block by block. Basically, he applied the old Pendergast community arrangement to war rather than politics.[20] Even though Boss Pendergast was in imposed political exile, his specter continued to loom over the former Tom's Town.

FURTHER LEGAL PROBLEMS

Pendergast contended with further legal problems after his sentencing for tax evasion. In the summer of 1939, a Jackson County grand jury had indicted Pendergast for bribery in connection with his receipt of the money from the insurance companies. Nothing came of the indictment. Authorities eventually dropped the charges in November 1940, citing a lack of evidence and bag man A. L. McCormick's refusal to testify. Another excuse given was that Pendergast's influence peddling, no matter how odious and reprehensible, constituted, rather than a crime in Missouri, a business deal between private

parties. This may have been stretching matters, but, given Pendergast's influence over the state judiciary, a conviction was probably an extremely remote
possibility. Various actions filed against him in Missouri for tax evasion never
went to trial.[21]

Another confrontation between Pendergast and Judge Merrill Otis arose.
In May of 1939, a three-judge court of Otis, Reeves, and Eighth Circuit
Court of Appeals Judge Kimbrough Stone ordered Milligan to conduct further
investigations. A year later, on July 13, 1940, a grand jury charged by Otis
returned two new indictments against Pendergast, Robert Emmet O'Malley,
and A. L. McCormick. The first count was for conspiring to obstruct justice,
the second for conspiracy to defraud the government. This was a belated
attempt to deal with the problem presented by Milligan's failure to clearly
inform the court at the time of Pendergast's May 1939 guilty plea that the
government wanted the sentence to reflect Pendergast's tax transgressions as
a whole and not simply those for the two years cited in the indictments. On
March 1, 1941, a visiting federal judge, A. Lee Wyman from South Dakota,
brought to Kansas City to hear the cases, officially dismissed the charges. In
regard to Pendergast, Wyman called Otis's charge to the grand jury prejudicial
and therefore grounds for throwing out the indictments.[22]

Otis had filed contempt proceedings against the three men relating to
the disposition of escrowed money in the fire-insurance-rate controversy
placed under court supervision. Pendergast, in an "Affidavit of Prejudice,"
then accused Otis of "personal bias and prejudice." A complex legal problem
arose. Otis wrote the contempt opinion for the three-judge court. But on
May 1, 1941, in a highly unusual letter, he asked the other two members of
the tribunal, Reeves and Stone, to issue the contempt opinion as a per curiam
opinion, meaning one without a stated author. Otis, who may have been
experiencing delusions of grandeur, believed himself out of favor with some
justices of the Supreme Court and said that an opinion signed by him would
be the equivalent of waving a red flag in the eyes of a wild bull. He candidly
admitted that his opinion had "some of the characteristics of a brief," which
he said was his purpose. He anticipated the action would go all the way to the
United States Supreme Court, which it did, so he made a suggestion, which
was followed, to appoint a special counsel to argue the case.[23]

In June 1941 the three-judge court sentenced Pendergast to two years in
prison on the contempt citation; its sentence was upheld by the Eighth Circuit
Court of Appeals. But on January 4, 1943, in *Pendergast v. United States*, the
Supreme Court reversed the Eighth Circuit in a six-to-one decision, primarily
on the grounds that the statute of limitations had expired. Supreme Court
Justice William O. Douglas wrote that in district court "the court asked the

district attorney whether contempt proceedings should be filed. About a year passed, when the court on May 30, 1940, requested the district attorney to institute contempt proceedings against petitioners."[24]

This indicated that there was at least a "gentlemen's agreement" between Milligan and Pendergast's attorney that Milligan would announce to the court at Pendergast's guilty plea to the tax evasion charges for 1935 and 1936 that no further criminal proceedings were to be instituted. Milligan indicated that he expected Otis to punish Pendergast for other misconduct, or at least to take his other misconduct into consideration: (1) nine years of tax evasion, totaling about as much money as for 1935 and 1936, (2) obstruction of justice, and (3) contempt of court. A delay of a year in answering the questions about the contempt proceedings suggests considerable embarrassment, torn between what counsel had been assured and the other consideration that Judge Otis had stated at the sentencing—that he had not taken into account uncharged crimes, which might have included misconduct as boss of Kansas City in addition to the specifics. Furthermore, it suggests that Otis was bending to the public criticism of him for imposing a "light" sentence.

The appeals court's decision in the contempt action confirmed that there was an undisclosed plea bargain that miscarried. That is, Milligan had expected the punishment of Pendergast to go beyond the original indictment, which, of course, Otis did not act out. Otis was apparently unaware of the agreement (although he doubtless suspected its existence, as most lawyers would, from the government's assurance that it would not prosecute for other crimes). Everyone was embarrassed by what happened, and Pendergast may have "lucked out."[25] So it could be argued that Pendergast won the final legal confrontation between himself and the federal court in western Missouri. But he already stood destroyed.

Several Kansas Citians, feeling that Pendergast, old and sick, had suffered enough, wrote to Judge Otis asking him to release Pendergast, to modify the terms of his probation, or even to help him gain executive clemency. The signers of the letter, almost all civic leaders, included banker James M. Kemper and real estate magnate J. C. Nichols. They called the probation unusually severe and oppressive. In his reply of August 13, 1943, Judge Otis noted that Pendergast had "neither whimpered nor complained nor asked concessions" and that he "literally, even meticulously" complied with his probation. Otis "respectfully" declined to make any changes, explaining, "When I imposed the sentence I took into consideration the two matters referred to in the petition, the age and the physical infirmity of the defendant, and assessed what I believed was a just punishment. I still think that was just."[26] Of course, the alternative to probation was three years in jail. Otis sent the letter on to Washington, D.C., and on November 17, 1943, the justice department declined to act on the clemency request. The letter ended efforts to change Pendergast's status. Still, the attempted intervention of prominent individuals in his behalf gave indication that even in disgrace, his name still counted for something in Kansas City.

CONTINUING TROUBLE FOR THE ORGANIZATION

Troubles mounted for the organization, which sorely missed the old boss's firm hand and political skills. A reorganization and strengthening of the welfare department in Kansas City deprived the machine of most of its local charitable and relief functions. Mayor John Gage won an easy reelection in 1942 as the candidate of the Citizens Association, a consolidated reform coalition established late in the previous year. In addition, the Pendergast faction received little recognition for helping in the war effort. A change in the city charter strengthened a merit system for city employees and restricted their political activities. Ward bosses appeared increasingly discontent. Shannon, who did not stand for reelection, died on March 28, 1943, after an illness of ten months, lessening the possibility of old-line Rabbits coming back to revitalize the machine fold. Roger T. Sermon, a Pendergast ally and Independence political leader, increasingly charted his own course. With Carrolla convicted and eventually deported to Sicily, the underworld rallied behind a new leader, Charles Binaggio, an unknown quantity. The new officials of the police department were ostentatiously anti-Pendergast. Money from graft and corruption stopped rolling into machine coffers.

The demise of the machine at the municipal level was an imminent possibility. A prophetic analysis in the *Star* in March of 1943 observed, "James M. Pendergast has carried on with what he had to work with. . . . Today Jim Pendergast undoubtedly will attempt to continue the role left to him. But many who have known 'Young Jim' long have doubted that his political appetite has been sharpened any in recent years; they feel he tries to carry on largely through loyalty to old friends of the faction."[27]

Tom Pendergast Jr. recalled that sometime in 1943 his father asked him to come over from his office to Ready Mixed for an afternoon meeting. Tom Jr. brought along Phil McCrory, his partner in the liquor business and a close family friend. They found Tom Sr. with several ward leaders. Tom Jr. explained, "They wanted to know if I would go on with J. P. like he had done under my father." Tom Jr. did not specify who he meant by "they," so his father's role over and above bringing the parties together remains unclear, but in effect, given Jim's leadership problems and indirection, Tom Jr. was offered a position under Jim Pendergast, who would remain as head of the organization. Tom Jr. turned the overture down, noting that Bernard Gnefkow, whom he hated with a passion, already functioned as number two man. Tom Jr. recalled, "I said no way, who are you kidding. J. P. has got B. G. If he steps down B. G. will step up, and it won't be too long before you all will be like Humpty Dumpty, nobody will be able to put you together again." If Tom Jr. had accepted a high position in the organization, a calling his father had trained him for, his heart would not have been in it. Throughout his life he remained a private man who stayed out of politics.[28]

After the meeting ended, Tom Jr. and McCrory drove back to their liquor company. McCrory observed, "Tom, you are right. Let it end and never change your mind, but if you should don't go as a 'Goat,' go as just a plain Democrat." Recalling that James Michael Pendergast had started the machine many decades earlier, McCrory observed, "It started with a JMP, let it end with a JMP."[29]

By the postwar period, reform government led by the Citizens Association had started to take hold in Kansas City.[30] A new mayor, William Kemp, elected in 1946, made his reputation fighting the Pendergast machine. Cookingham continued to enjoy a good image. He ran an efficient administration that was far less costly than in machine days and actually managed, helped by federal write-offs of relief money, to retire the city's astronomical debt in only six years. Prosperity continued following the war, reflected by changing interests. The politics of relief and concern over corrupt practices faded into the background. New issues involved proposals to pass bond issues for massive public improvement projects and to extend the municipal limits, especially by annexing territory north of the Missouri River. The business community, strongly backing Cookingham, sought to bury Pendergastism. Two *Kansas City Star* journalists, Henry C. Haskell Jr. and Richard B. Fowler, in their 1950 book *City of the Future: A Narrative History of Kansas City, 1850–1950*, summed up the machine as but a dark chapter in an ever-continuing march to glory by the city's business leadership, driven by a unique "Kansas City spirit." The editors labeled the Pendergast period "the tragic era."[31]

Jerome Walsh, an opponent of Pendergastism and an influential Democratic leader in Kansas City, put a slightly different twist on the business community and Boss Pendergast: "Pendergast himself moved among the business and professional men of his city as an accepted and respected equal, whose handshake and nod was a flattering unction to chamber of commerce presidents, newspaper publishers, professional and commercial leaders of all kinds, whose attendance at church and intoning of the ritual was punctilious and sincere. The hands of these sturdy gentry, pillars of society, were lifted high in horror when the extent of civic corruption became manifest following Pendergast's departure for Leavenworth."[32]

The Pendergast machine never recovered at the municipal level. The Rabbits fragmented, with the Gallagher family taking over the Independence wing of the faction. Many of the ward leaders defected to a new movement headed by Binaggio. The mobster, masquerading as a legitimate North Side political leader, wanted to reopen Kansas City to widespread vice. These plans were aborted with his sensational 1950 gangland-style murder. Afterwards, local organized criminals, increasingly allied with a national Mafia, turned to other means than direct political action to obtain their goals. Alex Presta, a former Binaggio ally, took over the Italian organization started by Johnny Lazia in the old North End.

Jim Pendergast engineered a comeback of sorts, for a few years regaining control of the Jackson County Court. He suffered a bad defeat in the 1954 county elections, followed by a devastating and final election debacle in 1956. By then, the machine had no obvious electoral power at any level—municipal, county, state, or national. Jim claimed that his Jackson Democratic Club, relegated to the status of a faction, continued to stand for the Democratic party in Kansas City. Few believed him, as the once-great Pendergast machine passed into history. When the modest and unassuming James Pendergast died in 1966, some four hundred mourners, including his old friend Harry Truman, attended his funeral.[33]

James Pendergast's Evaluation of Tom

On August 3, 1956, James Pendergast, in an unusual fifteen-minute filmed political address on local television, said that the word "Pendergastism" had no meaning and belonged to another era. Harry Truman introduced Jim, calling him a "man of integrity" and a "Christian gentleman."[34] With the tide of a forthcoming primary running strongly against him, Jim, in a sort of last hurrah, gave his evaluation of his uncle, Thomas J. Pendergast:

> Some very good things have been said about him—and some very bad things. . . . The record shows quite plainly that it all came to a tragic end for Tom Pendergast in 1939. It was a collapse brought on by forces so complex and so far-reaching as to defy a simple explanation—and certainly make a fool of anyone who attempts it. I am not the one to say on this occasion whether Tom Pendergast was part saint or part sinner—part benefactor or part boss—good Samaritan or mischief maker. I am not the one to say he was too merciful or too greedy, or whether he was all of these things or part of them or none of them. It is not for me to judge. That is the task of some greater power. But I have a personal opinion which I seek to impose on no one, but I know that I share it with many thousands of others. We have certain memories about him. We remember him for his kindness and

charity, his many gifts of food, clothing, coal and money to the needy poor. I feel with thousands of others that our town made substantial gains under Tom Pendergast.

Jim, observing that he was the only Pendergast remaining in Kansas City politics, bitterly denounced people who kept shouting, "Stop Pendergastism," without ever explaining what they wanted stopped. He said that such a cry by "certain individuals" was aimless and deceptive: "They say it in a way to make it appear there is some stain or stigma attached to it. But it is the simple tyranny of partisanship—the cry of a group of local conspirators who are trying to make the public believe in ghosts and witches, and thus divert attention from their own record in office." Jim failed to stop the references that, to the frustration of the Pendergast family, rolled down through the years to the "notorious Tom Pendergast," a phrase used twice in a single article in the *Star* in the fall of 1994. In a reply to Jim's 1956 speech, Richard H. Koenigsdorf, the executive vice-chairman of an anti-Pendergast coalition said it all: "Pendergastism is undimmed."[35]

JUDGE REEVES'S ANALYSIS OF TOM PENDERGAST

Judge Albert L. Reeves, who had openly defied the machine in performing his judicial duties, felt the methods employed by Tom Pendergast necessitated a clearly stated account for posterity. In an unpublished manuscript, "The Shame of a Great City," Reeves wrote a scathing "Pen Portrait of Thomas J. Pendergast," which borders on demonization:

> He thoroughly understood the psychology of the underworld and the habitues of the shadowy kingdom followed him blindly as well as devotedly. He protected them from prosecution for their misdeeds, and granted them commissions to sin against the laws of God and man. His past experience had qualified him to lead and rule the refuse in society. He understood the life of the brothel and houses of ill fame. . . . Election victories were made personal. He was in fact the victor—never his party. To achieve victory he marshalled and controlled every element of human society. . . . For window dressing and good appearance he enlisted the support of ambitious and pliable individuals who were willing to serve for the rewards of office. . . . He derived immense revenues from graft in public office, and from his levies on crime. To support his invisible government, he deemed it prudent to increase his power over elections and to take away every element of chance. . . . All citizens, to be secure, were forced to acknowledge the uncontrolled and despotic power of one man with his invisible empire. . . . He lived in luxury and wealth and reveled in his despotic power.[36]

Judge Reeves's analysis of T. J. Pendergast paralleled that of many honest people who knew him. They recognized his power and influence, but determined, as well, that there was a sinister element in his makeup and that he was utterly corrupt. Despite all his attempts, he failed to impress many people in the end as decent and upright in character. Writing in 1943, Rabbi Samuel Mayerberg defined Pendergast in relation to his background: "More than a flood of wealth, Pendergast enjoyed the enormous sense of power domination brought him. It flattered him, pleased his vanity, and removed a sense of social frustration, that must have developed as he grew from an obscure social stratum. He reveled in that power and the sense of superiority it brought him."[37]

PENDERGAST'S LEGACY

Pendergast seemed unconcerned about how history would judge him. During all his years in Kansas City, he raised not a single public monument to herald his accomplishments. One of the few honors he did accept was the Order of the Crown of Italy, bestowed in 1938 by the King of Italy for services to Kansas Citians of Italian lineage. For Pendergast, it was almost as if selling concrete and seeing his political fortunes prosper represented enough glory. One of the few times he let his guard down came in a 1933 interview, when, sounding like a typical urban booster, he spoke with passion about what he and his family had done for Kansas City: "I'll say that any unprejudiced man who comes here and investigates will say we have turned Kansas City from a town into a metropolitan city. Look at our streets and our parks and public buildings and everything! This is a metropolis—one of the greatest in the world!"[38]

His needs led him to acquire large sums of money, but he made no obvious effort to build a great family fortune. Instead, he spent his money to a lesser extent on conspicuous consumption and to a greater one on gambling. On the surface, he appeared a plunger, an image he tried to encourage. Actually, even taking into account his reckless spending on the horses, he often took calculated risks, many of which he had a high-percentage chance of winning. Given the opportunity, as in the case of elections, he fixed the results in his favor. He claimed to make snap decisions that he honored no matter what the consequences. This coincided with his contention that he always kept his word.

One must understand that Pendergast's vice connections flowed from his basic operating style. In the beginning, cooperating with criminals was the same as retaining hired hands—a way to facilitate getting things done. Later, the criminal aspect became a problem that he could not or would not shake. Once committed, he found himself drawn in deeper and deeper, with no point of return. Working with the underworld came back to haunt him, especially when he undertook his quest for respectability and the trappings of a life among the wealthy.

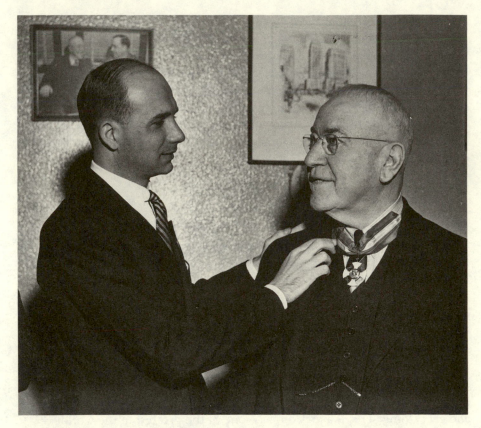

An Italian diplomat bestows the Order of the Crown of Italy on Tom Pendergast in 1936 in gratitude for his services to Kansas Citians of Italian lineage. (*Photograph courtesy the Jack Wally Collection, Western Historical Manuscript Collection, Kansas City, Mo.*)

What if there had been no Tom Pendergast? In all likelihood, there would have been nobody of a similar bent to step forward in Kansas City. The city would have been in the hands of lesser individuals. What if he had chosen a different path for himself? One must conclude that with such a combination of superb business acumen, outstanding political instincts, and exceptional ability, he would have succeeded even if he had been scrupulously honest and upright. Without qualification, Pendergast was a tremendously effective political operator, possibly a political genius. He had an understanding that few have ever had about how to build and maintain a large urban political organization. Perhaps Truman was not far from the mark when he once compared Stalin to Pendergast. Pendergast well realized that while it is nice to build a consensus by bringing together divergent elements into a whole, you cannot put a machine together that way. An iron will and a ruthless ability to keep people in line made it possible to help the needy and to push worthwhile civic endeavors.

Pendergast offered a well-ordered, if morally wide-open, city that demonstrated compassion to the poor. He sold his vision and followed up on promises. He was part of the ongoing political process of his day, and the public for the most part tolerated the excesses of his invisible government. He was very benevolent in his personal charitable pursuits, but it must be remembered that it was not his own money. Even considering all his complexities and flaws, there is no question that Pendergast ranks as one of the most significant forces in the building and shaping of modern Kansas City.

That is not to say that the boss was a positive force, nor is it clear that Tom's Town weathered the Great Depression better than other large cities. The population stagnated, actually suffering a net loss of almost six hundred people between 1930 and 1940. Economic indicators showed a general decline in commercial, transportation, and manufacturing activity. Given the realities of Pendergastism, new businesses—unless illegal—stayed away from Kansas City. The claim that a wide-open town helped commerce had a dubious ring, ignoring human costs. Just as it did in the nation as a whole, the economy in Kansas City bottomed out in 1933 and started to show signs of recovery by 1935, either because of or in spite of New Deal recovery programs.[39] Doubtless, welfare distribution was more efficiently organized in Kansas City than in many other cities. Indeed, New Deal social planners studied Pendergast's relief programs. While there can be no definitive answer to the question, the perception among most Kansas Citians of all races was that the policies of the Pendergast machine lessened the impact of the Great Depression in their city.

Almost inevitably, comparisons arise between Pendergast and Richard J. Daley, the mayor of Chicago from 1955 until his death in 1976. The leader of a highly visible Democratic machine, Daley had a public reputation that made him the opposite of the kindly boss in the novel *The Last Hurrah*, by Edwin O'Connor. Daley was of Irish descent in a city with a large Irish voting bloc. He ran Chicago with ruthless efficiency, punishing enemies and rewarding friends. Allegedly, he manipulated election results, going beyond herding voters to the polls, controlling voting stations, and using a vast and loyal army of political minions. Legend has it that he helped elect John F. Kennedy to the presidency in 1960 by fixing the Chicago vote. Daley gained great notoriety at the time of the 1968 Democratic National Convention in Chicago, during which the police force dealt brutally with demonstrators in Lincoln Park, in what the later Walker report described as a "police riot." While it was never proved, critics claimed that Daley had ties to the infamous Chicago crime syndicate.

Hardly any commentators outside Chicago had many positive things to say about Daley.[40]

What many people failed to understand was that Daley headed a machine in which power flowed from the bottom upward. This had been true since the origins of the machine in the mid-nineteenth century, when ward leaders put together a collective group to deal with the financing of internal improvements important to the city as a whole, such as bridges and systems of sewerage. As an operating principle, the ward leaders customarily selected a boss. In its modern manifestation, the machine survived a series of leadership changes: Mayor Anton J. Cermak, the combination of Mayor Edward J. Kelly and Patrick Nash, and Mayor Martin Kennelly. Hence, Daley, actually at one time considered a possible reformer, was the leader of a coalition, the Cook County Democratic Central Committee, akin to the old Soviet Politburo. Here was a marked difference from boss politics, Kansas City model.[41]

From its inception, the Pendergast faction was a family organization. By the beginning of the Great Depression, Thomas J. Pendergast, after the vanquishing of Shannon and the subjugation of Welch, reigned as supreme ruler. Despite the show for the general public, power in the Pendergast machine flowed from the top down. Unlike their counterparts in Chicago, many of whom had strong bases of support in African American, Irish, or Polish districts, the Kansas City ward captains owed their positions solely to Pendergast. They acted like what they were, middle managers, subject to dismissal or other forms of retribution if they got out of line and tried to pursue courses running counter to directives from 1908 Main. In actions as well as in fact, Pendergast was much more of a classic self-appointed political boss than Richard J. Daley.

Aside from Daley's coming after and Pendergast's coming before World War II, other contrasts between the two men make a valid comparison very thin at best. Pendergast generally stayed away from the limelight, unlike Daley, who sought publicity. Daley appeared at countless political affairs and openly tried to influence national policy, speaking out on issues such as policy toward Northern Ireland. In another different twist, in a period in which the federal government increasingly handled social services, Daley never depended on distributing welfare as a bedrock of his organization. While, like Pendergast, Daley exercised great local power, he never enjoyed nearly as much statewide dominance. In regard to vote fraud, Pendergast exercised far less restraint in influencing election results, fixing much larger and more blatant vote totals than Daley supposedly did. More fundamentally, Daley was far more disciplined in his private life. He lived without ostentation in an old Irish Chicago neighborhood, and he never had a financial vice like Pendergast's addiction to gambling. Finally, Daley stayed out of the penitentiary.

Nationally, Pendergast was one of the last of the great American political bosses of the pre-television era. That an important leader of his machine rose to the presidency served as a testimonial. On September 26, 1944, Truman, campaigning for vice president, told labor union members in a Kansas City speech, "I am a Jackson County organization Democrat and proud of it! That is the way I got to be a county judge, a senator, and the candidate for vice president."[42] The qualms he had expressed ten years earlier in his "Pickwick Papers" had evidently been suppressed.

President Truman's political enemies, as a matter of course, tried to tie him to the corruption of his Pendergast years. The greater amount of the political propaganda had overtly heavy-handed attributes, but in December 1951, *Chicago Tribune* anti–New Deal columnist Arthur Sears Henning took a more light-handed approach in "Santa Claus in Stripes!":

'Twas the night before Christmas in Washington's town,
Many creatures were stirring, of doubtful renown,
Subpoenas were hung by the chimney with care,
In the hope that the tax-fixer soon would be there. . . .
And there in the midst of the turmoil and fury
Was a bandwagon drawn by eight mules of Missouri,
With a driver in stripes like a wraith of the past;
One knew at a glance it was Boss Pendergast. . . .
Now up to the roof the Missouri mules flew
With the bandwagon, gifts, and Pendergast, too.
While the New and Fair Dealers were thirsting for cash
Down the chimney Boss Pendergast came in a flash.
He was tastefully dressed in stripes running around
And sported a number, black on a pale ground.
A bundle of gifts he unslung from his back;
And grinned as he opened and emptied his pack;
Presents for tax-fixing, contracts, and lending,
Quashing indictments and upping the spending,
Pardons, paroles, duces, tecums, and waivers,
Inside tips, influence, various favors. . . .
Then laying his finger aside of his nose,
With a meaningful nod up the chimney he rose
And was heard to exclaim with a wink and a leer,
"Merry Christmas, taxpayers, and Happy New Year."[43]

In October 1944, Pendergast, breaking a long silence about his post-prison affairs, granted an interview at Ready Mixed to Harry Wohle of the *St. Louis Star-Times*. Old, sick, and tired, the former boss may have thought it was time for some last words. In about as philosophical a mood as he ever was, he declared an end to his political career: "At seventy-two, it is too late to get back into politics, to start the day's work at five or six o'clock in the morning, to see my friends from morning until night. No. I am too old for that. But if I were a young man I would engage actively in politics again. Politics is a great game and I have enjoyed every minute of it." He said that all he intended to do in the future was engage in private business: "All I want to do is go ahead with my business here, to provide for my family and to take care of any poor friends as I did in the past. I'd like to do this for a long time to come." Then, growing serious, he observed, "I've had a good life. I got into trouble, but I am not blaming anybody but myself." There is little wonder that even his dedicated enemies found him both fascinating and inexplicable.[44]

Looking back over his career, Pendergast saw his greatest accomplishment as helping the poor: "I've done a lot for Kansas City—for the poor of Kansas City. I've done more for them than all the big shots and bankers, all of them put together. We used to take care of our poor, with coal and wood and food and rent, and we helped them in their trouble. We never asked the poor about their politics." Finally, he restated his favorite axiom: "And I've never broken my word. Put this down: I've never broken my word to any living human being I gave it to. That is the key to success in politics or anything else."[45]

Sarcastic enemies refused to give Pendergast his due for this attribute of keeping his word. They noted that he rarely gave his word and that when he did he sometimes did break it. An old acquaintance remembered Pendergast's pledge of his word differently. In 1994 Matt Devoe recalled, "In my estimation, he was an honorable person. Honorable, if he said yes he meant yes, if he said no he meant no." Back in 1934, another political lieutenant had discussed the boss's loyalty to his friends in earthier language: "He stays by his friends, and that's more than your white-bellied reformers will do."[46]

PENDERGAST'S FINAL YEARS

Pendergast, shorn of power, was a pitiful figure in his enforced obscurity and isolation. Few people showed compassion; he felt humiliated and alone. William Gilmer, one of the last Kansas City policemen hired by Pendergast, went to see him occasionally. Gilmer recalled, "Mr. Pendergast would look at me and say, 'Bill, where have all my old friends gone?' You know, I couldn't answer him."[47] In Pendergast's day, time in the penitentiary, especially for the few white-collar offenders, carried with it a terrible social stigma. To many people it made little difference that he was a professional politician rather than a Lazia, Carrolla, or Capone. Some family members thought that he had disgraced them, and many old associates shunned him. Perhaps the most personally galling part of his probation was the restriction on playing politics.

In an unanticipated irony, the proscription on betting on horse races proved to be no problem: the sport suspended operations during World War II.

During his final years, life for Tom Pendergast at his 5650 Ward Parkway mansion was an absolute disaster. He was far from the master of his own house, let alone a man plotting a political comeback. His continuing heart troubles prevented him from even going to his second-floor bedroom. His stomach condition presented further vexations. In effect, he found himself restricted to three downstairs rooms. At one point, Tom Jr. discovered him in pain and despair, relegated to a small cot in the laundry room. Tom Jr., horrified, moved his father to the Ambassador Hotel. He eventually returned home, but his wife moved out, taking her furs with her. In 1940, their daughter Aileen had married Thomas F. Houlihan, leaving only Tom and Carolyn at home. Houlihan was a businessman who owned Tom Houlihan's Mens Wear. Carolyn Pendergast, for whom the marriage had long been over, took an apartment at the Locarno Apartments at 225 Ward Parkway. Strangely, Johnny Lazia's widow, Marie, lived there too. Cynical gossips said that Carolyn left in disgust over Tom's resumption of gambling. True or not, it made a good story. Tom did not change a will he made in 1939; in it he bequeathed $100 each to their children and the rest of his estate to Carolyn.[48]

Tom handled his business and other outstanding affairs and obligations as best he could. He told close friends that he never doubted his ability to make money and that he intended to build a new fortune.[49] He became reflective about his career, reportedly concluding that Truman had betrayed him by not trying to help him, thus engineering his fall. He settled the last of his large federal tax liability by liquidating assets and through a $125,000 loan from Tom Jr. and Phil McCrory. When able, Pendergast attended morning mass at Visitation Church. "I have a humble and contrite heart," he said. He went with some regularity to his Ready Mixed office, where he was surprised on his seventy-second birthday on July 22, 1944, by several large floral displays from his employees. Although he avoided fraternal activities and social events, he never missed his required monthly probation meeting at the courthouse. He made his last appearance on January 15, 1945. Although obviously ill, he declined an offer by the parole officer to come to his house. For what turned out to be the last time, he talked briefly with reporters, expressing regret at the recent death of Judge Merrill Otis and calling him a fine and dedicated public servant.[50]

On Tuesday, January 23, 1945, Tom Pendergast suffered a heart attack in his Ready Mixed office. Rushed to Menorah Hospital, he failed steadily over the next few days. At 10:00 P.M. on Friday, January 26, he died of a massive coronary thrombosis. At his bedside the only family members present were his two daughters, Marceline and Aileen. Messages sent to summon Tom Jr.

Floral displays from employees decorate Pendergast's Ready Mixed office on the occasion of his seventy-second birthday on July 22, 1944. *(Photograph courtesy the Pendergast Collection)*

and Carolyn arrived too late. As the word spread, callers jammed the hospital switchboard to ask if the news was true.[51] The boss's faithful supporters had hoped he had not meant it when he said he had retired from politics. Some wishfully looked ahead to a resurrection of the great days of the Pendergast machine when his five years of probation expired at the end of May 1945. That was not to be.

Pendergast's funeral was on Monday, January 29, at Visitation Church. He rested in an open casket, his hands clasping a rosary, with a gold crucifix at his side. Seven hundred people filled the church, and several hundred more remained standing outside. More than a thousand sympathy cards were displayed by the casket. Sprays and easels of red roses, yellow pompons, pink azaleas, red and white carnations, and assorted other flowers transformed the rooms of the church. "The boys" from the First Ward sent an elaborate display of carnations, lilies, and orchids. Robert E. Hannegan of St. Louis, the chairman of the Democratic National Committee, dispatched peach gladioli. A procession of several priests from Kansas City parishes passed by the casket, flanked by mauve orchids and red roses. Members of the family and longtime retainers were the pallbearers.[52] Carolyn Pendergast was not present.

Msgr. Thomas B. McDonald, for thirty years Pendergast's priest, conducted a high mass and gave a brief eulogy. He emphasized "the good side of Tom Pendergast," mentioning his many charitable contributions and his role as a devout parishioner who regularly attended morning mass. According to Msgr. McDonald, "He just wanted to know if there was a human being who needed help. He had a noble heart. His word was his bond. If he was your friend he was a true friend. In regarding his life it would be well to recall the injunction, 'Let him who is without sin cast the first stone.'" Msgr. McDonald asked God to forget all Pendergast's faults, saying that he never maliciously injured the character of anyone.[53]

Conspicuously present among the mourners was Harry S. Truman, the new vice president of the United States. Truman made a quick flight from Washington to Kansas City in a U.S. Army bomber, arriving at the church minutes before the service and leaving shortly afterwards. Truman, who took heat from Republicans for attending the funeral of a convicted felon, said when he first heard of Tom's death that he was "as sorry as I can be," and that "he has always been my friend and I was his."[54] With time, Truman's words became part of the Truman legend, illustrating his willingness to take an unpopular course out of loyalty, while playing down Tom Pendergast's role in his rise to power. Tom Jr., believing that his father had been betrayed by Truman, bitterly wrote that he could not believe it when he saw the vice president making what he considered a grandstanding appearance, upstaging the family: "Who in the hell was he fooling. My family didn't know VP Truman." Tom Jr., feeling Truman had not raised a finger when his father got in trouble, considered him "like a cur dog that bites the hand that feeds him."[55]

A cortege of more than a hundred automobiles made the four-mile drive to Calvary Cemetery on Kansas City's South Side for the graveside service. Thomas Joseph Pendergast's final resting place is under a simple headstone, away from the West Bottoms, the North Side, and 1908 Main Street.

Epilogue

In the years following Pendergast's death, his immediate family gradually faded from the scene. His widow, Carolyn, after a lengthy illness with a viral infection, died with her children by her side at St. Mary's hospital on June 13, 1951.[1] Tragically, Carolyn's youngest daughter, Aileen Houlihan, died ten days later of leukemia at the age of thirty-two. She had one daughter.[2]

In 1965, Marceline and her husband, William E. Burnett, then living in southern California, faced public bankruptcy hearings in Los Angeles. The large inheritance from her mother long spent, Marceline testified in court that "bad investment and high living led to the financial failure."[3] She also stated that she had pawned her furs and her wedding silver to pay off debts. Marceline returned to Kansas City after the bankruptcy. She died in 1987, leaving one son, two daughters, and two grandchildren.

Thomas J. Pendergast Jr. owned and operated the City Beverage Company until 1965. He then retired to care for his wife, Mary Louise, whose health was failing. They had no children. After her death in 1975, Tom Jr. founded the Pendergast-Weyer Foundation, which contributes financial support to small Catholic schools in Missouri. Tom Jr. became a somewhat reclusive man, only emerging in the public eye when he felt he needed to protect the memory of his family. He eventually remarried, and upon his death on February 17, 1990, his wife, Beverly Burrus Pendergast, assumed the operation of the foundation. Beverly Pendergast died in December 1996.[4]

The fall of Thomas J. Pendergast and his Democratic machine put an end to open gambling and vice in Kansas City. Eventually, gaming operations such as illegal slot machines, card games, craps, and numbers running came to lurk in the shadowy realm of a powerful Kansas City underworld. The Jockey Club vanished, the horse track at Riverside met the bulldozer. Illegal betting on horse races also fell under the domain of organized crime. Prostitution, once an open and thriving enterprise, became relegated to small mob-controlled bordellos or pimp-dominated call girls working the streets. On the surface, a new morality reigned in Kansas City.

Fifty years after Pendergast's death, the hub of his machine, 1908 Main Street, sits empty. The building, once the seat of the most powerful political boss Missouri has ever seen and now designated as a local historical landmark, is in shameful disrepair. The neighborhood surrounding 1908 Main, currently referred to as the Crossroads District, has been recognized by the city council as Kansas City's only official adult entertainment district. Tom's old office now shares the neighborhood with "juice bars" and lap dancers.

A few miles to the west of 1908 Main sits the Woodlands, a grand horse and dog track. The racetrack, however, is losing ground to the slot machines, for, looking north, colorful riverboat casinos lit up like jewels in the night dot the banks of the Missouri River.[5] To the south, Brush Creek flows along the Plaza, Pendergast's Ready Mixed concrete that once lined the channel gone. Contrary to a long-standing and time-honored legend, no bodies were found when the old concrete was torn up and replaced for the new Kansas City River Walk. Finally, to the east of 1908 Main, city hall casts its long shadow, still operating under basically the same 1925 charter that allowed Pendergast to ultimately gain complete control of the city.

Kansas City's infrastructure is crumbling, and many middle- and working-class neighborhoods have deteriorated, some beyond saving. Racial anxiety sent many thousands of Kansas City residents scurrying to the suburbs following World War II. A wildly expensive, federally mandated school-desegregation initiative attempted to recapture the lost student population. Hundreds of millions of dollars in tax money flowed into the coffers, resulting in schools that look like palaces, with administrators paid like kings. Busing served to further fragment neighborhood cohesion, the dropout rate soared, and truancy was ignored. In the inner city a sense of neighborhood and community spirit has been lost. There are few block leaders, no recognizable ward captains, and abysmal turnouts for local elections at the precincts. Attempts by neighborhood volunteers and community activists to improve life and services in their communities are commonly stonewalled by the powers that be in city hall.

Corruption in city hall is reported by the news media on an all-too-regular basis, and some council members have been indicted for accepting bribes and pilfering city funds. When the fact that city funds had been criminally misspent by a councilwoman came to light in 1996, Mayor Emanuel Cleaver said, "Now people can join me and puke in unison, I am sick of this mess." In calling for an investigation of the corruption involved in awarding city contracts, Councilman Pat Danaher enjoined, "We need to find where the rats are, this place stinks."[6] The list of the fallen, disgraced, and implicated grows on a regular basis. The rats are in city hall.

Citizens' cries to clean up Kansas City often fall on deaf ears, and vital municipal functions such as road and bridge repair and neighborhood clean-ups are often superseded by tax expenditures for large-ticket items such as expanded arenas and convention centers. Comparisons between Pendergast's Kansas City and today's bewildering municipal government appear frequently in the daily newspapers. In your mind's eye, you can almost see Tom watching from the window of 1908 Main Street; you can almost hear him laughing.

Notes

Introduction

1. "Admission Summary," Notorious Offender Case Files, Records of the Bureau of Prisons, Record Group 129, National Archives, Washington, D.C. See Lawrence H. Larsen, "A Political Boss at Bay: Thomas J. Pendergast in Federal Prison."

2. *St. Louis Star-Times*, May 29, 1939; "Return," by Rob H. Webb, May 29, 1939, Notorious Offender Case Files, RG 129, NA-Wash.

3. James V. Bennett to Robert H. Hudspeth, June 1, 1939; Gordon Dean to "State Editor," June 2, 1939; Ed Meisburger to Bureau of Prisons, June 2, 1939, all in Notorious Offender Case Files, RG 129, NA-Wash.

4. Bennett to Hudspeth, May 24, 1939, Notorious Offender Case Files, RG 129, NA-Wash.

5. Quoted in Maurice M. Milligan, *Missouri Waltz: The Inside Story of the Pendergast Machine by the Man Who Smashed It*, 79. See William M. Reddig, *Tom's Town: Kansas City and the Pendergast Legend*, and Lyle W. Dorsett, *The Pendergast Machine*. Because of a copyright dispute over the use of the title *Missouri Waltz*, a later edition of Milligan's book, published in the same year as the original, 1948, bears the title *The Inside Story of the Pendergast Machine by the Man Who Smashed It*.

6. Quoted in *Missouri Democrat*, March 31, 1939.

7. See Eric Monkkonen, *The Local State: Public Money and American Cities*.

8. Ewing Young Mitchell, *The Four Horsemen of the Pendergast Machine*, 1944, "Pendergast, Thomas J.," Vertical File, Harry S. Truman Library (hereafter cited as HSTL), Independence, Missouri. The standard work on city elections is William A. Johnson, *Kansas City Votes, 1853–1979: Precinct Election Returns for the Offices of President, Governor, and Mayor*.

9. *Missouri Democrat*, May 5, 1933.

10. Judge Albert L. Reeves used the term "invisible government" in his unpublished "The Shame of a Great City," Albert L. Reeves Papers, Archives of the United States District Court for the Western District of Missouri (hereafter cited as A-WDM). The excesses of the machine are detailed throughout Milligan, *Missouri Waltz*.

11. Quoted in *Kansas City Times*, July 11, 1975; quoted in Jerome Beatty, "A Political Boss Talks about His Job," 108. On Pendergast's use of denicotinized cigarettes, see Abraham Sophian, M.D., to James Bennett, May 24, 1939, Notorious Offender Case Files, RG 129, NA-Wash.

12. Quoted in Beatty, "Political Boss Talks," 110. See also Milligan, *Missouri Waltz*, 211.

13. Jonathan Daniels, *The Man of Independence*, 278; President's Secretary's File, Papers of Harry S. Truman, HSTL (hereafter cited as "Pickwick Papers," which is the name given by Truman scholars of revealing comments the future president wrote for an undisclosed purpose, most in 1934, on stationery of the Pickwick Hotel in downtown Kansas City, where he sometimes stayed); *New York Herald-Tribune*, October 14, 1934.

14. *St. Louis Post-Dispatch*, September 12, 1937; "Psychiatric," "Admission Summary," Notorious Offender Case Files, RG 129, NA-Wash.

15. Rudolph H. Hartmann to Elmer Lincoln Irey, June 6, 1939, Notorious Offender Case Files, RG 129, NA-Wash.

16. A historian who studied appointments in Missouri during the New Deal concluded, "The evidence suggests that F.D.R. fully cooperated with Pendergast on matters of patronage" (J. Christopher Schnell, "New Deal Scandals: E. Y. Mitchell and F.D.R.'s Commerce Department," 371).

17. For the evolution of bossism, see such general accounts as Charles N. Glaab and A. Theodore Brown, *A History of Urban America*; David R. Goldfield and Blaine A. Brownell, *Urban America: A History*. Studies on the historical development of municipal government include Jon C. Teaford, *The Municipal Revolution in America: Origins of Modern Urban Government, 1650–1825*; Jon C. Teaford, *The Twentieth-Century City: Problem, Progress, and Reality*; Jon C. Teaford, *The Unheralded Triumph: City Government in America, 1870–1900*; John Fairlie, *Municipal Administration*; and Ernest S. Griffith, *The Modern Development of City Government in the United States and the United Kingdom*.

18. See Jerome Mushkat, *Tammany: The Evolution of a Political Machine, 1789–1865*; Zane Miller, *Boss Cox's Cincinnati: Urban Politics in the Progressive Era*; Melvin G. Holli, *Reform in Detroit: Hazen S. Pingree and Urban Politics*; Louis G. Geiger, "Joseph W. Folk v. Edward Butler, St. Louis, 1902"; Lloyd Wendt and Herman Kogan, *Bosses in Lusty Chicago*.

19. Quoted in *Missouri Democrat*, December 17, 1937. On the "community consensus," see William L. Riordan, *Plunkett of Tammany Hall: A Series of Very Plain Talks on Very Practical Politics*; Seymour Mandelbaum, *Boss Tweed's New York*; Samuel Hays, "The Politics of Reform in Municipal Government in the Progressive Era"; James Bryce, *The American Commonwealth*; Lincoln Steffens, *Shame of the Cities*; Bruce M. Stave, ed., *Urban Bosses, Machines, and Progressive Reformers*.

20. Newspaper clipping, "Debauchery of Law Held Greatest Threat to United States," May 20, 1938, n.p., attached to Administrative Form 61, Bureau of Prisons, June 6, 1939, Notorious Offender Case Files, RG 129, NA-Wash. Hoover's image has become so unfavorable since his death in 1972 that it is hard to convey the respect that he and the FBI received in the 1930s. "His Federal Bureau of Investigation was venerated like no other institution in a country where even Christianity and baseball have to tolerate disbelievers. . . . For most Americans Hoover's FBI was a national security blanket. . . . Hoover's popularity was so high above the political stage that he could comment on the struggle below, interpret the action to the audience, lead the crowd in cheers and catcalls, change the script when it pleased him, and intervene magisterially whenever one of his favorites faltered, all without exposing himself to the battering of political strife. By a quirk of the public psychology, Americans saw, when they looked

at Hoover, not a spokesman for a partisan political philosophy, but a suprapolitical national hero" (Richard Gid Powers, *G-Men: Hoover's FBI in American Popular Culture,* xi–xii). See Richard Gid Powers, *Secrecy and Power: The Life of J. Edgar Hoover.*

21. See Harold Zink, *City Bosses in the United States: A Study of Twenty Municipal Bosses;* M. Ostrogorski, *Democracy and the Party System;* George Reedy, *From the Ward to the White House: The Irish in American Politics;* Edward M. Levine, *The Irish and Irish Politicians.* Throughout the 1930s, S. J. Ray, a political cartoonist for the *Kansas City Star,* depicted Pendergast as a smug and greedy petty dictator (*Kansas City Star,* February 28, 1990).

22. Jack Beatty, *The Rascal King: The Life and Times of James Michael Curley;* Thomas H. O'Connor, *The Boston Irish: A Political History.*

23. David McCullough, *Truman,* 156–58.

24. Beatty, "Political Boss Talks," 31.

25. Robert B. Dishman, "Machine Politics—Kansas City Model," 1.

26. Charles N. Glaab, "Visions of Metropolis: William Gilpin and Theories of City Growth in the American West."

1. EARLY YEARS, 1872–1894

1. "Certificate of Baptism," Thomas J. Pendergast Jr. Papers, Western Historical Manuscript Collection, a Joint Collection of the University of Missouri and the State Historical Society of Missouri (hereafter cited as WHMC); quoted in *Kansas City Times,* November 30, 1979.

2. Reedy, *From the Ward to the White House,* 75–92.

3. Pendergast Family Records, Pendergast Papers, WHMC.

4. A standard local history is Elwood King, *History of Buchanan County and St. Joseph, Mo.: From the Time of the Platte Purchase to the End of the Year 1915;* see also Sheridan A. Logan, *Old Saint Jo: Gateway to the West, 1799–1932.* For the triumph of Kansas City in the westward-moving construction of the railroads, see Charles N. Glaab, *Kansas City and the Railroads: Community Policy in the Growth of a Regional Metropolis;* A. Theodore Brown, *Frontier Community: Kansas City to 1870.*

5. Pendergast family genealogy provided to the authors by Michael Pendergast.

6. Milligan, *Missouri Waltz,* 27–33; "Admission Summary," Notorious Offender Case Files, RG 129, NA-Wash. The *St. Joseph City Directory,* 1866, 1877, 1897, 1881–1882, 1889, contains information on Michael Pendergast's job history.

7. "Admission Summary," Notorious Offender Case Files, RG 129, NA-Wash.

8. Fred Slater to Lawrence H. Larsen, August 23, 1996; *St. Joseph City Directory,* 1878, 1887, 1899.

9. Milligan, *Missouri Waltz,* 32–33. *St. Joseph News-Press,* January 28, 1945; *Kansas City Star,* September 18, 1946.

10. "Admission Summary," Notorious Offender Case Files, RG 129, NA-Wash; photocopy of "Annual Register of the Webster School," 1879–1884, in authors' possession; Lew Larkin, "The Other Side of Tom Pendergast," 22; *St. Louis Star-Times,* February 2, 1945; the quote is in Milligan, *Missouri Waltz,* 33.

11. The most comprehensive account of James Pendergast's career is a 1960 master's thesis by Lyle W. Dorsett, "Alderman Jim Pendergast." Dorsett summarized his findings in a scholarly article with the same title. Considerable information can also be found in the early chapters of Dorsett, *Pendergast Machine,* and in Reddig, *Tom's Town.* Obituaries

include *Kansas City World,* November 11, 1911; *Kansas City Times,* November 11, 1911; *Kansas City Star,* November 11, 1911; *Kansas City Journal,* November 11, 1911. See Darrell Garwood, *Crossroads of America: The Story of Kansas City,* 170–76.

12. *Kansas City World,* November 16, 1901; *Political History of Jackson County: Biographical Sketches of Men Who Have Helped to Make It,* 183.

13. For information on the formation of Kansas City's economy, see Fredrick M. Spletstoser and Lawrence H. Larsen, *Kansas City: 100 Years of Business;* A. Theodore Brown and Lyle W. Dorsett, *K.C.: A History of Kansas City, Missouri;* Henry C. Haskell Jr. and Richard B. Fowler, *City of the Future: A Narrative History of Kansas City, 1850–1950.*

14. A good description of the demography of Jim Pendergast's part of town can be found in Dorsett's article "Alderman Jim" (1964), 4–5. See also Haskell and Fowler, *City of the Future,* 59–67.

15. The Climax story is in Reddig, *Tom's Town,* 25, and in Dorsett, *Pendergast Machine,* 4. The *Kansas City Business Directory* for 1880 lists John Porter as the proprietor of the American House, and the directory for 1881 lists the proprietor as James Pendergast. A student of West Bottoms affairs claimed that Pendergast's establishment was a "reputable place" and that "its genial host catered less to the traveling public than to the men who worked in the railroad yards and shops, the mills and the packing plants" (Reddig, *Tom's Town,* 26).

16. The police seldom entered establishments in the West Bottoms. According to the *1879 Kansas City Police Regulations,* officers could not enter "public houses, bawdy places, saloons, houses of assignation, or any other houses of public nature, unless called in officially." For the characteristics of the Kansas City force in 1880, see Lawrence H. Larsen, *The Urban West at the End of the Frontier.*

17. For a description of a "hell dance," see Lawrence H. Larsen and Nancy J. Hulston, "Through the Eyes of a Medical Student: A Window on Frontier Life in Kansas City, Missouri, 1870–1871," 432. Frontier Omaha, Nebraska, two hundred miles to the north rivaled Kansas City as an entertainment center (see Lawrence H. Larsen and Barbara J. Cottrell, *The Gate City: A History of Omaha,* 89–96). A member of the oldest profession who arrived in Kansas City in 1871 and became a well-known madam, not retiring until 1922, is the subject of a novel by Lenore Carroll, *Annie Chambers.*

18. According to the records of Mount St. Mary's Cemetery, Kansas City, Missouri, Jim bought lot 74 in section A on August 8, 1884.

19. Reddig, *Tom's Town,* 28–29; Dorsett, "Alderman Jim" (1964), 10.

20. Dorsett, *Pendergast Machine,* 7.

21. *Kansas City Times,* November 11, 1911. An article in the *Kansas City World,* November 16, 1901, reported that James Pendergast married "Mrs. Doerr, a widow," within a year of entering the saloon business. The son is mentioned in his will (*Kansas City Star,* November 14, 1911).

22. City directories list as living in the American House: Michael in 1887, Josephine in 1889, John in 1890, and Mary Anne in 1891. Margaret almost certainly stayed there prior to marrying a Kansas Citian. Michael is listed as a bartender in the 1887 directory and John in that for 1890. Michael is listed as a clerk in 1889.

23. Material on the 1889 charter can be found in Donald B. Oster, "Kansas City Charter Movements, 1905–1925."

24. Reddig, *Tom's Town,* 30.

25. Dorsett, *Pendergast Machine,* 9–10. The vote totals are in the *St. Louis Star-Times,* February 2, 1944. See also William Rufus Jackson, *Missouri Democracy: A History of the Party*

and Its Representative Members—Past and Present, 1:645–47; Kansas City Star, March 16, 17, April 6, 1892.

26. *Kansas City Star*, January 2, 22, 27, February 3, 1897.

27. Reddig, *Tom's Town*, 28–32; *Kansas City Journal*, November 11, 1911.

28. Editorial in the *Jackson Examiner*, November 17, 1911, "Pendergast, Thomas J.," Vertical File, HSTL.

29. Quoted in *Kansas City Times*, November 11, 1911.

30. *St. Joseph News-Press*, January 28, 1945.

31. Pendergast said he had four years of college, while prison examiners believed he had two ("Admission Summary," Notorious Offender Case Files, RG 129, NA-Wash). The information is in "Investigation and Conviction of Thomas J. Pendergast, Kansas City, Missouri. (Including Robert Emmett O'Malley, former Superintendent of Insurance, Kansas City, Missouri)," p. 21, Thomas J. Pendergast File, Papers of Henry J. Morgenthau Jr., Franklin D. Roosevelt Library (hereafter cited as FDRL), Hyde Park, New York. The *Kansas City World*, December 31, 1902, reported that Pendergast had attended Christian Brothers in St. Louis. The *St. Joseph News-Press*, January 28, 1945, said he had attended St. Mary's College "in Kansas" and a St. Joseph business college. Reddig, *Tom's Town*, 32, gave the same information as the *Kansas City Times*, January 27, 1945; *St. Louis Post-Dispatch*, January 27, 1945. Percy B. Sovey, "T. J. Pendergast: The Man Whose Word Is Good," wrote that he graduated from St. Mary's College in St. Marys, Kansas. The *St. Louis Star-Times*, February 2, 1945, said he matriculated at St. Mary's in Marysville, Kansas. According to Beatty, "Political Boss Talks," he graduated from Christian Brothers in St. Joseph and from St. Mary's College in St. Marys, Kansas. Milligan, *Missouri Waltz*, 31–32, said that Pendergast did not go to St. Mary's College, St. Marys, Kansas. A Truman biographer wrote in 1962, "Though he later claimed he was a college man and a big league baseball prospect, Tom had little schooling" (Alfred Steinberg, *The Man from Missouri: The Life and Times of Harry S. Truman*, 68).

32. Fred Slater to Lawrence H. Larsen, August 3, 1996.

33. *St. Joseph City Directory*, 1890, 1891, 1892, 1893, 1894; quoted in *St. Joseph News-Press*, January 28, 1945.

34. *St. Joseph Daily News*, December 29, 1902. Mary Pendergast did not leave a will ("Petition for Refusal of Mary Pendergast, Deceased," Thomas J. Pendergast, petitioner, April 7, 1909, Clerk's Office, Buchanan County Court, St. Joseph).

2. APPRENTICESHIP, 1895–1910

1. Quoted in *St. Joseph News-Press*, January 28, 1945. See *Kansas City Times*, January 27, 1945. An account of Pendergast's baseball career in the *Kansas City Star* on April 7, 1939, describes him as a "brilliant infielder" with "magnificent and sure hands," but a "buckshot arm," who could hit the long ball.

2. See the chapters "Metropolitan Aspirations" in Brown and Dorsett, *K.C.*, 99–130, and "The 1900s: Out of Fire and Flood" in Haskell and Fowler, *City of the Future*, 89–102. Of considerable use is material in *Kansas City as It Is* (no author listed) and Robert H. Ferrell, *Harry S. Truman: A Life*.

3. Daniel Serda, *Boston Investors and the Early Development of Kansas City, Missouri*; Spletstoser and Larsen, *Kansas City*; William S. Worley, *Development of Industrial Districts in the Kansas City Region: From the Close of the Civil War to World War II*.

4. Spletstoser and Larsen, *Kansas City*; see Haskell and Fowler, *City of the Future*, 79–80.

5. Brown and Dorsett, *K.C.*, 15; Dorsett, *Pendergast Machine*, 19–21; *Kansas City Journal*, November 11, 1911. See Seymour Mandelbaum, *Boss Tweed's New York*. Mandelbaum argued that a boss was able to form ties with all segments of society and to create community consensus.

6. *Kansas City World*, May 15, 1902; George Creel and John Slavens, *Men Who Are Making Kansas City: A Biographical Dictionary*; Milligan, *Missouri Waltz*, 48; "Admission Summary," Notorious Offender Case Files, RG 129, NA-Wash; Reddig, *Tom's Town*, 32–33; *Kansas City Times*, January 27, 1945.

7. Quoted in Dorsett, *Pendergast Machine*, 43. George Creel, *Rebel at Large: Recollections of Fifty Crowded Years*, 50–51; *Ghosts in the Heart of America: Daylight Ghosts in Kansas City*, 6; Garwood, *Crossroads of America*, 181.

8. Quoted in Dishman, "Machine Politics—Kansas City Model," 21; *Kansas City World*, May 18, 1902; *Kansas City Times*, January 27, 1945; *St. Louis Post-Dispatch*, February 2, 1945; Dorsett, *Pendergast Machine*, 44–46.

9. Tom Pendergast, quoted in Dishman, "Machine Politics," 21; *Kansas City Star*, June 12, 1938.

10. Dishman, "Machine Politics," 21; Milligan, *Missouri Waltz*, 47.

11. Quoted in Reddig, *Tom's Town*, 96.

12. Quoted in "Carbon Copy of a Story," Richard A. Fowler to James A. Reed, July 26, 1929, James A. Reed Papers, WHMC. For Reed obituaries, see *Kansas City Times*, September 9, 1944; *New York Times*, September 9, 1944.

13. Quoted in "Carbon Copy of a Story," 2, Reed Papers, WHMC.

14. Quoted ibid., 4; *Kansas City Star*, January 4, 1897.

15. Quoted in "Carbon Copy of a Story," 1, Reed Papers, WHMC; Notation, "A.G.S.," July 29, Reed Papers, WHMC.

16. Dorsett, "Alderman Jim" (1964), 10; Milligan, *Missouri Waltz*, 47–48. The activities of Pendergast family members are mentioned in the *St. Joseph News-Press*, January 28, 1945.

17. Quoted in Dorsett, *Pendergast Machine*, 30. See also Dorsett, "Alderman Jim" (1964), 13.

18. Reddig, *Tom's Town*, 35–37; *Kansas City Times*, March 29, 1943; *Kansas City Star*, March 29, 1943; Charles P. Blackmore, "Joseph B. Shannon: Political Boss and Twentieth Century 'Jeffersonian.'"

19. For instance, see Milligan, *Missouri Waltz*, 69; Dorsett, *Pendergast Machine*, 141; Reddig, *Tom's Town*, 33–37; *Missouri Democrat*, October 21, 1927.

20. Quoted in *Political History of Jackson County*, 58.

21. Quoted ibid., 238–39.

22. See Dorsett, *Pendergast Machine*, 33–34; Reddig, *Tom's Town*, 82–85.

23. Quoted in *Kansas City Journal*, November 11, 1911; Milligan, *Missouri Waltz*, 71–72.

24. *Kansas City Journal*, December 11, 1911.

25. Milligan, *Missouri Waltz*, 59–64.

26. Quoted in "Carbon Copy of a Story," 4, Reed Papers, WHMC. See *Political History of Jackson County*, 55; Lee Meriwether, *Jim Reed: Senatorial Immortal*.

27. *Kansas City Journal*, July 26, 1902.

28. Quoted in "Carbon Copy of a Story," 4, Reed Papers, WHMC; *Kansas City Star*, November 9, 1904; Dishman, "Machine Politics," 22.

29. Creel and Slavens, *Biographical Dictionary*.

30. *Kansas City Star*, n.d., copy, Robert M. Wedow Collection, WHMC; quoted in *Kansas City World*, May 18, 1902.

31. *Kansas City Star*, November 3, 1902; *Kansas City World*, December 31, 1902; *Kansas City Star*, November 5, 1902; *Political History of Jackson County*, 183.

32. *Kansas City Rising Son*, October 25, 1906.

33. *Kansas City World*, August 5, 1904.

34. Quoted in *Kansas City Times*, March 15, 1900, November 11, 1911; *Kansas City Star*, March 9, 1910.

35. Quoted in *Kansas City Times*, November 11, 1911.

36. Quoted in *Kansas City Journal*, November 11, 1911.

37. Quoted in *Kansas City Times*, November 11, 1911.

38. "Proof of Will of James Pendergast Deceased," County Clerk's Office, Jackson County, Missouri.

39. *Kansas City Times*, November 11, 1911. A New Left interpretation of James Pendergast's career claims that he fought against a corporate capitalistic "new order" in Missouri that used force to destroy traditional values: "Recognizing the essential military nature of the conflict, Pendergast based his organization on the police department" (David Thelen, *Paths of Resistance: Tradition and Dignity in Industrializing Missouri*, 22).

40. See Haskell and Fowler, *City of the Future.*

41. Quoted in *Kansas City Star*, April 13, 1996, January 22, 1897.

42. See Reddig, *Tom's Town*, 37–48; Haskell and Fowler, *City of the Future*, 64–67.

43. Milligan, *Missouri Waltz*, 48–49.

44. *St. Louis Star-Times*, "Rise and Fall of Boss Tom," February 3, 1945; *Dictionary of American Biography*, 3d supp., s.v. "Pendergast, Thomas J."; recorder of deeds to N. R. Timmons, June 2, 1939, Notorious Offender Case Files, RG 129, NA-Wash.

45. Beatty, "Political Boss Talks," 110; *Kansas City Star*, June 13, 1951. A writer in the *Missouri Democrat*, January 27, 1933, commented on Beatty's article, "The story was fairly accurate except that the writer failed to grasp the fact that Pendergast is not a 'boss' but a leader of the Democratic organization in Kansas City."

46. "Preliminary Social Abstract," Notorious Offender Case Files, RG 129, NA-Wash; "Confidential Report for Client Only, re: Margaret Ann Geivett," April 30, 1966, in possession of Beverly Pendergast Estate. Margaret Ann Geivett was the daughter of Carolyn Pendergast.

47. *Kansas City World*, August 5, 1904; portions of Polk's *Kansas City Directory*, Pendergast Papers, WHMC; Reddig, *Tom's Town*, 137.

48. Portions of downtown Kansas City business directory, Pendergast Papers, WHMC; quoted in *Kansas City Star*, April 17, 1936, April 7, 1939.

49. *Kansas City World*, August 5, 1904.

50. Portions of downtown Kansas City business directory, Pendergast Papers, WHMC.

51. *St. Louis Post-Dispatch*, September 12, 1937.

52. Quoted in Reddig, *Tom's Town*, 72.

53. *St. Louis Star-Times*, February 2, 1945.

3. RISE, 1911–1925

1. See Haskell and Fowler, *City of the Future*, 102–13; and William H. Wilson, *The City Beautiful Movement in Kansas City.*

2. Haskell and Fowler, *City of the Future*, 119–21; William S. Worley, *J. C. Nichols and the Shaping of Kansas City*.

3. Marjorie Beach, *The Mayor's Wife: Crusade in Kansas City*, 25.

4. Portions of downtown Kansas City business directory, Pendergast Papers, WHMC.

5. See map "Ward Boundaries, 1904–12" in Dorsett, *Pendergast Machine*, 36.

6. *Kansas City Star*, April 17, 1936.

7. Quoted ibid., January 3, 1939.

8. Ibid.; Dorsett, *Pendergast Machine*, 63; Reddig, *Tom's Town*, 104–15; *Ghosts in the Heart of America*, 6–7; quoted in *Kansas City Journal*, July 28, 1913. Under a new law, the county marshal appointed Michael Pendergast to the office of County License Inspector. According to a newspaper account, "The new official will not only have charge of the license applications of the more than six hundred saloons of Jackson County but will inspect pool halls and all other places which require a license to do business" (*Jackson Examiner*, April 4, 1913).

9. *Kansas City Journal*, March 18, 1913.

10. Quoted ibid., October 7, 1913.

11. Quoted ibid.

12. Beach, *Mayor's Wife*, 22, 36.

13. Quoted in *Kansas City Journal*, February 18, 1916.

14. Dorsett, *Pendergast Machine*, 59–61; *Kansas City Star*, July 8, 1914.

15. *Kansas City Star*, June 12, 1914.

16. Quoted ibid., June 20, 1914; ibid., March 30, 1914.

17. See Dorsett, *Pendergast Machine*, 61.

18. Both quotes are from the *Kansas City Journal*, January 10, 1913.

19. Quoted in *Kansas City Star*, June 10, 1915.

20. *Kansas City Journal*, August 30, 1913.

21. Ibid., March 6, 8, 1914; April 8, 16, 21, 1914. The statue had been unveiled in 1913 before a crowd of three thousand admirers. As the city grew, expressways built around the monument cut it off from all except the most resolute visitor. It fell into disrepair and was the target of vandals. After a time in storage, it was reset in 1966 in a secluded part of Mulkey Square near its original location. In 1990, following an eighteen-month restoration project, the statue was moved with appropriate ceremonies emphasizing Jim Pendergast's Irish roots to a new location in Case Park overlooking the West Bottoms. See *Kansas City Times*, October 18, 22, 1988, and September 27, 1989; *Kansas City Star*, February 11, 1987, April 26, 1990; *New York Times*, April 30, 1990; Barbara Magerl, "The Other Pendergast," 14–15.

22. *Kansas City Journal*, August 8, 1914.

23. Ibid., August 13, 1914.

24. Quoted ibid., January 10, 1915; Reddig, *Tom's Town*, 82–83.

25. Quoted in *Kansas City Journal*, January 10, 1915.

26. Ibid., January 12, 1915.

27. Quoted ibid., February 19, 1915; February 20, 1915.

28. Quoted ibid. According to Reddig, a calculating Tom Pendergast was seeking to change the Fifty-Fifty to seventy-thirty in his favor and had been looking for an excuse to pick a fight (*Tom's Town*, 83–84).

29. Quoted in *Kansas City Post*, May 3, 1915; *Kansas City Journal*, May 4, 1915.

30. Quoted in *Kansas City Post*, May 4, 1915.

31. Reddig, *Tom's Town*, 84.

32. Quoted in *Kansas City Post*, May 4, 1915.

33. *Kansas City Journal*, February 20, April 1, 1916; Reddig, *Tom's Town*, 84–85; Dorsett, *Pendergast Machine*, 66–67.

34. Dorsett, *Pendergast Machine*, 69–70.

35. *Kansas City Journal*, February 18, 1916.

36. Quoted ibid. See *Kansas City Times*, January 27, 1945.

37. *Ghosts in the Heart of America*, 6; *Kansas City Star*, March 18, 1984.

38. Reeves, "Shame," 41–42, Reeves Papers, A-WDM.

39. Ibid., 62–65; *Kansas City Star*, November 8, 1918.

40. Quoted in Reeves, "Shame," 65, Reeves Papers, A-WDM; *Kansas City Star*, November 6, 10, 22, 1918.

41. Reeves, "Shame," 67, Reeves Papers, A-WDM.

42. *Kansas City Star*, September 4, 1929.

43. See ibid., October 12, 1912. William Ross, who continued his association with Pendergast into Prohibition, died in an automobile accident in 1928 while on the way to a construction site.

44. Ibid., March 18, 1914, November 9, 1996; Reddig, *Tom's Town*, 88; *Kansas City in Caricature*, 267.

45. "Wine List, Jefferson Hotel, Kansas City, Missouri," Pendergast Papers, WHMC.

46. Quoted in Reddig, *Tom's Town*, 88; *Kansas City Star*, July 27, 1914.

47. "Admission Summary," Notorious Offender Case Files, RG 129, NA-Wash. Pendergast may have held it against Miles Bulger that he did not come to see him while he was recovering from his ear operation (*Kansas City Star*, January 3, 1939).

48. Reddig, *Tom's Town*, 93; *T. J. Pendergast Wholesale Liquor Co. vs. Howell* (1920), L and E, 255-KC, United States District Court for the Western District of Missouri, Records of District Courts of the United States, RG 21, National Archives—Central Plains Region (hereafter cited as NA-CPR), Kansas City, Missouri.

49. Quoted in *St. Louis Post-Dispatch*, September 12, 1937.

50. See Milligan, *Missouri Waltz*, 223.

51. See Richard L. Miller, *Harry S. Truman: The Rise to Power*; Daniels, *Man of Independence*; McCullough, *Truman*; Ferrell, *Truman: A Life*; Alonzo L. Hamby, *Man of the People: A Life of Harry S. Truman*; Truman, "Pickwick Papers," Truman Papers, HSTL. In the draft of a letter apparently never sent to Margaret Truman, Tom Pendergast Jr. wrote, "I know it must have galled your father to take this help from my father, when he would rather have taken it from Mike and his son Jim Pendergast, but that is the way the cookies broke. I am sure Mr. T. took a lot of heat from your mother and you because he had to take help from Tom, who your father felt was a cross he had to bear if he wanted to be elected even dog catcher" (Pendergast Jr., "The Other Side of the Coin," Pendergast Papers, WHMC). Margaret Truman contended that her father did not go "hat in hand to Tom Pendergast," claiming, "In mid-1921 when Truman and Jacobson's haberdashery was flourishing, Mike appeared on the customer's side of the counter one day and asked Dad if he would like to run for judge of the county court for the eastern district. My father politely declined to commit himself. It was obvious to him—and to just about everyone else—that the Pendergasts needed Harry S. Truman at least as much as he needed them" (Margaret Truman, *Harry S. Truman*, 61–62).

52. For a summary of Truman's career written before he was a world figure, see Jackson, *Missouri Democracy*, 3:731–33. During the fall 1922 campaign, more than fourteen thousand men, women, and children attended a Klan rally at the Convention Hall, in which

none of the participants wore sheets (*Kansas City Star*, October 29, 1922). Most of the rhetoric was directed against Shannon and Pendergast. To the tune of "Good-by Mule with the Old Hee Haw," the crowd sang, "Good-by Tom and good-by Joe, you and Reed will have to go." In the election, a Klan candidate for circuit judge drew slightly more than 16,000 of some 90,000 votes cast (*Kansas City Star*, November 8, 1922).

53. Truman, "Pickwick Papers," Truman Papers, HSTL; Ferrell, *Truman: A Life*, 96–98; McCullough, *Truman*, 159–96.

54. Truman, "Pickwick Papers," Truman Papers, HSTL. As for running as a Republican, Margaret Truman wrote, "To my father, being a Democrat was an article of faith. He could not run on a Republican ticket if an angel on high appeared with a flaming sword and ordered him to do so. He supported the Pendergasts because they were Democrats and they supported him for the same reason" (*Harry S. Truman*, 65).

55. Papers concerning his service as mayor, 1924–1931, are in the Albert I. Beach Papers, WHMC.

56. Reddig, *Tom's Town*, 112–14; Dorsett, *Pendergast Machine*, 71–73; Truman, "Pickwick Papers," Truman Papers, HSTL; Ferrell, *Truman: A Life*, 100–103; Hamby, *Man of the People*, 118–27; *Kansas City Star*, November 6, 1924.

57. Quoted in Reddig, *Tom's Town*, 114–15; *Kansas City Star*, September 1, 1929.

58. *Kansas City Times*, March 8, 1924.

59. Miles Bulger to Lloyd C. Stark, July 30, 1938, Lloyd Crow Stark Papers, WHMC; *Kansas City Star*, January 3, 1939.

60. Haskell and Fowler, *City of the Future*, 111–12.

61. Ibid., 112–13; Reddig, *Tom's Town*, 53–54.

62. Quoted in Reddig, *Tom's Town*, 116; Walter Matscheck, "Kansas City Adopts the Manager Plan," 20. See Oster, "Kansas City Charter Movements."

63. Walter Matscheck, "Kansas City Tries to Improve the Manager Plan," 617–20. See Dorsett, *Pendergast Machine*, 78–79.

64. Quoted in Reddig, *Tom's Town*, 117; A. Theodore Brown, *Politics of Reform: Kansas City's Municipal Government, 1925–1950*, 34.

65. Quoted in Reddig, *Tom's Town*, 122.

66. Henry Jost to Joseph Shannon, July 12, 1939, Henry Jost Papers, WHMC.

67. Reddig, *Tom's Town*, 122; Dorsett, *Pendergast Machine*, 79–80.

68. Reddig, *Tom's Town*, 122; quoted in Alan Hynd, *The Giant Killers*; Beach, *Mayor's Wife*, 177–79.

69. Minutes of the Public Service Institute, January 11, 1926, Civic Research Institute Records, WHMC. The Public Service Institute, named the Civic Research Institute after 1941, continued to study city government and to fund research projects. Matscheck left town to take a position in New York in 1936.

4. POWER, 1926–1932

1. Quoted in Beatty, "Political Boss Talks," 110.

2. Quoted ibid., 112–13.

3. Samuel J. Crumbine, *Frontier Doctor*, 234–36.

4. Ibid., 236.

5. Ibid., 237.

6. Quoted in Beatty, "Political Boss Talks," 111.

7. Quoted ibid., 110, 108.
8. See *Kansas City Post,* December 26, 1927; *Kansas City Journal,* December 26, 1927; *Kansas City Star,* December 25, 1929; *Kansas City Times,* December 26, 1929. On December 23, 1929, the *Star* reported that T. J. Pendergast was planning his nineteenth dinner. The *St. Louis Globe-Democrat,* December 7, 1930, said that the "broken derelicts of the North Side" were part of "his smooth-working political organization, are registered, and live in great numbers in the cheap lodging houses of that section in campaign season." A machine paper gave wide coverage (*Missouri Democrat,* December 22, 1933, December 23, 1934).
9. Larkin, "Other Side of Tom Pendergast," 23–24; *Ghosts in the Heart of America,* 6–7. During the depths of the Great Depression, the Pendergast machine handed out several thousand meal tickets a day for use at the City Mission (*Kansas City Star,* March 19, 1934).
10. Quoted in *Missouri Democrat,* January 3, 1933.
11. *Kansas City Star,* December 25, 1930.
12. *Tom's Town,* 131–32; *New York Times,* February 21, 1932; Ralph Coghlan, "Boss Pendergast: King of Kansas City, Emperor of Missouri"; *St. Louis Globe-Democrat,* December 7, 1930; Larkin, "Other Side of Tom Pendergast," 25. By 1995 the building was an abandoned and boarded-up ruin (*Kansas City Star,* July 19, 1995).
13. Quoted in Reddig, *Tom's Town,* 131. See *St. Louis Globe-Democrat,* December 7, 1930; *Kansas City Star,* September 24, 1994.
14. Quoted in *Kansas City Star,* September 24, 1994.
15. Quoted ibid.
16. *Kansas City Star,* April 21, 1956; quoted in *Kansas City Star,* May 13, 1995; *Kansas City Times,* January 27, 1945.
17. Quoted in *St. Louis Post-Dispatch,* September 12, 1937. In regard to selecting candidates, a Springfield and Greene County attorney recalled, "The best Circuit Court Judge Greene County had ever had was probably Warren L. White, who served the longest term ever as Circuit Judge (36 years). His father had been a Missouri Supreme Court Judge and Judge White aspired to that office also. He went, hat in hand, to seek Pendergast's support, but the support had already been pledged to someone else and Judge White never attained his goal" (John K. Hulston to Nancy J. Hulston, January 15, 1997).
18. Quoted in Nathan W. Pearson Jr., *Goin' to Kansas City,* 88.
19. James A. Reed to Thomas J. Pendergast, June 10, 1930 (Grover Calmessee), April 22, 1930 (Tim Hallissey), November 12, 1931 (Harry Daly), November 3, 1934 (J. J. Brink), April 3, 1934 (Mrs. John Scott), March 28, 1929 (Joseph Neschese), Reed Papers, WHMC; James A. Reed to Albert O. Blakey, December 20, 1934, Reed Papers, WHMC. See *Kansas City Times,* April 21, 1936.
20. Thomas J. Pendergast to James A. Reed, n.d., Reed Papers, WHMC. Pendergast wrote another "Ruth J. Rubel" letter, calling her a "young lady," to Governor Guy Park: "While not actively engaged in political work, she has a large acquaintance among a certain class of people in Kansas City who are influential" (n.d., Guy Park Papers, WHMC).
21. Reddig, *Tom's Town,* 133.
22. *Kansas City Star,* September 13, 1927; Reddig, *Tom's Town,* 135–36. See *Kansas City Times,* July 28, 1927, June 8, 1931, July 9, 1935; *Kansas City Journal,* June 26, 1935.
23. Quoted in *Kansas City Star,* September 13, 1927.

24. Quoted ibid.

25. Quoted ibid.

26. Robert Pearson and Brad Pearson, *The J. C. Nichols Chronicle: The Authorized Story of the Man, His Company, and His Legacy*, 141–42.

27. *Kansas City Star*, September 30, 1928.

28. See Milligan, *Missouri Waltz*, 88.

29. Quoted in Milligan, *Missouri Waltz*, 91; *Kansas City Star*, September 4, 1929.

30. Quoted in *Kansas City Times*, January 27, 1945.

31. *Kansas City Star*, September 24, 1994; *St. Louis Post-Dispatch*, September 12, 1937; Reddig, *Tom's Town*, 134–35.

32. Reddig, *Tom's Town*, 135; newspaper clipping, "Intelligence Unit," Notorious Offender Case Files, RG 129, NA-Wash; quoted in *Kansas City Star*, September 24, 1994; quoted in *St. Louis Post-Dispatch*, January 27, 1945; unidentified newspaper editorial, Reed Papers, WHMC. See *Kansas City Star*, October 15, 1929.

33. Doyle Patterson, conversation with Lawrence H. Larsen, November 1995; Matt Devoe, interview by Nancy J. Hulston, April 15, 1994, A-WDM; quoted in *St. Louis Post-Dispatch*, September 12, 1937; Mary Phillips to Barbara J. Larsen, October 29, 1993.

34. Matt Devoe, interview, A-WDM; *St. Louis Post-Dispatch*, September 12, 1937; *Kansas City Star*, September 24, 1994.

35. Quoted in *Kansas City Star*, September 4, 1929. Earl Quinn, who was convicted of the murder of two women schoolteachers, confessed to the robbery shortly before his execution (*Missouri Democrat*, December 1, 1933).

36. *Kansas City Star*, June 23, 1951.

37. Quoted in *Kansas City Star*, June 4, 1989; *Kansas City Star*, April 24, 1935; Matt Devoe, interview, A-WDM.

38. *Kansas City Star*, September 2, 1929.

39. Quoted in Larkin, "Other Side of Tom Pendergast," 25.

40. "Confidential Report for client only, re: Margaret Ann Geivett," April 20, 1966, Pendergast Papers, WHMC.

41. Margaret Geivett to Thomas J. Pendergast Jr., April 21, 1967, Pendergast Papers, WHMC.

42. Ibid.

43. *Time*, April 18, 1936, 45.

44. Ready Mixed was a well-run company (Dun and Bradstreet, Audit Report, Edward J. Dillon & Co. to Board of Directors, January 18, 1939, "Ready Mixed Concrete Company, Kansas City, Missouri, Examination of Books and Records, January 1, 1937 to January 31, 1937," A-WDM). Mike Ross died of a stroke in 1937 (*Missouri Democrat*, September 3, 1937). Quoted in *Kansas City Star*, April 7, 1939.

45. Matt Devoe, interview, A-WDM. As early as 1929, Mayor Albert Beach accused Ready Mixed of rigged bidding (*Kansas City Times*, September 15, 1929).

46. Quoted in Reddig, *Tom's Town*, 137.

47. *Directory of Kansas City Missouri*, 1937. Milligan, in *Missouri Waltz*, 189–94, admitted that federal agents found it impossible to uncover all of Pendergast's business connections. See "Statement of Facts to the Court," 6, *United States v. Pendergast* (1939), C, 14,567-KC, RG 21, NA-CPR; *Kansas City Times*, January 27, 1945.

48. Quoted in *Kansas City Star*, March 2, 1934.

49. Hynd, *Giant Killers*, 192–93.

50. Quoted in *Kansas City Times*, March 20, 1930. See the *Times*, January 22, February 17, 1930; *Kansas City Star*, March 15, 18, 1930.

51. Quoted in *Kansas City Times*, March 20, 1930.

52. Quoted ibid., March 21, 1930.

53. Quoted in "City a Business Success," n.d., Wedow Collection, WHMC.

54. *St. Louis Globe-Democrat*, December 7, 1930.

55. Reddig, *Tom's Town*, 179–85; Dorsett, *Pendergast Machine*, 107–8; Truman, *Harry S. Truman*, 70–73; Miller, *Truman: Rise to Power*, 222–24; Hamby, *Man of the People*, 147–55.

56. Chamber of Commerce of Greater Kansas City, *Where These Rocky Bluffs Meet: Including the Story of the Kansas City Ten-Year Plan*, 170; quoted in Garwood, *Crossroads of America*, 310. In 1937 machine officials successfully mediated a local strike against the six Katz drugstores (*Missouri Democrat*, July 9, 1937).

57. Truman, "Pickwick Papers," Truman Papers, HSTL. Kansas City Republicans praised Truman's policies, noting that the cost for concrete on rural Jackson County projects was $2.36 per yard, compared to $3.75 per yard in the city (*Kansas City Times*, January 22, 1930). See Ferrell, *Truman: A Life*, 108–15; McCullough, *Truman*, 173–78; Hamby, *Man of the People*, 152–60. According to Truman, Pendergast, calling him the "contrariest man in the state of Missouri," told him, "You carry out the agreement you made with the people of Jackson County" (quoted in Harry S. Truman, *Memoirs*, 1:141).

58. *Kansas City Times*, January 28, 1945; meeting with William H. Becker, October 2, 1987, A-WDM; *St. Louis Post-Dispatch*, January 27, 1945; Dorsett, *Pendergast Machine*, 95; Milligan, *Missouri Waltz*, 99–100; quoted in McCullough, *Truman*, 193–94.

59. Quoted in *Springfield Daily News*, August 17, 1935.

60. Quoted in *St. Louis Post-Dispatch*, September 12, 1937.

61. A gradual shift to FDR, who needed more than two-thirds of the vote to win, began on the second ballot, leading to his fourth ballot victory. According to manager James Farley, "Missouri gave us the largest increase, thanks to the friendship of Tom Pendergast of Kansas City and other Missouri leaders who were friendly. While loyal to Jim Reed, they knew he had no chance and were gradually coming over to the Roosevelt camp" (James A. Farley, *Behind the Ballots: The Personal History of a Politician*, 86–87). See also James A. Farley, *Jim Farley's Story: The Roosevelt Years*, 22; McCullough, *Truman*, 195.

62. Larkin, "Other Side of Tom Pendergast," 25.

63. Quoted in *Kansas City Star*, September 13, 1931.

64. Quoted in *St. Joseph News-Press*, January 28, 1945.

65. *Kansas City Star*, January 10, 1933; Schnell, "New Deal Scandals," 370–71; *Missouri Democrat*, October 27, 1933.

66. Reddig, *Tom's Town*, 132; Beatty, "Political Boss Talks," 111–12; Pearson, *Goin' to Kansas City*, 90.

67. *St. Louis Post-Dispatch*, September 12, 1937; *Kansas City Star*, May 21, 1939. In advance of the 1934 city election, the machine ordered all city employees to contribute 40 percent of their weekly salaries and county workers to give 22.5 percent of their weekly salaries for a designated campaign period to raise a $100,000 special campaign chest (*Kansas City Star*, February 15, 1934).

68. Lyle W. Dorsett, "Kansas City Politics: A Study of Boss Pendergast's Machine." See *Kansas City Star*, April 24, 1965.

69. A journalistic analysis noted, "For the first time the big G.O.P. Negro precincts went Democratic. This is explained by the Democrats, and most Republicans, to have been due chiefly to the unrelenting activity of the police against a certain element

of the Negroes. It was the persistence of Chief Miles's campaign against the 'crap shooters' that turned many formerly Republican votes to the Democratic column, they say" (*Kansas City Times*, March 27, 1930). Franklin recognized Pendergast's ability and appeal: "If Pendergast were arbitrary and arrogant, or dumb and destructive, he would not have grown to be the state and national figure he has become. There had to be something in the man to keep on accumulating confidence" (*Kansas City Call*, January 18, 1936).

70. Quoted in *St. Louis Post-Dispatch*, September 12, 1937.
71. Quoted in Beatty, "Political Boss Talks," 112.
72. See Patricia Mooney Melvin, *The Organic City: Urban Definition and Neighborhood Organization*.
73. Quoted in Beatty, "Political Boss Talks," 112. See *Time*, April 18, 1936, 45.
74. Quoted in *Kansas City Star*, May 13, 1995.
75. Beatty, "Political Boss Talks," 112.
76. Quoted ibid.; *Ghosts in the Heart of America*, 12.
77. Quoted in *St. Louis Post-Dispatch*, September 12, 1937.
78. Quoted in Hugh B. Downey, memorandum, January 24, 1978, Pendergast Papers, WHMC.
79. Howard F. Sachs, interview by Lawrence H. Larsen, December 1996. Alex Sachs was Howard Sachs's father. See Daniels, *Man of Independence*, 160.
80. *Kansas City Star*, May 13, 1995.
81. Reddig, *Tom's Town*, 165–66; quoted in *Missouri Democrat*, August 25, 1933.
82. Herb Phipps, *Bill Kyne of Bay Meadows: The Man Who Brought Horse Racing Back to California*, 27–28.
83. Program, Riverside Jockey Club, 1937 Meeting, Pendergast Papers; *Kansas City Times*, January 27, 1945; *Kansas City Star*, April 7, 1939; quoted in Phipps, *Bill Kyne of Bay Meadows*, 28.
84. *New York Times*, February 21, 1932; *Kansas City Times*, January 27, 1945; Truman, "Pickwick Papers," Truman Papers, HSTL.
85. *Kansas City Times*, June 8, 1931. On July 9, 1935, the *Times* reported the Pendergasts' return on the French liner *Normandie*. See *St. Louis Post-Dispatch*, September 12, 1937; *New York Times*, July 9, 1935.
86. Long, considered a classic demagogue by his enemies, had a political objective, hoping to rise to the presidency by promoting his Share the Wealth program. Both as a governor and as a U.S. senator, he dominated Louisiana for more than a decade and was a growing force in Washington prior to his 1935 assassination. Langer, less well known, turned the populist Nonpartisan League in North Dakota into an organization dedicated to his own aggrandizement. In the Great Depression, he had a controversial tenure as governor and narrowly avoided going to the penitentiary on a federal charge. Elected to the Senate in 1940, he died in office in 1958. See T. Harry Williams, *Huey Long*; Lawrence H. Larsen, "United States v. Langer, et al.: The U.S. District Attorney's Files."

5. DEBACLE, 1933–1938

1. Milligan, *Missouri Waltz*, 12; Larsen and Cottrell, *Gate City*, 183; *St. Louis Post-Dispatch*, December 9, 1934; Dorsett, *Pendergast Machine*, 88–89; *Ghosts in the Heart of America*,

24; *St. Louis Star-Times,* February 2, 1945; *New York Herald Tribune,* October 14, 1934. Elmer Irey said in 1945 about Kansas City under T. J. Pendergast's yoke, "No city in the United States, before or since, was ever the locale of such open and widespread corruption as was the Kansas City of the Pendergast regime" (Hynd, *Giant Killers,* 158). Tom Dennison, a former Colorado dance hall proprietor, ran a Prohibition-era political machine in Omaha. Dennison did not engage in wholesale vote fraud, but he did promote a wide-open town in which he acted as power broker between the business community and the local vice interests (Orville Menard, *Political Bossism in Mid-America: Tom Dennison's Omaha, 1900–1933*).

2. Milton Rakove, *Don't Make No Waves—Don't Back No Losers: An Insider's Analysis of the Daley Machine,* 23–26; Creel, *Rebel at Large,* 355. A reporter thought the $20 million figure was too high (*Kansas City Star,* April 12, 1939).

3. See John M. Findlay, *People of Chance: Gambling in American Society from Jamestown to Las Vegas.*

4. "American Gambling: Half of the Nation Made Bets in 1938," 46–47. In 1997 the legal "tourism and leisure time industry" (gambling) in Kansas City had a reported 7,936 slot machines and 448 table games located in five casinos (*Kansas City Star,* January 16, 1997). In 1933 a state grand jury claimed that Kansas City had 38 gambling halls and 2,000 slots (*Missouri Democrat,* September 15, November 15, 1933).

5. Article on 1930s vice in *Kansas City Star,* January 24, 1993; Samuel S. Mayerberg, *Chronicle of an American Crusader,* 117.

6. See *Kansas City Star,* April 18, 1994.

7. Quoted in *Kansas City Star,* April 18, 1991; Lawrence H. Larsen, *Federal Justice in Western Missouri: The Judges, the Cases, the Times,* 168–69; meeting with William H. Becker, October 2, 1987, A-WDM.

8. Quoted in *Kansas City Star,* April 13, 1939; *Kansas City Star,* April 19, 1939; John O. McWilliams, *The Protectors: Harry J. Anslinger and the Federal Bureau of Narcotics, 1930–1962,* 146; Harry J. Anslinger and Will Oursler, *The Murderers.*

9. Quoted in *New York Herald-Tribune,* March 13, 1938; quoted in *Missouri Democrat,* October 13, 1933.

10. Franklin Driggs, "Kansas City and the Southwest"; Dorsett, *Pendergast Machine,* 88–89; Katherine Wilson Frohoff, "In Search of Kansas City Jazz"; Ross Russell, *Jazz Style in Kansas City and the Southwest; Kansas City Star,* February 8, 1993. Kansas City had long been a center for musical pursuits. Because of its centrality and exceptional transportation network, the city was the headquarters for vaudeville and theatrical circuits. Many musicians working in traveling shows used the city as a base, and enough stayed permanently to start a conservatory that became the present conservatory at the University of Missouri–Kansas City. At the turn of the century, Kansas City had enough musical talent to staff two local opera companies. The jazz musicians, even though they came to town for different reasons, were very much in the musical traditions of Kansas City.

11. See Janet Bruce, *The Kansas City Monarchs: Champions of Black Baseball.*

12. *Kansas City Star,* November 14, 1996. On the formation of the African American community, see Dwayne R. Martin, "The Hidden Community: The Black Community of Kansas City, Missouri, during the 1870s and 1880s."

13. No African American served on either the Kansas City school board or city council until the 1960s. An ordinance in 1961 desegregated hotels, and a public accommodation act narrowly passed by a citywide vote in 1964. An African American,

Emanuel Cleaver, was elected mayor in 1991 and reelected in 1995. In 1990, Kansas City's population of 435,146 included 128,768 black people; a total of 200,508 black people lived in the metropolitan area of 1,506,250 people.

14. Johnson, *Kansas City Votes*. For Welch's role, see *Kansas City Star*, April 17, 1936.
15. Quoted in Reddig, *Tom's Town*, 216–17.
16. Quoted in *Kansas City Star*, November 22, 1964.
17. Quoted in *Kansas City Star*, May 22, 1932; *Kansas City Times*, June 1, 1932; Mayerberg, *Chronicle*, 131.
18. Quoted in Reddig, *Tom's Town*, 219; *Kansas City Star*, March 22, 1934; *Missouri Democrat*, March 24, 1934.
19. Truman, "Pickwick Papers," Truman Papers, HSTL.
20. Reeves, "Shame," 32, Reeves Papers, A-WDM.
21. Ibid., 32–33.
22. Unidentified writer to James Reed, May 10, 1928, Reed Papers, WHMC; *Kansas City Times*, May 23, 1928; Mitchell, *Four Horsemen*, "Pendergast, Thomas J.," Vertical File, HSTL. See Reddig, *Tom's Town*, 159–60; Mayerberg, *Chronicle*, 116.
23. Unidentified writer to James Reed, May 10, 1928, Reed Papers, WHMC.
24. It may have been a somewhat stormy relationship. According to Marjorie Beach, Lazia once hit Pendergast over the head with a chair (Beach, *The Mayor's Wife*, 208).
25. *Kansas City Times*, May 23, 1928.
26. Milligan, *Missouri Waltz*, 103–7. See "Transcripts of Records and Briefs," *Lazia vs. United States*, C, no. 10019, May Term, 1934, United States Court of Appeals for the Eighth Circuit, Records of United States Courts of Appeals, RG 276, NA-CPR.
27. For the rise of Weissman, see Reddig, *Tom's Town*, 160–68. For his demise, see *Kansas City Times*, October 29, 1930; *Kansas City Star*, October 29, 1930; May 5, 1931. See *Missouri Democrat*, September 15, 1933.
28. Milligan, *Missouri Waltz*, 18–19; Mayerberg, *Chronicle*, 115; Steinberg, *Man from Missouri*, 101–2.
29. See Albert L. Reeves to Maurice Milligan, October 30, 1936, in Reeves, "Shame," 71–79, Reeves Papers, A-WDM.
30. Quoted in Milligan, *Missouri Waltz*, 115; Reddig, *Tom's Town*, 257–59; Dorsett, *Pendergast Machine*, 127; "Conspiracy to Deliver a Federal Prisoner: 'The Kansas City Massacre,'" May 29, 1940, Federal Bureau of Investigation, Non-Record, NA-CPR. Questions concerning the crime and the perpetrators continued to be of interest decades later (see *Kansas City Star*, June 12, 1995).
31. Larsen, *Federal Justice*, 167; quoted in *Kansas City Times*, March 5, 1935; Miller, *Truman: Rise to Power*, 253; Hamby, *Man of the People*, 170–71. In 1993, a Kansas City author concluded that a vast conspiracy and cover-up existed involving Johnny Lazia, J. Edgar Hoover, Kansas City police and machine officials, and many career criminals, plus numerous others, and that "the sad reality of this is that powerful men controlled the outcome of this event from the beginning" (L. R. [Larry] Kirchner, *Triple Cross Fire!: J. Edgar Hoover and the Kansas City Union Station Massacre*, 158; McCullough, *Truman*, 201).
32. See *Missouri Democrat*, September 15, 1933.
33. Quoted in *St. Louis Star-Times*, January 25, 1934; quoted in *Kansas City Star*, March 26, 1934. See Reddig, *Tom's Town*, 224–37; Mayerberg, *Chronicle*, 141–42; Brown, *Politics of Reform; Ghosts in the Heart of America*, 9.
34. *Kansas City Star*, March 6, 13, 20, 22, 26, 27, 1934.

35. Meeting with William H. Becker, October 2, 1987, A-WDM.
36. Reddig, *Tom's Town*, 237–43; Milligan, *Missouri Waltz*, 138–43; *Kansas City Times*, March 28, 1934; *Kansas City Star*, March 28, 1934; *New York Times*, April 8, 1934; *Kansas City Post*, March 28, 1934.
37. *Kansas City Star*, March 28, 1934; *New York Times*, April 8, 1934.
38. Quoted in *Missouri Democrat*, March 23, 30, April 20, 1934.
39. Quoted in *Kansas City Star*, June 25, 1994.
40. Reddig, *Tom's Town*, 244–46.
41. Quoted in *Kansas City Star*, June 25, 1994.
42. Phone conversation, Thomas J. Pendergast and unidentified man, probably 1934, wiretap of Jefferson Democratic Club, Marr Sound Archives, Miller Nichols Library, University of Missouri–Kansas City.
43. Quoted in *Kansas City Star*, April 17, 1936; *Kansas City Post*, April 17, 1936.
44. Beatty, "Political Boss Talks," 113. In late 1934, Pendergast admitted he wrote the letter. See *St. Louis Star-Times*, December 1, 1934; *Kansas City Star*, March 6, 1935.
45. Quoted in *Kansas City Post*, July 10, 1934. *Kansas City Times*, July 11, 1934; *Kansas City Star*, July 10, 1934; Reddig, *Tom's Town*, 261–63; Hamby, *Man of the People*, 193; Steinberg, *Man from Missouri*, 101–2. There is an account of the murder in the *Kansas City Star*, March 18, 1984.
46. See *Kansas City Star*, July 12, 1934.
47. *Missouri Democrat*, July 13, 1934.
48. *Kansas City Times*, July 11, 12, 13, 1934. Six years later, a suspect, St. Louis hoodlum Jack Gregory, may have been the victim of a revenge killing by Lazia associates. According to a report in the *Kansas City Times*, November 16, 1940, "The underworld whispers have it that Gregory was horribly tortured, killed, his body encased in concrete and dumped into the Missouri River." See *Kansas City Kansan*, July 14, 1934; *Kansas City Journal*, July 14, 1934. Charles Carrolla also went by the name of Charles Carollo.
49. Quoted in *Kansas City Star*, June 25, 1994. Aylward campaigned for Truman. In a speech praising the roads and buildings Truman constructed during Truman's tenure, Aylward said, "They are monuments to Judge Truman's executive ability, to his honesty, to his efficiency in the administration of a public trust. Not a hint of scandal, of extravagance, of favoritism has ever been made against him in the construction of those highways and the expenditure of the vast sums entrusted to his hands" (Papers of James P. Aylward, HSTL).
50. Quoted in *Missouri Democrat*, May 11, 1934; *Missouri Democrat*, May 18, 1934.
51. Timothy K. Evans, "'This Certainly Is Relief!': Matthew S. Murray and Missouri Politics during the Depression"; Dorsett, *Pendergast Machine*, 111–12; Reddig, *Tom's Town*, 271. See Lyle W. Dorsett, *Franklin D. Roosevelt and the City Bosses*; Ferrell, *Truman: A Life*, 114–16.
52. Quoted in *New York Times*, July 9, 1935.
53. Mayerberg, *Chronicle*, 109–10; meeting with William H. Becker, October 2, 1987, A-WDM; *Kansas City Times*, May 15, 1936.
54. Quoted on keeping books in Reddig, *Tom's Town*, 124; quoted on partnership in *Time*, April 11, 1938.
55. *New York Herald-Tribune*, March 13, 1938.
56. Quoted in *Kansas City Star*, October 23, 1991; Reddig, *Tom's Town*, 183. The 1990s flood-control project for Brush Creek, far more vast and expensive than that of the

1930s, had imperfect results, with the media and others sarcastically renaming the stream "Flush Creek" (see *Kansas City Star,* October 30, 1995).

57. Newspaper clipping, n.d., n.p., A-WDM; Milligan, *Missouri Waltz,* 200–201; Reddig, *Tom's Town,* 278–79; Pendergast Jr., "Other Side of the Coin," Pendergast Papers, WHMC.

58. Quoted in *St. Louis Post-Dispatch,* October 17, 1935. Ferrell, *Truman: A Life,* 142–44, deals with Truman's role in the selection. See Reddig, *Tom's Town,* 279–80; Dorsett, *Pendergast Machine,* 119–21.

59. For a biography of Stark see *Kansas City Star,* November 8, 1936.

60. Quoted in *St. Louis Post-Dispatch,* September 12, 1937; quoted in *Kansas City Star,* April 1, 1938.

61. Reddig, *Tom's Town,* 278. In 1933, a machine spokesman said that Pendergast's "rugged constitution" had speeded his prolonged recovery from an unspecified "serious illness," possibly a heart attack (*Missouri Democrat,* April 28, 1933).

62. Reddig, *Tom's Town,* 281; Dorsett, *Pendergast Machine,* 134; Ferrell, *Truman: A Life,* 141.

63. Quoted in Reddig, *Tom's Town,* 281.

64. Sovey, "T. J. Pendergast," 4–5. According to Albert Reeves, one of the boss's tactics was to have writers in machine publications bestow on him "God-like qualities" (Reeves, "Shame," 51, Reeves Papers, A-WDM). See Dorsett, *Pendergast Machine,* 83–84.

65. Pendergast's health problems are the subject of an article in the *Kansas City Star,* August 2, 1936. See the *Star,* November 23, 25, 26, July 5, 1937; *Kansas City Times,* September 10, 12, 1936. In the summer of 1937, Pendergast went to Colorado Springs on an extended, health-related vacation. He weighed approximately 210 pounds, up from 180 pounds the previous fall.

66. A Republican chairman of the Kansas City Board of Election Commissioners had removed thousands of nonexistent voters from the registration lists prior to Albert Beach's election as mayor in 1924. An election commissioner wrote the new mayor, "I am proud to know that I played a small part in bringing about the results, especially in our dealings with the north-end ghost vote" (Eugene N. Blake to Albert I. Beach, April 26, 1924, Beach Papers, WHMC).

67. The registration and voting process is explained in *Ghosts in the Heart of America,* 10–11; Reddig, *Tom's Town,* 286; Milligan, *Missouri Waltz,* 134–38; *Kansas City Star,* March 13, 1934.

68. Quoted in *Kansas City Star,* September 13, 1931.

69. W. W. Filkin to Lloyd Stark, January 25, 1938, Stark Papers, WHMC.

70. Mitchell, *Four Horsemen,* "Pendergast, Thomas J.," Vertical File, HSTL.

71. Quoted in Reddig, *Tom's Town,* 282–83; Pendergast Jr., "Other Side of the Coin," Pendergast Papers, WHMC. The *Kansas City Star* warned about the election on November 1, 1936, and Pendergast issued a statement published in the newspaper on December 15, 1936.

72. Quoted in Reeves, "Shame," 68, Reeves Papers, WHMC.

73. Larsen, *Federal Justice,* 127–30; Albert L. Reeves, "Judge Albert L. Reeves—Early History," Reeves Papers, WHMC.

74. Larsen, *Federal Justice,* 131–33.

75. Merrill E. Otis, *In the Day's Work of a Federal Judge: A Miscellany of Opinions, Addresses and Extracts from Opinions and Addresses,* 163–65.

76. Mitchell, *Four Horsemen,* "Pendergast, Thomas J.," Vertical File, HSTL; Larsen, *Federal Justice,* 170–75; Dorsett, *Pendergast Machine,* 121–23; Reddig, *Tom's Town,* 285–90; Reeves, "Shame," 76–79, Reeves Papers, A-WDM.

77. *St. Louis Post-Dispatch*, April 16, 1939.
78. Milligan, *Missouri Waltz*, 4; Larsen, *Federal Justice*, 169–70; Reeves, "Shame," 73–74, Reeves Papers, A-WDM.
79. Quoted in *Kansas City Star*, December 14, 1936. See Larsen, *Federal Justice*, 172.
80. "Memorandum," August 19, 1939, *United States v. Pendergast*, 28 F. Supp. 601 (W.D.Mo., 1939); Larsen, *Federal Justice*, 180.
81. Reeves, "Shame," 86–93, Reeves Papers, A-WDM; Milligan, *Missouri Waltz*, 162–63.
82. Quoted in *Kansas City Star*, May 23, 1938.
83. Milligan, *Missouri Waltz*, 165; *Ghosts in the Heart of America*, 27; McCullough, *Truman*, 235–36.
84. *Kansas City Star*, March 21, 28, 1938.
85. Coghlan, "Boss Pendergast"; *Kansas City Star*, November 11, 1936.
86. Story in *Kansas City Times*, March 15, 1971.
87. Reeves, "Shame," 111–12, Reeves Papers, A-WDM.
88. Farley, *Jim Farley's Story*, 108.
89. Larsen, *Federal Justice*, 175.
90. U.S. Congress, Senate, *Congressional Record*, 75th Cong., 1st sess. (February 15, 1938), pp. 1962–64. Excerpts from the speech are quoted in many places. See Larsen, *Federal Justice*, 175–76; Reddig, *Tom's Town*, 292; Ferrell, *Truman: A Life*, 145–46; Truman, *Harry S. Truman*, 114–16; Miller, *Truman: Rise to Power*, 299–304; Hamby, *Man of the People*, 230–32; McCullough, *Truman*, 237.
91. Reeves, "Shame," 262, Reeves Papers, A-WDM; Reddig, *Tom's Town*, 292.
92. Hamby, *Man of the People*, 203–4; Miller, *Truman: Rise to Power*, 263–64, 275; Thomas J. Pendergast to Harry S. Truman, February 16, 1935, May 5, 1935, June 13, 1938, February 1, 1938, Truman Senatorial Papers, HSTL; Truman, "Pickwick Papers," Truman Papers, HSTL.
93. Quoted in Steinberg, *Man from Missouri*, 153. See the chapter "Senator from Pendergast," in Harold F. Gosnell, *Truman's Crises: A Political Biography of Harry S. Truman*, 112–23, and McCullough, *Truman*, 239.

6. DOWNFALL, 1935–1939

1. Reddig, *Tom's Town*, 278; Elmer Irey and William Slocum, "How We Smashed the Pendergast Machine," 67–68. Pendergast is quoted in the *Kansas City Star*, April 7, 1939.
2. See Milligan, *Missouri Waltz*, 169–87; Larsen, *Federal Justice*, 181–82.
3. "Investigation and Conviction," 10, June 2, 1939, Pendergast File, Morgenthau Papers, FDRL; Reddig, *Tom's Town*, 275–79.
4. "Investigation and Conviction," 16, June 2, 1939, Pendergast File, Morgenthau Papers, FDRL. A summary of the investigation is in "Statement of Facts to the Court," *United States v. Pendergast* (1939), C, 14,567-KC, RG 21, NA-CPR. See also *Kansas City Star*, May 22, 1939.
5. "Investigation and Conviction," 16, June 2, 1939, Pendergast File, Morgenthau Papers, FDRL. The transaction is summarized in Reddig, *Tom's Town*, 276–77.
6. "Investigation and Conviction," 16–17, June 2, 1939, Pendergast File, Morgenthau Papers, FDRL.
7. Ibid., 17.
8. "Statement of Facts to the Court," 6, *United States v. Pendergast* (1939), C, 14,567-KC, RG 21, NA-CPR; *Kansas City Star*, April 7, 1939.

9. "Investigation and Conviction," 17, June 2, 1939, Pendergast File, Morgenthau Papers, FDRL.

10. Ibid., 18.

11. Ibid.

12. Ibid.

13. "Statement of Facts to the Court," 10, *United States v. Pendergast* (1939), C, 14,567-KC, RG 21, NA-CPR.

14. "Investigation and Conviction," 11, June 2, 1939, Pendergast File, Morgenthau Papers, FDRL.

15. Quoted ibid.

16. "Statement of Facts to the Court," 12, *United States v. Pendergast* (1939), C, 14,567-KC, RG 21, NA-CPR. See Judge Arthur Wood's comments praising Irey in "Transcript of Minutes," United States Board of Parole, November 4, 1939, Notorious Offender Case Files, RG 129, NA-CPR.

17. "Investigation and Conviction," 11, June 2, 1939, Pendergast File, Morgenthau Papers, FDRL. A memorandum seemed to express concern over the security of the records: "In October 1937, the Pendergast returns were called into Washington by Deputy Commissioner Russell, who apparently had it in mind that the direct investigation of these returns, when made, should be made by agents from outside the St. Louis division" ("Re: Pendergast Case, Memorandum for the Secretary," April 10, 1939, Pendergast File, Morgenthau Papers, FDRL).

18. Quoted in *Kansas City Times*, April 8, 1939.

19. Quoted in *St. Louis Post-Dispatch*, September 12, 1937.

20. Quoted ibid.

21. Quoted ibid.

22. *Kansas City Star*, August 7, 1937; *Missouri Democrat*, July 30, October 22, 1937; quoted in *Missouri Democrat*, November 12, 1937.

23. "Re: Pendergast Case, Memorandum for the Secretary," April 10, 1939, Pendergast File, Morgenthau Papers, FDRL.

24. Farley, who discussed the Missouri split with FDR in 1938, recalled, "He concluded by saying Stark and T.J. Pendergast would have a battle for control this fall and the Governor might win" (Farley, *Jim Farley's Story*, 134).

25. Reeves, "Shame," 90–92, Reeves Papers, A-WDM.

26. *Missouri Democrat*, March 25, 1938.

27. Quoted in *Kansas City Star*, April 1, 1938; quoted in Reddig, *Tom's Town*, 305; *Time*, April 11, 1938. Reformer Samuel S. Mayerberg said, "We set to work for the 1938 election and won a partial victory. We elected two members to Council in spite of the fact that the election board had insufficient time to remove all the ghost votes and to install sufficient reliable tellers and judges" (Mayerberg, *Chronicle*, 142). Stark praised his own election board, saying he was "deeply gratified" by the conduct of the canvass (quoted in *Kansas City Star*, March 30, 1938). A *Star* front-page story said the election proved "some of the axioms of every day politics, among them that the unorganized cannot beat the organized; that votes count more than a ribbon of words and that politics is a year round game" (*Kansas City Star*, March 30, 1938).

28. Quoted in *Denver Post*, June 18, 1938; quoted in *Missouri Democrat*, April 8, 1938.

29. John W. Oliver to Howard F. Sachs, memorandum, "Questions Posed for Becker/ Oliver Session on the 1930s—Kansas City," February 4, 1987, pp. 11–12, A-WDM.

30. Meeting with William H. Becker, October 2, 1987, A-WDM. In Merle Miller, *Plain Speaking: An Oral Biography of Harry S. Truman*, 151, Truman is quoted as saying, "Lloyd Stark is a no good son of a bitch, and I don't care what anyone says."

31. William H. Becker, interview by Fredrick Spletstoser, April 17, 21, May 12, June 16, July 7, 28, 1989, pp. 130–31, A-WDM.

32. Ibid., 129–30.

33. "Statement of Facts to the Court," 13–16, *United States v. Pendergast* (1939), C, 14,567-KC, RG 21, NA-CPR; meeting with William H. Becker, October 2, 1987, A-WDM.

34. "Statement of Facts to the Court," 15–16, *United States v. Pendergast* (1939), C, 14,567-KC, RG 21, NA-CPR; *Kansas City Star*, December 27, 1974.

35. "Investigation and Conviction," 4–8, June 2, 1939, Pendergast File, Morgenthau Papers, FDRL; Reeves, "Shame," 281, Reeves Papers, A-WDM.

36. *St. Louis Post-Dispatch*, November 26, 1939; *Kansas City Times*, January 27, 1945.

37. *St. Louis Post-Dispatch*, November 26, 1939; Reeves, "Shame," 283, Reeves Papers, A-WDM.

38. Reeves, "Shame," 278, Reeves Papers, A-WDM.

39. Milligan, *Missouri Waltz*, 183.

40. Charles O'B. Berry to Elmer Irey, March 18, 1939, Pendergast File, Morgenthau Papers, FDRL.

41. Quoted in Reddig, *Tom's Town*, 327; Reeves, "Shame," 286, Reeves Papers, A-WDM.

42. Quoted in *St. Louis Post-Dispatch*, April 8, 1939, and in *Kansas City Star*, April 7, 1939. Truman later wrote, "I realized that attempts would be made to link my name with the misdeeds and misfortunes of Pendergast and to make it appear that I was the product of a corrupt political machine. This did not bother me personally, because I had an unblemished record to point to" (Truman, *Memoirs*, 1:159). Truman refused to repudiate Pendergast. Truman's daughter recalled that "one day in 1939" she heard her father tell a *Kansas City Star* reporter, "I'm not a rat who deserts a sinking ship" (Truman, *Harry S. Truman*, 117). See Miller, *Truman: Rise to Power*, 313.

43. Harry S. Truman to Alex Sachs, April 19, 1939, President's Personal File, HSTL. The reference was to an Olsen and Johnson comic stage show. See Hamby, *Man of the People*, 233.

44. *Kansas City Star*, April 9, 15, 29, 1939; *Missouri Democrat*, April 21, 1939.

45. The rumor circulated in Kansas City legal circles (William Collinson to Howard F. Sachs, September 13, 1988, A-WDM).

46. "Investigation and Conviction," 7, June 2, 1939, Pendergast File, Morgenthau Papers, FDRL; *Kansas City Post*, April 29, 1938.

47. "Transcript of Testimony Given by Thomas J. Pendergast, Jr.," Intelligence Unit, Internal Revenue Service, April 18, 1939, Pendergast Papers, WHMC.

48. "Investigation and Conviction," 21, June 2, 1939, Pendergast File, Morgenthau Papers, FDRL; *Kansas City Star*, May 1, 2, 5, 6, 1939; Reeves, "Shame," 282, Reeves Papers, A-WDM.

49. "Investigation and Conviction," 21, June 2, 1939; Rudolph H. Hartmann to Elmer Irey, June 6, 1939, Pendergast File, Morgenthau Papers, FDRL; *Kansas City Star*, April 27, 1939.

50. Quoted in Milligan, *Missouri Waltz*, 199; *Kansas City Star*, May 19, 21, 22, 1939; *Kansas City Times*, May 20, 1939. See Larsen, *Federal Justice*, 182–85.

51. *Kansas City Star*, May 22, 1939; *Kansas City Times*, May 23, 1939.

52. Quoted in *Kansas City Star,* May 22, 1939. This was the first time the public heard of the extent of Pendergast's illness.
53. "Statement of Facts to the Court," 19, *United States v. Pendergast* (1939), C, 14,567-KC, RG 21, NA-CPR.
54. Ibid., 19–20; *Kansas City Star,* May 22, 1939.
55. Quoted in Milligan, *Missouri Waltz,* 200–201.
56. Reeves, "Shame," 287, Reeves Papers, A-WDM.
57. "The Applicable Principles," *United States v. Pendergast* (1939), C, 14,567-KC, RG 21, NA-CPR; McCullough, *Truman,* 239–40.
58. "The Applicable Principles," *United States v. Pendergast* (1939), C, 14,567-KC, RG 21, NA-CPR. See *Kansas City Star,* May 22, 1939.
59. "Sentence," *United States v. Pendergast* (1939), C, 14,567-KC, RG 21, NA-CPR. See Larsen, *Federal Justice,* 183–84; Reddig, *Tom's Town,* 329; quoted in *Kansas City Star,* April 17, 1993.
60. Quoted in newspaper clipping "Pendergast's Stooge Guilty," May 27, 1939, n.p., Division of Press Intelligence, Bureau of Prisons, Notorious Offender Case Files, RG 129, NA-Wash; "Memorandum," August 19, 1939, *United States v. Pendergast,* 28 F. Supp. 601 (W.D.Mo., 1939). See Reddig, *Tom's Town,* 378. The litigation continued for many more years (*Kansas City Times,* October 8, 1958).
61. *Kansas City Times,* May 23, 1939.
62. *St. Louis Globe-Democrat,* May 23, 1939; *St. Louis Star-Times,* May 23, 1939; *St. Joseph Gazette,* May 23, 1939; *St. Louis Post-Dispatch,* May 23, 1939. See E. R. Schauffler, "The End of Pendergast," 18–23; Beverly Smith, "Good-by Boss."
63. "Memorandum," August 19, 1939, *United States v. Pendergast,* 28 F. Supp. 601 (W.D.Mo. 1939).
64. Ibid. John W. Oliver recalled that Kansas City reformers made good use in political speeches of Judge Otis's words: "I gave a number of those speeches and wrote other speeches for others to give" (John W. Oliver to Howard F. Sachs, memorandum, February 7, 1987, p. 12, A-WDM).
65. "Memorandum," August 19, 1939, *United States v. Pendergast,* 28 F. Supp. 601 (W.D.Mo. 1939).
66. *Kansas City Post,* April 5, 1939.
67. See Lawrence H. Larsen and Nancy J. Hulston, "Criminal Aspects of the Pendergast Machine."

7. PRISON, 1939–1940

1. Justin K. Fuller, M.D., memorandum, June 1, 1939, Notorious Offender Case Files, RG 129, NA-Wash. See Larsen, "Political Boss at Bay."
2. James V. Bennett to Frank Murphy, memorandum, June 2, 1939, Notorious Offender Case Files, RG 129, NA-Wash.
3. C. H. Waring, M.D., to Justin K. Fuller, M.D., June 3, 1939, Notorious Offender Case Files, RG 129, NA-Wash; ibid. See also "Clinical Record," June 2, 3, 1939, Notorious Offender Case Files, RG 129, NA-Wash.
4. Waring to Fuller, June 3, 1939; Lawrence P. Engle, M.D., to C. H. Waring, M.D., memorandum, "Re: History of heart attack, T. J. Pendergast," June 7, 1939, in Robert H. Hudspeth to James Bennett, June 7, 1939; James Bennett to Frank Murphy, June 2, 1939, all in Notorious Offender Case Files, RG 129, NA-Wash.

5. "Record of Interviews and Visits," Thomas J. Pendergast, n.d.; Robert H. Hudspeth to James Bennett, June 5, 1939, both in Notorious Offender Case Files, RG 129, NA-Wash.

6. "Official News Bulletin," June 5, 1939, Department of Justice; James Bennett, telegram to Ed Meisburger, *Kansas City Journal,* June 5, 1939, both in Notorious Offender Case Files, RG 129, NA-Wash.

7. D. J. Daley, M.D. to C. H. Waring, M.D., June 8–10, 12–17, 19–24, 26–27, 30, July 10, 1939; C. H. Waring, M.D. to Robert H. Hudspeth, June 10, 1939; Robert H. Hudspeth to James Bennett, July 1, 1939, all in Notorious Offender Case Files, RG 129, NA-Wash. See *Kansas City Journal,* June 5, 1939.

8. "Psychological," "Admission Summary," Notorious Offender Case Files, RG 129, NA-Wash.

9. Ibid.

10. Justin K. Fuller to C. H. Waring, June 5, 1939, Notorious Offender Case Files, NA-Wash.

11. Robert Hudson, M.D., "Medical Aspects of Tom Pendergast," 1–6, University of Kansas Medical Center Archives, Kansas City, Kansas.

12. Ibid, 6.

13. D. J. Daley to C. H. Waring, July 10, 1939, Notorious Offender Case Files, NA-Wash.

14. "Summary of Account," July 17, 1939; "Educational Department Report," n.d.; "List of Relatives and Requested Visitors"; MKR to W. T. Hammack, July 10, 1939; "Confidential Work Report to the United States Board of Parole," August 18, 1939, all in Notorious Offender Case Files, RG 129, NA-Wash.

15. Thomas J. Pendergast to United States Board of Parole, June 28, 1939; "Parole Progress Report," both in Notorious Offender Case Files, RG 129, NA-Wash.

16. "Report on Convicted Prisoner by United States Attorney," signed by Maurice Milligan and Merrill E. Otis, June 20, 1939, Notorious Offender Case Files, RG 129, NA-Wash. See Maurice Milligan to Myrl Alexander, September 23, 1939, Notorious Offender Case Files, RG 129, NA-Wash.

17. "Memorandum," August 19, 1939, *United States v. Pendergast,* 28 F. Supp. 601 (W.D.Mo., 1939).

18. Reeves, "Shame," 270–71, Reeves Papers, A-WDM.

19. Quoted in *Kansas City Star,* October 28, 1939.

20. C. H. Waring to N. R. Timmons, October 30, 1939, Notorious Offender Case Files, RG 129, NA-Wash.

21. "Memorandum," Bennett to attorney general, November 3, 1939, Notorious Offender Case Files, RG 129, NA-Wash.

22. "Transcript of Minutes," United States Board of Parole, November 4, 1939, Notorious Offender Case Files, RG 129, NA-Wash.

23. Judge Arthur Wood, in lengthy remarks attached to the "Transcript of Minutes," recommended a denial of parole (ibid.).

24. "Order of the Denial, Adjourned Case," November 21, 1939, and "In re: Thomas J. Pendergast, Reg. NA 55295; cross-section of press commentary," Division of Press Intelligence, Notorious Offender Case Files, RG 129, NA-Wash. The *Kansas City Star,* October 31, 1939, ran a story on the then impending parole hearing.

25. *Kansas City Star,* January 7, 1940. See Milligan, *Missouri Waltz,* 203–4.

26. Quoted in *Kansas City Star,* January 30, 1991.

27. Charles O'B. Berry to W. R. Woolf, January 17, 1940, Notorious Offender Case Files, RG 129, NA-Wash.

28. James Bennett to Robert H. Hudspeth, January 25, 1940, Notorious Offender Case Files, RG 129, NA-Wash.

29. W. Harold Lane to Charles O'B. Berry, January 17, 1940; Robert H. Hudspeth to James Bennett, January 22, 1940; "Record of Interviews and Visits," Thomas J. Pendergast, n.d., all in Notorious Offender Case Files, RG 129, NA-Wash.

30. J. Edgar Hoover to Matthew F. McGuire, memorandum, June 13, 1940, Notorious Offender Case Files, RG 129, NA-Wash. McGuire was the assistant to the attorney general. The memo was forwarded to James Bennett, who wrote across the bottom, "Released May 30—as widely published in news. No action." Hoover quoted an informant: "Warden Hudspeth may be treating Pendergast as any other prisoner; I wouldn't know, but the big Jersey horse books—which continue to operate in spite of the Department of Justice—tell me that considerable money is being wired out of Leavenworth daily in Pendergast's name, though not such large sums as he used to drop. As infatuated a horse-player as Pendergast will go on playing unless you lock him up in solitary."

31. "Medical Release Report," April 15, 1940, "Medical Certificate of Departing Prisoners," May 27, 1940, both in Notorious Offender Case Files, RG 129, NA-Wash.

32. "Copy of Certificate of Payment of Fine," April 29, 1940; Robert H. Hudspeth to A. L. Arnold, April 30, 1940; Vice President, Ready Mixed Concrete Co., to U.S. Board of Parole, July 2, 1939, all in Notorious Offender Case Files, RG 129, NA-Wash. A job was available for Pendergast "anytime" at Ready Mixed.

33. See Kansas City Star, April 10, 1940, and Milligan, Missouri Waltz, 201.

34. "Certificate of Conditional Release," May 30, 1940, Notorious Offender Case Files, RG 129, NA-Wash; Kansas City Times, May 30, 1940; Kansas City Star, May 30, 1940.

35. Mattie Acock to Office of Parole Executive, May 22, 1939, Notorious Offender Case Files, RG 129, NA-Wash. The date and return address, "Leets Station, Box 7928," Kansas City, Missouri, were curious enough—May 22 was the day of the guilty plea and sentencing, and "Leets" probably should have been "Leeds"—that the handwritten letter to "Secretary to the President" was passed on by the White House to the Bureau of Prisons with the notation "RE: Requests parole of Mr. Tom Pendergast; he is a good man—trouble was caused by Governor Stark." See Ruby M. Carr to Mattie Acock, June 24, 1939, Notorious Offender Case Files, RG 129, NA-Wash. Carr was acting parole executive.

8. FINAL DAYS, 1940–1945

1. See Reddig, Tom's Town, 354–56; Kansas City Star, December 6, 1936.

2. Kansas City Star, March 30, 31, 1966; Kansas City Times, March 29, 1966; Milligan, Missouri Waltz, 242–43.

3. Pendergast Jr., "Other Side of the Coin," Pendergast Papers, WHMC.

4. Kansas City Journal, November 3, 1939; Denver Post, June 18, 1939; Kansas City Star, May 21, 1939; Galen Johnson, "Policing in Kansas City: Reform, Reorganization, and the Crime Fighting Image"; Reddig, Tom's Town, 320–21.

5. Lear B. Reed, Human Wolves: Seventeen Years of War on Crime, 178.

6. Ibid., 226. See Missouri Democrat, July 14, 1939.

7. Reed, *Human Wolves*, 228.

8. Ibid., 243–44.

9. Ibid., 259–63.

10. *Time*, April 24, 1939; *Missouri Democrat*, May 2, 1939.

11. Henry Jost to Joseph Shannon, July 12, 1939, Jost Papers, WHMC. Many decades later an editorial in a Kansas City newspaper directed against "apologists" for T. J. Pendergast concluded, "Tax money came in—and got lost in a labyrinth understood only by Pendergast's lackeys. It was a terrible way to run a city" (*Kansas City Star*, November 25, 1990). See Reddig, *Tom's Town*, 335–36.

12. Reddig, *Tom's Town*, 337–38; *Kansas City Times*, March 29, 1943; Mayerberg, *Chronicle*, 143–46. See Brown, *Politics of Reform*.

13. Joseph Shannon to Henry Jost, January 8, 1937, Jost Papers, WHMC.

14. Reddig, *Tom's Town*, 339; *Kansas City Times*, November 9, 1939; *Kansas City Journal*, November 10, 1939; quoted in *Missouri Democrat*, November 17, 1939; *Kansas City Star*, January 5, 1940.

15. Eloise Conner, who helped organize women into a reform organization, the Charter party, recalling that every election meeting started with the admission that the goal was clean government and not patronage, remembered, "But the minute we won my telephone rang like crazy. Everybody that we had worked with wanted a job. I couldn't believe it. It thoroughly disillusioned me with politics" (*Kansas City Star*, March 30, 1996). See Mayerberg, *Chronicle*, 142–46; Joseph L. Adams Jr., "Reformer—Kansas City Style"; *Kansas City Star*, June 12, 1990.

16. Quoted in *Missouri Democrat*, March 15, 1940.

17. Quoted in *Kansas City Times*, May 26, 1988. For the background of Cookingham's appointment, see Reddig, *Tom's Town*, 338–39.

18. Henry Jost to Charles S. Keith, December 29, 1939, Jost Papers, WHMC.

19. See Larsen, *Federal Justice*, 193.

20. See Fredrick M. Spletstoser, "A City at War: The Impact of World War Two on Kansas City."

21. *Kansas City Times*, January 27, 1945; Reddig, *Tom's Town*, 377–78; *Kansas City Kansan*, November 19, 1940.

22. *United States v. Pendergast*, 35 F. Supp. 593 (W.D.Mo., 1940); *United States v. Pendergast*, 39 F. Supp. 189 (W.D.Mo., 1941).

23. Merrill E. Otis to Kimbrough Stone and Albert L. Reeves, May 1, 1941, Open Court Files, JC, USDC-WM, RG 21, A-CPR.

24. *O'Malley v. United States*, 128 F. 2d. 676 (8th Cir. 1942); *Pendergast v. United States*, 317 U.S. 412 (1943). See *Kansas City Times*, January 27, 1945.

25. Howard F. Sachs to Lawrence H. Larsen, November 1995, A-WDM.

26. Daniel M. Lyons to Merrill E. Otis, August 10, 1943, Merrill E. Otis to Davis, August 13, 1943, *United States v. Pendergast* (1943), C, 14,458-KC, USDC-WM, RG 21, NA-CPR.

27. *Kansas City Star*, March 18, 1943.

28. Pendergast Jr., "Other Side of the Coin," Pendergast Papers, WHMC. Gnefkow did not become head of the organization until twenty-three years later (*Kansas City Star*, April 13, 1976). Thomas Pendergast Jr., who died on February 17, 1990, zealously guarded his father's memory. In 1965, 1967, and 1980 he took legal action against taverns he felt traded on and tarnished the Pendergast name and invaded the privacy of the Pendergast family.

29. Quoted in Pendergast Jr., "Other Side of the Coin," Pendergast Papers, WHMC.
30. On the evolution of reform government, see *Kansas City Star*, May 3, 1966; *Kansas City Times*, May 26, 1988.
31. Haskell and Fowler, *City of the Future*, 131.
32. Jerome Walsh, "A Special Book Review," 12b.
33. *Kansas City Times*, August 4, 1956; *Kansas City Star*, March 30, 1966.
34. Quoted in *Kansas City Times*, August 4, 1956.
35. Jim Pendergast quoted ibid.; *Kansas City Star*, Sunday magazine section, October 9, 1994; Richard Koenigsdorf quoted in *Kansas City Times*, August 4, 1956. See *Kansas City Star*, May 21, 1989, for a story on controversy over T. J. Pendergast's legacy. Pendergast's "ghost in politics" was commented on in the *Kansas City Star*, May 16, 1992. See *Kansas City Star*, April 23, 1989, November 25, 1990; Tom Bogdon, "Will the *Star* Ever Forgive the Pendergasts?" A front-page article in the *Kansas City Star*, April 14, 1996, made a most unusual use of the Pendergast legend: "Other than the shock of white hair and crisp business suits, James B. Nutter Sr. bears little physical resemblance to legendary Kansas City political boss Tom Pendergast. However, his role as king maker has some people now comparing the towering mortgage banker to the squat power broker who dominated Kansas City politics and politicians in the 1920s and '30s." On May 16, 1982, as part of a cautionary tale warning against a return of Pendergastism, a *Star* editorialist quoted a former assistant of Maurice Milligan, "They're always out there. The ones who live for power and will do anything to get it. The names and faces change from one generation to the next. But they're there, always waiting."
36. Reeves, "Shame," 27–30, Reeves Papers, A-WDM.
37. Mayerberg, *Chronicle*, 111.
38. *Kansas City Star*, April 12, 1938; Milligan, *Missouri Waltz*, 105; quoted in Beatty, "Political Boss Talks," 110.
39. In 1935, journalist Lorene Hickok, an unofficial investigator who reported directly to relief administrator Harry Hopkins, and hence to FDR, reported after a short visit to Kansas City that the department stores were busy, that there were too few jobs available for people seeking work, and that drought conditions were bad in Kansas— hardly new or startling information (Richard Lowitt and Maurine Beasley, *One Third of a Nation: Lorene Hickok Reports on the Great Depression*, 336, 357).
40. The standard popular account is Mike Royko, *Boss: Richard J. Daley of Chicago*. See Rakove, *Don't Make No Waves*; Roger Biles, *Richard J. Daley: Politics, Race, and the Governing of Chicago*.
41. Robin L. Einhorn, *Property Rules: Political Economy in Chicago, 1833–1872*; Harold F. Gosnell, *Machine Politics: Chicago Model*; Charles E. Merriam, *Chicago: A More Intimate View of Urban Politics*; Lloyd Wendt and Herman Kogan, *Big Bill of Chicago*; Wendt and Kogan, *Bosses in Lusty Chicago*.
42. Mitchell, *Four Horsemen*, "Pendergast, Thomas J.," Vertical File, HSTL.
43. *Chicago Tribune*, December 24, 1951.
44. Quoted in Reddig, *Tom's Town*, 385.
45. Quoted ibid. A scholarly history of Missouri that appeared in 1962 played down Pendergast's importance: "The influence of the Kansas City organization from 1930 to 1940, outside Kansas City, has been vastly exaggerated: the toughness of the Kansas City toughs has been emphasized, the heroism of the people who opposed the 'machine' has been publicized, often by the heroes themselves, all for the sake of

making a good newspaper story or providing material for an interesting lecture, until a balanced view of Missouri politics in the era has become difficult if not impossible to achieve" (Edwin McReynolds, *Missouri: A History of the Crossroads State,* 50).

46. Matt Devoe, interview, A-WDM; quoted in *New York Herald-Tribune,* October 14, 1934.
47. *Kansas City Star,* April 2, 1994. Quoted in *Kansas City Times,* April 21, 1986.
48. Pendergast Jr., "Other Side of the Coin," Pendergast Papers, WHMC; *Kansas City Star,* September 24, 1994.
49. *Kansas City Star,* January 27, 1945.
50. Quoted in *St. Louis Post-Dispatch,* January 27, 1945; Pendergast Jr., "Other Side of the Coin," Pendergast Papers, WHMC; Reddig, *Tom's Town,* 378.
51. *Kansas City Times,* January 27, 1945; *Kansas City Star,* January 27, 1945.
52. *St. Louis Post-Dispatch,* January 29, 1945.
53. Quoted in *St. Louis Post-Dispatch,* January 29, 1945.
54. Quoted in *Kansas City Star,* January 27, 1945.
55. Pendergast Jr., "Other Side of the Coin," Pendergast Papers, WHMC. Truman, asked while on vacation in Naples, Italy, about his appearance at Pendergast's funeral, reiterated, "I made a statement at the time that he was always my friend, and I stand by him. I've always done that with all my friends. When your friends are in trouble, that's when they need your help; not when they're on top of the heap" (quoted in *Kansas City Times,* May 22, 1956). Truman's daughter wrote in 1972, "Dad's presence at the funeral meant a great deal to Mr. Pendergast's family, and that is all Dad cared about" (Truman, *Harry S. Truman,* 203). See McCullough, *Truman,* 236; Hamby, *Man of the People,* 287; Miller, *Plain Speaking,* 196, 384–85.

EPILOGUE

1. *Kansas City Star,* June 13, 1951.
2. Ibid., June 23, 1951.
3. *Kansas City Times,* July 9, 1965.
4. *Kansas City Star,* February 18, 1990.
5. The first riverboat opened in 1994, and by 1997 gambling boats were taking in several hundred million dollars annually. A feature story reported, "Kansas City has never seen the likes of it. Boss Tom Pendergast's free-wheeling '30s might have come close. But nothing like this" (*Kansas City Star,* March 9, 1997).
6. Quoted in *Kansas City Star,* December 7, 1996; quoted in *Kansas City Star,* December 13, 1996.

Bibliography

COMMENTARY ON SOURCES

The three basic books on the Pendergast machine are William M. Reddig, *Tom's Town: Kansas City and the Pendergast Legend* (1947); Maurice M. Milligan, *Missouri Waltz: The Inside Story of the Pendergast Machine by the Man Who Smashed It* (1948); and Lyle W. Dorsett, *The Pendergast Machine* (1968). Milligan was the United States Attorney who helped bring the machine down, and Reddig was a journalist for the *Kansas City Star.* Both their accounts, within fairly obvious limitations, are primary in character. Dorsett's history is the standard scholarly study. Much useful information can be found in Samuel S. Mayerberg, *Chronicle of an American Crusader* (1944); Alan Hynd, *The Giant Killers* (1945); Marjorie Beach, *The Mayor's Wife: Crusade in Kansas City* (1953); A. Theodore Brown, *The Politics of Reform: Kansas City's Municipal Government, 1925–1950* (1958); and Lawrence H. Larsen, *Federal Justice in Western Missouri: The Judges, the Cases, the Times* (1994). Two general histories of Kansas City are Henry C. Haskell Jr. and Richard B. Fowler, *City of the Future: A Narrative History of Kansas City, 1850–1950* (1950), and A. Theodore Brown and Lyle W. Dorsett, *K.C.: A History of Kansas City, Missouri.* (1978). Harry S. Truman's career in Kansas City and Jackson County politics is considered in Jonathan Daniels, *The Man of Independence* (1950); Margaret Truman, *Truman* (1972); David McCullough, *Truman* (1992); Robert H. Ferrell, *Harry S. Truman: A Life* (1994); and Alonzo L. Hamby, *Man of the People: A Life of Harry S. Truman* (1995). A comprehensive, very well researched book is Richard L. Miller, *Harry S. Truman: The Rise to Power* (1986). Of numerous articles dealing with Thomas J. Pendergast and his organization, two of special worth are Jerome Beatty, "A Political

Boss Talks about His Job" (1933) and Lyle W. Dorsett, "Kansas City Politics" (1966).

Primary material can be found in a number of places. The extensive Robert M. Wedow Collection contains typed copies of newspaper articles on Pendergast covering his entire political career. The papers of Henry Jost, mayor of Kansas City from 1912 to 1916, include scrapbooks of political articles. The Thomas J. Pendergast file in the "Vertical File" at the Harry S. Truman Library has media material running from the 1910s to the 1990s. Truman reflected on his Pendergast association in his "Pickwick Papers"— notes written on stationery from the Pickwick Hotel—also on file at the Truman Library. The papers of two Missouri governors, Guy Park and Lloyd Crow Stark, view Pendergastism from differing standpoints. Many patronage letters to and from Pendergast are in the James A. Reed Papers. The Thomas J. Pendergast Jr. Papers relate primarily to family affairs. Albert L. Reeves's Papers contain a copy of his unpublished memoir, "The Shame of a Great City," which deals in part with the unsavory side of Pendergastism. Investigative reports in the Henry J. Morgenthau Jr. Papers trace in detail Pendergast's commission of a serious crime. Federal court and prison records are crucial to understanding Pendergast. The locations of these records and private papers are given in the Archives and Manuscript Collections section at the end of this bibliography.

There apparently are no Thomas J. Pendergast Papers as such, but from his correspondence with others, from formal interviews he granted favored reporters, from extensive newspaper coverage of his daily activities, and from his prison psychiatric and other evaluations, it is clear that he was not the kind of personality who put his innermost thoughts down on paper or who would digress to writing about sunsets or even commenting on the pressing issues of the day. To everyone outside his immediate family, he was as much all business as possible, revealing little beyond what he wanted people to see.

This bibliography, intended to help guide future researchers, while not exhaustive, lists books, articles, manuscripts, and archives found of use in producing this book.

BOOKS AND ARTICLES

Adams, Joseph L., Jr. "Reformer—Kansas City Style." Master's thesis, University of Missouri–Kansas City, 1971.

Alexander, Henry M. "The City Manager Plan in Kansas City." *Missouri Historical Review* 34 (January 1940): 145–56.

"American Gambling: Half of the Nation Made Bets in 1938." *Life* 6 (February 6, 1939): 45–52.

Anslinger, Harry J., and Will Oursler. *The Murderers.* New York: Farrar, Straus, and Cudahy, 1961.

Armstrong, O.K. "Crusade in Kansas City." *This Week* (March 13, 1938): 12–13.

Beach, Marjorie. *The Mayor's Wife: Crusade in Kansas City.* New York: Vantage, 1953.

Beatty, Jack. *The Rascal King: The Life and Times of James Michael Curley, 1874–1958.* Reading, Mass.: Addison-Wesley, 1992.

Beatty, Jerome. "A Political Boss Talks about His Job." *American Magazine* 115 (February 1933): 31, 108–13.

Biles, Roger. *Richard J. Daley: Politics, Race, and the Governing of Chicago.* De Kalb: Northern Illinois University Press, 1995.

Blackmore, Charles P. "Joseph B. Shannon: Political Boss and Twentieth-Century 'Jeffersonian.'" Ph.D. diss., Columbia University, 1954.

Bogdon, Tom. "Will the *Star* Ever Forgive the Pendergasts?" *View* (May 16–May 29, 1990), 2.

Brown, A. Theodore. *Frontier Community: Kansas City to 1870.* Columbia: University of Missouri Press, 1963.

———. *The Politics of Reform: Kansas City's Municipal Government, 1925–1950.* Publication 116. Kansas City: Community Studies, 1958.

Brown, A. Theodore, and Lyle W. Dorsett. *K.C.: A History of Kansas City, Missouri.* Boulder: Pruett Publishing, 1978.

Brownell, Blaine A., and Warren E. Stickle, eds. *Bosses and Reformers: Urban Politics in America, 1880–1920.* Boston: Houghton Mifflin, 1973.

Bruce, Janet. *The Kansas City Monarchs: Champions of Black Baseball.* Lawrence: University Press of Kansas, 1985.

Bryce, James. *The American Commonwealth.* New York: Macmillan, 1888.

Carroll, Lenore. *Annie Chambers.* Wichita: Watermark Press, 1989.

Chamber of Commerce of Greater Kansas City. *Where These Rocky Bluffs Meet, Including the Story of the Kansas City Ten-Year Plan.* Kansas City: Smith-Grieve's, 1938.

Coghlan, Ralph. "Boss Pendergast: King of Kansas City, Emperor of Missouri." *Forum* 97 (February 1937): 67–72.

Creel, George. *Rebel at Large: Recollections of Fifty Crowded Years.* New York: G. P. Putnam's Sons, 1947.

Creel, George, and John Slavens. *Men Who Are Making Kansas City: A Biographical Dictionary.* Kansas City: Hudson-Kimberly, 1902.

Crumbine, Samuel J. *Frontier Doctor.* New York: Dorrance, 1948.

Daniels, Jonathan. *The Man of Independence.* Philadelphia: Lippincott, 1950.

Dickey, W. S., Clay Manufacturing Co. *Kansas City as It Is.* Kansas City: Union Bank Note Co., 1904.

Dishman, Robert B. "Machine Politics—Kansas City Model." Master's thesis, University of Missouri–Columbia, 1940.

Dorsett, Lyle W. "Alderman Jim Pendergast." Master's thesis, University of Kansas City, 1962.

———. "Alderman Jim Pendergast." *Missouri Historical Society Bulletin* 21 (October 1964): 3–16.

———. *Franklin D. Roosevelt and the City Bosses.* Port Washington, N.Y.: Kennikat Press, 1977.

———. "Kansas City Politics: A Study of Boss Pendergast's Machine." *Arizona and the West* 8 (spring 1966): 107–18.

———. *The Pendergast Machine.* 1968. Reprint, Lincoln: University of Nebraska Press, 1980.

Driggs, Franklin. "Kansas City and the Southwest." In *Jazz: New Perspectives on the History of Jazz by Twelve of the World's Foremost Jazz Critics and Scholars,* edited by Nat Hentoff and Albert McCarthy. 1959. Reprint, New York: Da Capo, 1975.

Dunar, Andrew J. *The Truman Scandals and the Politics of Morality.* Columbia: University of Missouri Press, 1984.

1879 Kansas City Police Regulations. Kansas City Police Department, 1879.

Einhorn, Robin L. *Property Rules: Political Economy in Chicago, 1833–1872.* Chicago: University of Chicago Press, 1991.

Ellis, Roy. *A Civic History of Kansas City, Missouri.* Springfield, Mo.: Elkins-Sawyer, 1930.

Evans, Timothy K. "'This Certainly Is Relief!': Matthew S. Murray and Missouri Politics during the Depression." *Missouri Historical Society Bulletin* 28 (July 1972): 219–33.

Fairlie, John. *Municipal Administration.* New York: Macmillan, 1901.

Farley, James A. *Behind the Ballots: The Personal History of a Politician.* New York: Harcourt, Brace, 1938.

———. *Jim Farley's Story: The Roosevelt Years.* New York: Whittlesey House, 1948.

Ferrell, Robert H. *Harry S. Truman: A Life.* Columbia: University of Missouri Press, 1994.

———, ed. *Dear Bess: The Letters from Harry to Bess Truman, 1910–1959.* New York: Norton, 1983.

———, ed. *Off the Record: The Private Papers of Harry S. Truman.* New York: Harper and Row, 1980.

Findlay, John M. *People of Chance: Gambling in American Society from Jamestown to Las Vegas.* New York: Oxford University Press, 1986.

Frohoff, Katherine Wilson. "In Search of Kansas City Jazz." *Perspectives* 6 (spring 1996): 3–5.

Garwood, Darrell. *Crossroads of America: The Story of Kansas City.* New York: Norton, 1948.

Geiger, Louis G. "Joseph W. Folk *v.* Edward Butler, St. Louis, 1902." *Journal of Southern History* 28 (November 1962): 438–49.

Ghosts in the Heart of America: Daylight Ghosts in Kansas City. N.p., 1938.

Glaab, Charles N. *Kansas City and the Railroads: Community Policy in the Growth of a Regional Metropolis.* Madison: State Historical Society of Wisconsin, 1962.

———. "Visions of Metropolis: William Gilpin and Theories of City Growth in the American West." *Wisconsin Magazine of History* 45 (autumn 1961): 21–31.

Glaab, Charles N., and A. Theodore Brown. *A History of Urban America.* New York: Macmillan, 1967.

Goldfield, David R., and Blaine A. Brownell, *Urban America: A History.* 2d ed. Boston: Houghton Mifflin, 1990.

Gosnell, Harold F. *Machine Politics: Chicago Model.* Chicago: University of Chicago Press, 1937.

———. *Truman's Crises: A Political Biography of Harry S. Truman.* Westport, N.Y.: Greenwood Press, 1980.

Gottfried, Alex. *Boss Cermak of Chicago.* Seattle: University of Washington Press, 1962.

"The Governor of Missouri Helps Indict the Boss of Kansas City and Becomes a Presidential Possibility." *Life* 6 (April 24, 1939): 15–16.

Green, George Fuller. *A Condensed History of the Kansas City Area: Its Mayors and Some V.I.P.'s.* Kansas City: Lowell Press, 1968.

Griffith, Ernest S. *The Modern Development of City Government in the United States and the United Kingdom.* London: Oxford University Press, 1927.

Grothaus, Larry. "Kansas City Blacks, Harry Truman, and the Pendergast Machine." *Missouri Historical Review* 69 (October 1974): 65–82.

Hamby, Alonzo L. *Man of the People: A Life of Harry S. Truman.* New York: Oxford University Press, 1995.

Haskell, Henry C., Jr., and Richard B. Fowler. *City of the Future: A Narrative History of Kansas City, 1850–1950.* Kansas City: Kansas City Star Co. and Glenn Publishing, 1950.

Hays, Samuel. "The Politics of Reform in Municipal Government in the Progressive Era." *Pacific Northwest Quarterly* 55 (October 1964): 157–69.

Holli, Melvin G. *Reform in Detroit: Hazen S. Pingree and Urban Politics.* New York: Oxford University Press, 1969.

Hynd, Alan. *The Giant Killers.* New York: R. M. McBride, 1945.

Irey, Elmer, and William Slocum. "How We Smashed the Pendergast Machine." *Coronet* 23 (December 1947): 67–76.

Jackson, William Rufus. *Missouri Democracy: A History of the Party and Its Representative Members—Past and Present.* 3 vols. Chicago: S. J. Clarke, 1935.

Johnson, Galen. "Policing in Kansas City: Reform, Reorganization, and the Crime Fighting Image." Master's thesis, University of Missouri–Kansas City, 1991.

Johnson, William A. *Kansas City Votes, 1853–1979: Precinct Election Returns for the Offices of President, Governor, and Mayor.* Kansas City: The Committee for Urban and Public Affairs, University of Missouri–Kansas City, 1981.

Kansas City in Caricature. Kansas City: Howard G. Bartling, 1912.

King, Elwood. *History of Buchanan County and St. Joseph, Mo.: From the Time of the Platte Purchase to the End of the Year 1915.* St. Joseph: History Publications Co., 1915.

Kirchner, L. R. *Triple Cross Fire!: J. Edgar Hoover and the Kansas City Union Station Massacre.* Kansas City: Janlar Books, 1993.

Larkin, Lew. "The Other Side of Tom Pendergast." *Missouri Life* 5 (January–February 1978): 21–26.

Larsen, Lawrence H. *Federal Justice in Western Missouri: The Judges, the Cases, the Times.* Columbia: University of Missouri Press, 1994.

———. "A Political Boss at Bay: Thomas J. Pendergast in Federal Prison." *Missouri Historical Review* 86 (July 1992): 396–417.

———. "United States v. Langer, et al.: The U.S. District Attorney's Files." *North Dakota History* 51 (spring 1984): 4–13.

———. *The Urban West at the End of the Frontier.* Lawrence: The Regents Press of Kansas, 1978.

Larsen, Lawrence H., and Barbara J. Cottrell. *The Gate City: A History of Omaha.* 1982. Reprint, Lincoln: University of Nebraska Press, 1997.

Larsen, Lawrence H., and Nancy J. Hulston. "Criminal Aspects of the Pendergast Machine." *Missouri Historical Review* 91 (January 1997): 168–80.

———. "Through the Eyes of a Medical Student: A Window on Frontier Life in Kansas City, Missouri, 1870–1871." *Missouri Historical Review* 83 (summer 1994): 430–45.

Levine, Edward M. *The Irish and Irish Politicians.* Notre Dame, Ind.: University of Notre Dame Press, 1971.

Logan, Sheridan A. *Old Saint Jo: Gateway to the West, 1799–1932.* St. Joseph: Sublet Foundation, 1979.

Lowitt, Richard, and Maurine Beasley. *One Third of a Nation: Lorene Hickok Reports on the Great Depression.* Urbana, Ill., 1981.

McCullough, David. *Truman.* New York: Simon and Schuster, 1992.

McReynolds, Edwin. *Missouri: A History of the Crossroads State.* Norman: University of Oklahoma Press, 1962.

McWilliams, John O. *The Protectors: Harry J. Anslinger and the Federal Bureau of Narcotics, 1930–1962.* Newark: University of Delaware Press, 1990.

Magerl, Barbara. "The Other Pendergast." *Kansas City* (January 1992): 14–15.

Mandelbaum, Seymour. *Boss Tweed's New York.* New York: J. Wiley, 1965.

Martin, Dwayne R. "The Hidden Community: The Black Community of Kansas City, Missouri, during the 1870s and 1880s." Master's thesis, University of Missouri–Kansas City, 1982.

Mason, Frank. *Truman and the Pendergasts.* Evanston: Regency Books, 1963.

Matscheck, Walter. "Kansas City Adopts the Manager Plan." *National Municipal Review* 14 (April 1925): 207–8.

———. "Kansas City Tries to Improve the Manager Plan." *National Municipal Review* 14 (October 1925): 617–20.

Mayerberg, Samuel S. *Chronicle of an American Crusader.* New York: Block Publishing, 1944.

Melvin, Patricia Mooney. *The Organic City: Urban Definition and Neighborhood Organization, 1880–1920.* Lexington: University Press of Kentucky, 1987.

Menard, Orville. *Political Bossism in Mid-America: Tom Dennison's Omaha, 1900–1933.* Lanham, Md.: University Press of America, 1989.

Meriwether, Lee. *Jim Reed: Senatorial Immortal.* Webster Grove, Mo.: International Mark Twain Society, 1948.

Merriam, Charles E. *Chicago: A More Intimate View of Urban Politics.* New York: Macmillan, 1929.

Miller, Merle. *Plain Speaking: An Oral Biography of Harry S. Truman.* New York: Berkeley Publishing, 1974.

Miller, Richard L. *Harry S. Truman: The Rise to Power.* New York: McGraw-Hill, 1986.

Miller, Zane. *Boss Cox's Cincinnati: Urban Politics in the Progressive Era.* New York: Oxford University Press, 1968.

Milligan, Maurice M. *Missouri Waltz: The Inside Story of the Pendergast Machine by the Man Who Smashed It.* New York: C. Scribner's Sons, 1948.

Mitchell, Franklin D. *Embattled Democracy: Missouri Democratic Politics, 1919–1932.* Columbia: University of Missouri Press, 1968.

Monkkonen, Eric H. *The Local State: Public Money and American Cities.* Berkeley: University of California Press, 1996.

Munroe, Mary Norris. "Opposition to the Pendergast Machine, 1925–1934." Master's thesis, Georgetown University, 1955.

Mushkat, Jerome. *Tammany: The Evolution of a Political Machine, 1789–1865.* Syracuse: Syracuse University Press, 1971.

O'Connor, Edwin. *The Last Hurrah*. Boston: Little, Brown, 1956.

O'Connor, Thomas H. *The Boston Irish: A Political History*. Boston: Northwestern University Press, 1995.

Oster, Donald B. "Kansas City Charter Movements, 1905–1925." Master's thesis, University of Kansas City, 1962.

Ostrogorski, M. *Democracy and the Party System*. New York: Macmillan, 1910.

Otis, Merrill E. *In the Day's Work of a Federal Judge: A Miscellany of Opinions, Addresses and Extracts from Opinions and Addresses*. Edited by Alexander M. Meyer. Kansas City: Brown-White, 1937.

Pearson, Nathan W., Jr. *Goin' to Kansas City*. Urbana: University of Illinois Press, 1987.

Pearson, Robert, and Brad Pearson. *The J. C. Nichols Chronicle: The Authorized Story of the Man, His Company, and His Legacy*. Lawrence, Kans.: Country Club Plaza Press, 1994.

Phipps, Herb. *Bill Kyne of Bay Meadows: The Man Who Brought Horse Racing Back to California*. South Brunswick, N.J.: A. S. Barnes, 1978.

Political History of Jackson County: Biographical Sketches of Men Who Have Helped to Make It. Kansas City: Marshall and Morrison, 1902.

Powell, Eugene James. *Tom's Boy Harry: The First Complete Authentic Story of Harry Truman's Connection with the Pendergast Machine*. Jefferson City: Hawthorn, 1948.

Powers, Richard Gid. *G-Men: Hoover's FBI in American Popular Culture*. Carbondale: Southern Illinois State University Press, 1983.

———. *Secrecy and Power: The Life of J. Edgar Hoover*. New York: Free Press, 1987.

Price, Ogle W. *The Federal Government in Greater Kansas City: History of the Federal Government in Greater Kansas City and Directory of Federal Officials and Agencies, May 23, 1939*. Vol. 1, *Kansas City: Greater Kansas City Federal Business Association*. Leavenworth, Kans.: Federal Prison Industries, Inc., Press, 1938.

Rakove, Milton. *Don't Make No Waves—Don't Back No Losers: An Insider's Analysis of the Daley Machine*. Bloomington: Indiana University Press, 1975.

Reddig, William M. *Tom's Town: Kansas City and the Pendergast Legend*. 1947. Reprint, Columbia: University of Missouri Press, 1986.

Reed, Lear B. *Human Wolves: Seventeen Years of War on Crime*. Kansas City: Brown-White-Lowell Press, 1941.

Reedy, George. *From the Ward to the White House: The Irish in American Politics*. New York: C. Scribner's Sons, 1991.

Riordan, William L. *Plunkett of Tammany Hall: A Series of Very Plain Talks on Very Practical Politics*. New York: McClure, Phillips, 1905.

Royko, Mike. *Boss: Richard J. Daley of Chicago*. New York: Dutton, 1971.

Russell, Ross. *Jazz Style in Kansas City and the Southwest*. Berkeley: University of California Press, 1971.

Schauffler, Edward R. "The End of Pendergast." *Forum* 102 (July 1939): 18–23.

Schnell, J. Christopher. "New Deal Scandals: E. Y. Mitchell and F.D.R.'s Commerce Department." *Missouri Historical Review* 69 (July 1975): 357–75.

Serda, Daniel. *Boston Investors and the Early Development of Kansas City, Missouri.* Kansas City: Midwest Research Institute, 1992.

Smith, Beverly. "Good-by Boss." *American Magazine* 128 (August 1939): 18–19, 124–25.

Sovey, Percy B. "T. J. Pendergast: The Man Whose Word Is Good." *Democracy* (July 1935): 4–5.

Spletstoser, Fredrick M. "A City at War: The Impact of World War Two on Kansas City." Master's thesis, University of Missouri–Kansas City, 1971.

Spletstoser, Fredrick M., and Lawrence H. Larsen. *Kansas City: 100 Years of Business.* Kansas City: Kansas City Journal, 1988.

Stave, Bruce M., ed. *Urban Bosses, Machines, and Progressive Reformers.* Lexington, Mass.: D. C. Heath, 1972.

Steffens, Lincoln. *Shame of the Cities.* New York: Hill and Wang, 1963.

Steinberg, Alfred. *The Bosses.* New York: Macmillan, 1972.

————. *The Man from Missouri: The Life and Times of Harry S. Truman.* New York: G. P. Putnam's Sons, 1962.

Teaford, Jon C. *The Municipal Revolution in America: Origins of Modern Urban Government, 1650–1825.* Chicago: University of Chicago Press, 1975.

————. *The Twentieth-Century City: Problem, Progress, and Reality.* Baltimore: Johns Hopkins University Press, 1986.

————. *The Unheralded Triumph: City Government in America, 1870–1900.* Baltimore: Johns Hopkins University Press, 1984.

Thelen, David. *Paths of Resistance: Tradition and Dignity in Industrializing Missouri.* New York: Oxford University Press, 1986.

Truman, Harry S. *Memoirs.* Vol. 1, *Year of Decisions,* and vol. 2, *Years of Trial and Hope.* Garden City, N.Y.: Doubleday, 1955, 1956.

Truman, Margaret. *Harry S. Truman.* 1972. Reprint, New York: Avon Books, 1993.

Walsh, Jerome. "A Special Book Review." *Kansas City Bar Bulletin* 24 (May 1948): 12a–12d.

Wendt, Lloyd, and Herman Kogan. *Big Bill of Chicago.* Indianapolis: Bobbs-Merrill, 1953.

————. *Bosses in Lusty Chicago.* Bloomington: University of Indiana Press, 1967.

Whitney, Carrie Westlake. *Kansas City, Missouri: Its History and Its People, 1808–1908.* Chicago: S. J. Clark Publishing, 1908.

Williams, T. Harry. *Huey Long.* New York: Alfred A. Knopf, 1969.

Wilson, William H. *The City Beautiful Movement in Kansas City.* Columbia: University of Missouri Press, 1964.

Worley, William S. *Development of Industrial Districts in the Kansas City Region: From the Close of the Civil War to World War II.* Kansas City: Midwest Research Institute, 1993.

————. *J. C. Nichols and the Shaping of Kansas City.* Columbia: University of Missouri Press, 1990.

Zink, Harold. *City Bosses in the United States: A Study of Twenty Municipal Bosses.* Durham, N.C.: Duke University Press, 1930.

ARCHIVES AND MANUSCRIPT COLLECTIONS

National Archives of the United States

A. Central Plains Region, Kansas City, Missouri
Record Group 21, Records of District Courts of the United States
    Western District of Missouri:
        Kansas City Division
            United States District Court Records
                Criminal Cases, 1879–1961
Record Group 276, Records of United States Courts of Appeals
    Eighth Circuit:
        Criminal Cases

B. National Archives, Washington, D.C.
Record Group 129, Records of the Bureau of Prisons
    Notorious Offender Case Files
        Thomas J. Pendergast

C. Franklin D. Roosevelt Library, Hyde Park, N.Y.
    Papers of Henry J. Morgenthau Jr.
        Thomas J. Pendergast File

D. Harry S. Truman Library, Independence, Missouri
    Papers of James P. Aylward
    Papers of Harry S. Truman
        President's Personal File
        President's Secretary's File
        Senatorial File
    Library Vertical File
        Pendergast, Thomas J.

Archives of the United States District Court for the Western District of Missouri
    Historical Files
    Albert L. Reeves Papers

Marr Sound Archives, General Library, University of Missouri– Kansas City
    Casimir Welch Wire Tap

Western Historical Manuscript Collection, a Joint Collection of the University of Missouri and the State Historical Society of Missouri
    Columbia:
        Guy Park Papers
        Lloyd Crow Stark Papers
    Kansas City:
        Albert I. Beach Papers
        The Civic Research Institute Records
        Henry Jost Papers
        Thomas J. Pendergast Jr. Papers
        James A. Reed Papers
        Robert M. Wedow Collection

University of Kansas Medical Center Archives, Kansas City, Kansas
    Robert Hudson, M.D., Papers

Index